D1590979

The Terrific Kemble

PN
2598
Kemble, Frances Anne, 1809- 1893 .K4
A33
1978

The Terrific Kemble

A Victorian Self-Portrait
from the writings of Fanny Kemble

Introduced and edited by

ELEANOR RANSOME

'I went a couple of nights since to a little party . . . I met everyone, including the terrific Kemble herself, whose splendid handsomeness of eye, nostril and mouth were the best things in the room.' – *Henry James, December 29th, 1872*

HAMISH HAMILTON
London

DALE H. GRAMLEY LIBRARY
SALEM COLLEGE
WINSTON-SALEM, N. C.

First published in Great Britain 1978
by Hamish Hamilton Limited
90 Great Russell Street London WC1B 3PT

Copyright © 1978 by Eleanor Ransome

British Library Cataloguing in Publication Data

Kemble, Fanny
   The Terrific Kemble.
   1. Kemble, Fanny 2. Actresses – Great Britain – Biography
   I. Title   II. Ransome, Eleanor
   792′.028′0924   PN2598.K4

   ISBN 0–241–89884–6

Phototypeset by Western Printing Services Ltd, Bristol
Printed and bound in Great Britain by
Redwood Burn Ltd, Trowbridge and Esher

Contents

Illustrations

Between pages 144 *and* 145

Introduction

This is not another biography of Fanny Kemble, actress and much more besides. It is a self-portrait: here she speaks for herself, tells her own story.

Fanny's journals, letters and memoirs were first published a hundred years ago, and some of them much earlier even than that. With one exception, none has since been reprinted. They make good reading, not only because they reveal an entertaining and complex character, but also because they vividly reflect the contemporary scene during a life which spanned almost the whole of the nineteenth century. Born in 1809, only four years after the Battle of Trafalgar and when Napoleon's armies still ranged undefeated over the continent of Europe, Frances Anne Kemble died within five years of Queen Victoria's jubilee in 1897.

Henry James remarked after her death that she 'had, in two hemispheres, seen everyone and known everyone, had assisted at the social comedy of her age'[1] – a true enough comment but one which suggests a butterfly existence among the famous and the fashionable. In fact, she had seen the social miseries of her age as well as its splendours and had also marvelled at its scientific discoveries and tremendous feats of engineering. Her observant eye absorbed everything; her ready pen recorded every last detail.

*

Few women can have known such changes and contrasts or possessed so diverse a personality. Though Fanny's stage career was brief, it is as an actress that she is still remembered in this country almost a century and a half after she first stumbled, nearly dead with fright, on to the stage of Covent Garden Theatre. Yet from the beginning she disliked and distrusted the acting profession. In America, where she spent half her life, she is better known as a passionate opponent of slavery. Yet, having

[1] *Essays in London*, p. 120.

unwittingly married into a slave-owning family, she never, until the cause was fought and nearly won, paraded her convictions in the open or made public the trauma of her experiences among the slaves whose labour provided her husband's wealth.

Sometimes she lived in luxury, consorting with the rich and great; at others she endured months, even years, of solitude and penury. A stage celebrity when scarcely out of her teens, she dropped into obscurity, faced a brief notoriety and eventually became a celebrity once more. She knew great happiness and great sorrow.

The author of her entry in the *Dictionary of National Biography* put her down as 'a sparkling, saucy and rather boisterous personality', as indeed she was, but he ignored the deeply thoughtful and serious side of her nature which was as much a part of her as the fun and drama. Her daughter's husband recalled the author of *Uncle Tom's Cabin* remarking that 'I guess that mother-in-law of yours would make six clever women and then there would be a remnant';[2] and another friend whom Fanny visited when she was unwell was pleased to see her but wondered aloud if she were really fit enough to receive 'as many people as you are'. Always passionate and uncompromising, often impulsive and downright tactless, her innumerable acquaintances in every walk of life delighted in her company although, it must be admitted, there were some who found her intolerably overbearing. She made many deep and lasting friendships. Ironically, the only one of her close relationships to fail was the closest of all – her marriage. Yet she never allowed her younger daughter's unequivocal support for her father's views on slavery to come between them.

*

For a generation before Fanny's birth the Kembles had been Britain's foremost theatrical family. Adored by their public, highly respected and eminently respectable, they had come far since Roger Kemble, hairdresser turned strolling player, had married his manager's daughter in the 1770s. Of the twelve children born to these young 'rogues and vagabonds' as they barnstormed their way round the country one achieved immortality – Sarah Siddons, Fanny's aunt and the original of Reynolds' Tragic Muse, and two became famous – her uncle, John Philip Kemble and her father, Charles. The two brothers, educated for

[2] Leigh, *Other Days*, p. 215.

the priesthood in France, each in turn rebelled and took to the road with companies of wandering actors. Both eventually achieved success in the capital, Charles being the less gifted but nevertheless 'a very gentlemanly and useful performer with a handsome face and a general air of the graceful and romantic'.[3] Off stage he was a cultivated and kindly man. Fanny was devoted to him.

'The Kembles', wrote Leigh Hunt in his autobiography many years after the dynasty had passed its long pre-eminence, 'were received everywhere among the truly best circles; that is to say, where intelligence was combined with high breeding; and they deserved it: for whatever difference of opinion may be entertained as to the amount of genius in the family, nobody who recollects them will dispute that they were a remarkable race, dignified and elegant in manners, with intellectual tendencies and in aspect very like what has been called "God Almighty's Nobility".'[4]

*

Fanny's parents were comfortably off. Her childhood was spent in a series of pleasant houses with a sufficiency of servants and there was money enough to give her brothers a good education and to send her to schools in France. Her father, however 'gentlemanly and useful' an actor he may have been, was no businessman, and after taking over his brother's sixth-share in the Covent Garden theatre soon found himself in serious financial difficulties. Faced with apparently immediate ruin, salvation seemed to lie in putting his daughter on the stage. The girl was eager to help; she would have become a governess if needs must.

So, with no training but an inborn talent and with little rehearsal, Fanny made her début as leading lady in *Romeo and Juliet* on October 5th, 1829.

She was a month short of twenty; she took the town by storm. Audiences hailed her as a second Mrs. Siddons – though, to be sure, a candid family friend observed that she was the Tragic Muse seen 'through the diminishing end of an opera glass'. Her performances, as her mother frequently reminded her, were unequal – sometimes very good, sometimes pretty bad. Still, she was young and attractive. She was a Kemble and, most important, she faced no competition: since the retirement of her

[3] Leigh Hunt, *Dramatic Criticism*, p. 105.
[4] *Autobiography*, pp. 152–3.

formidable Aunt Sarah seventeen years previously no actress of any distinction had appeared on the London stage. The public and the critics – or most of them – loved her and for a time at least Covent Garden was saved.

Fanny's new career lasted for only five years, three in England and two on a money-making tour of America which ended with her unfortunate marriage to the slave-owning Philadelphian, Pierce Butler. When, twelve years later, she perforce returned to the stage after leaving her husband, the passage of time had by no means reconciled her to the profession; but happily she was soon to find a more congenial occupation. For the next twenty years she was able to earn a comfortable living by giving public readings of Shakespeare's plays before enraptured audiences on both sides of the Atlantic.

Nobody who heard her ever forgot the experience. Dressed in rich scarlet, black velvet or white satin according to which play she was reading and sitting at a plain table with her book open on a lectern before her, she could conjure up tempests, pageants and battles; somehow she seemed almost to become Lear, Henry V, Prospero or Macbeth. On one occasion a small child was so overcome by Portia's command to Shylock to 'have by some surgeon to stop his wounds lest he do bleed to death' that she buried her face in her hands crying, 'I don't want to look! I can't bear to see him cut off the pound of flesh.'[5]

*

Thus, in her early forties, Fanny Kemble at last found her true dramatic vocation. To her other undoubted vocation – writing – she never seriously bent her mind. It is a pity that she did not, for she was a natural writer who lacked only the self-discipline and self-criticism which might have made her a considerable and not merely a prolific and entertaining one. From childhood to old age words poured from her pen as easily and naturally as water from a tap. At the age of seventeen she wrote in a single evening the last long act of a blank-verse tragedy. At eighty she had her first novel published. She always, in her own words, 'scribbled verse without stint or stay'. Insipid as her poems may now appear, her contemporaries enjoyed them – though discriminating critics such as Robert Browning were less enthusiastic: 'I had no conception Mrs. Butler could have written anything so mournfully mediocre . . . to go as near flattery as I can. With the exception of

[5] Craven: *La Jeunesse de Fanny Kemble*, p. 12.

three or four pieces respectable from their apparent earnestness, all that album writing . . . descriptions without colour, songs without tunes.'[6]

Such strictures cannot be made upon the letters, journals and memoirs on which this book is based. When writing for herself or her friends Fanny was an acute observer and lively reporter of the passing scene, although sometimes inclined to dramatise and elaborate. A more important failing was that, like most Victorians, she was verbose – often excessively so. To be sure, she was herself aware of her tendency to over-write: 'My sentences are the comicallest things in the world', she admitted, 'the end forgets the beginning and the whole is a perfect labyrinth of parentheses within parentheses.' Yet Fanny's very verbosity is one of her chief charms. Gifted with apparently total recall, she could never resist chasing off after whatever hare of a reflection or reminiscence that came into her mind as she wrote. In recounting her sensational début at Covent Garden, for instance, she stopped tantalisingly short of the climax for a fifty-page digression into any number of by-ways – the correct attire for Juliet, the ludicrously unsuitable costumes worn by Garrick and Mrs. Siddons, the idiosyncracies of long-forgotten actors and actresses, the convoluted love-affairs of Sir Thomas Lawrence and goodness knows what else besides.

No wonder then that Fanny's various autobiographical writings run to well over a million words. The books appeared over a period of more than forty years, starting with the controversial journal of the American tour with her father which led up to her marriage. Then came an account of a year in Italy after leaving her husband; the diary of her traumatic experience of slavery on the Butler plantations in Georgia (written a quarter of a century earlier), and finally the three series of *Records* compiled in retirement from some thousands of letters interspersed with numerous afterthoughts, comments and recollections.

In extracting what might be called 'the best of Fanny Kemble' from these many lengthy publications, I found myself faced with two main problems. With space for less than a tenth of the originals, the first was obviously the daunting decision about what should be included and what reluctantly omitted from so huge a mass of material packed with so much of real interest. Other editors would no doubt have produced very different books, perhaps emphasising more strongly than I have Fanny's

[6] *Letters of Robert Browning and Elizabeth Barrett Barrett*, Vol. II, p. 389.

religious and philosophical side, or her ecstatic love of nature, or her hatred of slavery. While reflecting all these and many other aspects of her complicated character, I have followed the chequered course of her life and also included much that may seem merely ephemeral, amusing or even trivial, but which I enjoyed and which shed light on the times in which she lived, the people she knew and the events she witnessed.

My second problem was the obverse of the first. For all her enormous output there are a number of gaps in Fanny's *Records*. Some periods of her life are only sparsely covered, and she herself deliberately suppressed all but the most indirect references to her marital difficulties although they had been common knowledge at the time of her divorce. Without going into the details of all the ramifications of her stormy and fluctuating relationship with her husband, I have where necessary briefly sketched in the background to the letters she continued to write even during the worst of her troubles – letters no less engrossing for the unmentioned heartbreak that lay behind them.[7]

*

Even the extracts from Fanny's voluminous output included in this book often proved far too long for full verbatim quotation, but I have been able to save several thousand words by eliminating many of her repetitive 'labyrinths of parentheses' and by cutting out large numbers of her proliferating and often pleonastic adjectives. In this essential foreshortening the convention of indicating omissions by rows of dots has had to be abandoned: otherwise the book might have appeared to be suffering from a severe case of black measles. Occasionally sentences or more extensive passages have been transposed and here and there a few words added for the sake of coherence, but nowhere has the sense of the original been changed or falsified.

The later comments and notes with which Fanny filled out her letters and journals are throughout identified by prefixing them with (*Records*). Passages which start with the date on the left-hand margin are taken from the journals. In the case of letters, the address and the introductory 'Dear . . .' are given only when the context demands them. My own occasional interpolations are enclosed in square brackets.

*

[7] For a full account of Fanny's fourteen years of marriage, see the recent biographies by Constance Wright and Dorothy Marshall.

I am not Frances Anne Kemble's biographer and have not set out to evaluate her, examine her motives, explain her actions or pass judgment on her virtues and failings. I have simply tried to distil the essence of an exceptional woman from her own always highly individual and characteristic writings.

London, 1977

Eleanor Ransome

Part One

CHAPTER 1

A Sunny but Stubborn Child
1809–1821

The heyday of the Kemble dynasty on the English stage had ended nearly two generations before Fanny began preparing her letters and journals for publication in the 1870s. Yet the memory of its long reign must still have remained so vividly alive that she could take it for granted that she could start her book with no more than a passing reference to her father's family and embark forthwith on the equally interesting but less well-known story of her mother's childhood and background.

Whatever qualities of mind or character I inherit from my father's family I am persuaded that I am more strongly stamped with those I derive from my mother, a woman who, possessing no specific gift in such perfection as the dramatic talents of the Kembles, had in a higher degree than any of them the peculiar organisation of genius. To the fine senses of a savage rather than a civilised nature, she joined an acute instinct of criticism in all matters of art, and a general quickness and accuracy of perception, and a brilliant vividness of expression that made her conversation delightful. Had she possessed half the advantages of education which she and my father laboured to bestow on us, she would, I think, have been one of the most remarkable persons of her time.

My mother was the daughter of a Frenchman whose father, a Monsieur de Fleury, adopted and gave his children the name of Decamp; my grandmother was the daughter of a farmer in the neighbourhood of Berne. From her birthplace you could see the great Jungfrau range of the Alps, and I sometimes wonder whether it is her blood in my veins that so loves and longs for those supremely beautiful mountains.

Not long after his marriage my grandfather went to Vienna, where my mother was born, and named after the great Empress-King who was her godmother, Maria-Theresa. In Vienna Mr. Decamp made the acquaintance of a young English

nobleman, Lord Malden (afterwards the Earl of Essex), who, with
an enthusiasm more friendly than wise, eagerly urged the young
Frenchman to come and settle in London, where his talents as a
draughtsman and musician, combined with the protection of
such friends as he could not fail to find, would easily enable him
to maintain himself and his young wife and child.

In an evil hour my grandfather accepted this advice. It was the
time when the emigration of the French nobility had filled London with objects of sympathy, and society with sympathisers
with their misfortunes. Among the means resorted to for assist-
ing the many interesting victims of the Revolution were representations, given under the direction of Le Texier, of Berquin's
and Madame de Genlis' juvenile dramas by young French
children. Their performances, combined with his own extraordinary readings, became one of the fashionable frenzies of the
day.

Among the little actors of Le Texier's troupe, my mother
attracted the greatest share of public attention by her beauty and
grace and the truth and spirit of her performance.[1]

The little French fairy was eagerly seized upon by admiring fine
ladies and gentlemen, and snatched up into their society where
she was fondled and petted and played with; passing whole days
in Mrs. Fitzherbert's drawing-room, and many a half-hour on the
knees of her royal and disloyal husband, the Prince Regent, one
of whose favourite jokes was to place my mother under a huge
glass bell, made to cover some large group of Dresden china,
where her tiny figure and flashing face produced an even more
beautiful effect than the costly work of art whose crystal covering
was made her momentary cage.

I have often heard my mother refer to this season of her childhood's favouritism with the fine folk of that day, one of her most
vivid impressions of which was the extraordinary beauty of person and royal charm of manner and deportment of the Prince of
Wales and – his enormous appetite: enormous perhaps after all
only by comparison with her own, which he compassionately
used to pity, saying frequently when she declined the delicacies

[1] Marie-Thérèse Decamp, born in 1774, could hardly have acted as a small child
before French émigrés. No doubt Fanny, writing as she approached old age and
looking back to events a hundred years past, somehow identified her mother's
stories with the talk she must frequently have heard – or half heard – about the
French Revolution, still, after all, a living memory in her childhood. Marie-
Thérèse's parentage and successes as a child actress are, however, fully cor-
roborated from other sources.

that he pressed upon her, 'Why, you poor child! Heaven has not blessed you with an appetite.'

Meantime, while the homes of the great and gay were her constant resort, the child's home was becoming sadder and her existence and that of her parents more precarious and penurious day by day. From my grandfather's first arrival in England his chest had suffered from the climate; the instrument he taught was the flute, and it was not long before disease of the lungs rendered that industry impossible. He endeavoured to supply its place by giving French and drawing lessons; and so struggled on, under the dark London sky and in the damp, smoky, foggy atmosphere, while the poor foreign wife bore and nursed four children.

How far my mother was hurt by the combination of circumstances that influenced her childhood, I know not. As I remember her, she was a frank, fearless and unworldly woman. How much the passionate, vehement, susceptible and most suffering nature was banefully fostered at the same time, I can better judge from the sad vantage ground of my own experience.

After six years of bitter struggle my grandfather died of consumption, leaving a widow and five children, of whom the eldest, my mother, not yet in her teens, became from that time the breadwinner and sole support.

After her marriage [in 1806] my mother remained but a few years on the stage. She had a fine and powerful voice and a rarely accurate musical ear; her figure was beautiful and her face very handsome and strikingly expressive; and [though of French parentage] she talked better, with more originality and vivacity than any Englishwoman I have ever known: to which good gifts she added that of being a first rate cook. And oh, how often and how bitterly, in my transatlantic household tribulations, have I deplored that her apron had not fallen on my shoulders or round my waist![2]

I was born on the 27th November, 1809, in Newman Street, Oxford Road [now Oxford Street], the third child of my parents, whose eldest died in infancy.

I have heard that, before we left our residence there, my father was convicted of having planted in my baby bosom the seeds of

[2] 'She is a most entertaining woman, shrewd and droll' wrote Henry Greville in his *Diary* (p. 43); and Edward Fitzgerald, the translator of Omar Khayyam remembered that 'my Mother always said that your Mother was by far the most witty, sensible and agreeable woman she knew'. (*Letters of Edward Fitzgerald to Fanny Kemble*, p. 62.)

personal vanity by having an especially pretty lace cap at hand in the drawing room, to be immediately substituted for some more homely daily adornment when I was exhibited to his visitors. In consequence, perhaps, of which I am a disgracefully dress-loving old woman of near seventy, one of whose minor miseries is that she can no longer find *any* lace cap whatever that is pretty and becoming to her grey head.

Our next home was at a place called Westbourne Green, now absorbed into endless avenues of 'palatial' residences. At this period of my life, I have been informed, I began to be exceedingly troublesome and unmanageable, my principal crime being a general audacious contempt for all authority, coupled with a sweet-tempered indifference to all punishment. I never cried, I never sulked, I never resented, lamented or repented either my ill-doings or their consequences.

Once some malefaction was met with an infliction of bread and water which I joyfully accepted, observing, 'Now I am like those poor dear French prisoners that everybody pities so.' Mrs. Siddons at that time lived next door to us; she came in one day when I had committed some of my daily offences against manners or morals and I was led into her awful presence to be admonished by her. Melpomene, the Tragic Muse, took me upon her lap and, bending upon me her 'controlling frown', discoursed to me of my evil ways in those accents which curdled the blood of the poor shopman of whom she demanded if the printed calico she purchased of him 'would wash'. The tragic tones pausing, in the midst of the impressed and impressive silence of the assembled family, I tinkled forth, 'What beautiful eyes you have!'', all my small faculties having been absorbed in those magnificent orbs.

A dangerous appeal, of a higher order, to the effect: 'Fanny why don't you pray to God to make you better?' immediately received the conclusive reply, 'So I do, and He makes me worse and worse.'

My aunt Adelaide, or Dall as we all called her, my mother's sister, lived with us, I believe, ever since I was born. Her story was as sad a one as could well be, yet she was one of the happiest persons I have ever known, as well as one of the best. Obliged to earn her bread, she had gone upon the stage under the kindly protection of Mr. Stephen Kemble, my father's brother, who lived for many years at Durham and was manager of the theatre there.

In his company my aunt Dall found employment, and in his daughter (also called Fanny) an inseparable friend and companion. My aunt lived with Mr. and Mrs. Kemble, and I suppose that a merrier life than that of these lasses, in the midst of their quaint theatrical tasks and homely household duties, was seldom led by two girls in any sphere of life. They made pies and puddings and patched and darned in the mornings; and by dint of paste and rouge, in dresses executed by themselves, became heroines in the evenings; and withal were well conducted good young things, full of the irresponsible spirits of their age and turning alike their hard homework and light stage labour into fun.

Two young men, officers of a militia regiment, became admirers of the young country actresses. Fanny Kemble's suitor, Robert Arkwright, had certainly no pretensions to dignity of descent, and the old Derbyshire barber, Sir Richard, or his son could hardly have stood out long upon that ground, though the immense wealth realised by their ingenuity and industry was abundant worldly reason for objections to such a match, no doubt.[3] However that may be, the opposition was eventually overcome. To the others a far different fate was allotted. The young man who addressed my aunt was sent for by his father, a wealthy Yorkshire squire, who, upon his son's refusing to give up his mistress, instantly assembled all the servants and tenants and declared that the young gentleman was illegitimate and thenceforth disinherited and disowned. He enlisted and went to India and never saw my aunt again.

So Adelaide Decamp came and lived with us and was the good angel of our home. With only the small pittance my father was able to give her, she spent her whole life in the service of my parents and their children, and lived and moved and had her being in a serene atmosphere of cheerful, self-forgetful content that was heroic in its absolute unconsciousness. Whenever anything went wrong, however, and she was 'vexed past her patience', she used to sing: it was the only indication by which we ever knew that she was out of sorts.

When she was seven Fanny was sent away to school for the second time. She had already spent a year at an aunt's 'fashionable

[3] Richard Arkwright (1732–1792). Before becoming an engineer and inventing the waterframe which, with Hargreaves' spinning jenny, revolutionised the manufacture of cotton goods, he 'amassed a little money by dealing in human hair and dying it by a process of his own'. (*Encyc. Brit.*)

establishment for the education of young ladies' in Bath. This time her destination was the formidable Mme. Faudier's school across the channel in Boulogne.

What I learned there, except French, which I could not help learning, I know not. I was taught music, dancing and Italian, and the small seven-year old beginnings of such particular humanities I mastered with tolerable success, but if I may judge from the frequency of my *pénitences*, humanity in general was not instilled in me without considerable trouble. I was a sore torment, no doubt, to poor Madame Faudier, who on being once informed by some alarmed passers-by in the street that one of her 'demoiselles' was perambulating the roof, exclaimed, in a paroxysm of rage and terror, 'Ce ne peut être que cette *diable* de Kemble,' and sure enough it was I.

Having committed I know not what crime, I had been thrust into a lonely garret, where I discovered a ladder to a trap door and was presently out on a sort of stone coping which ran round the steep roof. Snatched away from this perilous delight, I was forthwith plunged into the dark cellar. I suppose I suffered a martyrdom of fear, for I remember thirty years afterwards having this cellar and my misery in it brought to mind with intense vividness while reading in Hugo's *Notre Dame* poor Esmeralda's piteous entreaties for deliverance from her underground prison.

Less justifiable than banishment to lonely garrets or dark incarceration in cellars was another device adopted to impress me with the evil of my ways. There was to be an execution of some wretched malefactor who was condemned to be guillotined, and I was told that I should be taken to see this supreme act of legal retribution in order that I might know to what end evil courses conducted people. Whether it was ever intended that I should witness this ghastly spectacle, or whether it was expressly contrived that I should come too late, I know not. Certain it is that when I was taken to the Grande Place the slaughter was over; but I saw the guillotine, and gutters running red with what I was told was blood; all of which lugubrious objects no doubt had their due effect upon my poor childish imagination, with a benefit to my moral nature which I should think highly problematical.

The only agreeable impression I retain of my schooldays at Boulogne is that of the long half-holiday walks we were allowed to indulge in. Not the two-and-two dreary daily procession round the ramparts, but the disbanded freedom of the sunny afternoons spent in gathering wild flowers along the pretty secluded valley of the Liane, through which no iron road then bore its thundering freight.

I left Boulogne when I was almost nine years old and returned home, where I remained upwards of two years before again being sent to school. During this time we lived chiefly at a place called Craven Hill, Bayswater. My mother always had a detestation of London, which I have cordially inherited. She perpetually yearned for the fresh air and the quiet of the country. Occupied as my father was, however, this was an impossible luxury, and my poor mother escaped as far as her circumstances would allow from London by fixing her home at the place I have mentioned. In those days Tyburn turnpike, of nefarious memory, still stood at the junction of Oxford Road and the Edgware Road, and between the latter and Bayswater open fields stretched on one side of the high road; and on the other the untidy, shaggy selvage of Hyde Park; not trimmed with shady walks and flower borders and smooth grass and bright iron railings as now.

Even the most modest of the houses in Craven Hill had pretty gardens in front and behind which cheated my poor mother with a make-believe of being in the country. Infinite were her devices for making these dwellings of ours pleasant beyond what could have been thought possible. She had a peculiar taste and talent for furnishing and fitting up; her zeal was great for frequenting sales where she picked up at reasonable prices quaint pieces of old furniture. Nobody ever had such an eye for the disposal of every article in a room. However, she also had a rage for moving her furniture which never allowed her to let well alone. We never knew when we might find the rooms in a perfect chaos of disorder, while my mother, crimson and dishevelled with pushing and pulling the chairs, table and sofa hither and thither, was breathlessly organising new combinations. Nor could anything be more ludicrous than my father's piteous aspect, on arriving in the midst of this *remue-ménage* for the twentieth time, exclaiming in dismay, 'Why, bless my soul! What has happened to the rooms *again!*'

To my father, the five mile walk from Covent Garden to Craven Hill was a heavy increase to his almost nightly work in the theatre. It was perhaps the inconvenience of this process that led to us taking, in addition to our 'rural' residence, a lodging in Soho. While we were there, my uncle Kemble came for a short time to London from Lausanne where he had fixed his residence

– compelled to live abroad under penalty of seeing the private fortune he had realised by a long life of hard professional labour swept into the ruin of Covent Garden theatre, of which he was part proprietor. And I always associate this, my only recollection of his venerable white hair and beautiful face, full of an expression of most benign dignity, with the earliest mention I remember of that luckless property which weighed like an incubus upon my father all his life, and the ruinous burden of which both I and my sister successively endeavoured in vain to prop.

The Covent Garden theatre of which John Philip Kemble had become part owner in 1803 burned to the ground five years later, and all its contents, including Handel's great organ, valuable manuscripts and opera scores by Handel and Arne, were totally destroyed. By a prodigious effort cash was raised for its rebuilding, and a year later another far finer theatre rose from the ashes. The new magnificence cost dear, and accordingly the price of boxes was raised by a shilling to 7s. and of seats in the pit by sixpence to 4s.

An outraged public was not prepared to tolerate such extortion; nor did it like the new boxes and seating arrangements. So vociferous were the protests on the opening night that scarcely a word uttered by John Kemble and Sarah Siddons in Macbeth *could be heard for the shouts, boos, moans, hisses and catcalls. But 'both went steadily through their parts to the end. The extraordinary spectacle was presented of that great play being acted by such great players entirely in dumb show, while at every lull the fine tones of the great actress were heard distinctly as she calmly pursued her course'.* [4] *Scarcely a word could be heard at any performance for nearly three months thereafter. The organisers of the O.P. (Old Price) Riots were well organised: an O.P. song and dance was composed and repeatedly performed inside and outside the theatre; people wore O.P. badges in their hats; O.P. medallions were struck in copper and silver; the barracking persisted. Only when the prices were reduced and John Kemble made a public apology was peace restored. After so calamitous an initial setback, and with the retirement of its chief attraction, Mrs. Siddons, only three years later, John Kemble never succeeded in making the theatre pay. In spite of attempts to draw the crowds by extravagant spectacles such as jousts on horseback, performing animals, packs of hounds chasing across the stage and a production of* Bluebeard *enhanced by a whole circus troupe, the debts continued to mount, and he retired defeated in*

[4] Percy Fitzgerald: *The Kembles*, Vol. II, p. 124.

1817. During the visit to London here described by Fanny he made over his share in Covent Garden to his brother.

My father received the property with cheerful courage and not without sanguine hopes of retrieving its fortunes: instead of which it destroyed him and his family. Of the eighty thousand pounds which my uncle sank in endeavouring to sustain it, nothing remained to us after my father's death.

His sister, Mrs. Whitelock [who had been for many years on the American stage] came to live with us for some months at Craven Hill. She was a worthy but exceedingly ridiculous woman, in whom the strong peculiarities of her family were so exaggerated that she really seemed like a living parody or caricature of all the Kembles.

She was a larger and taller woman than her sister, Mrs. Siddons, with handsome features, too strongly marked for a woman, and with an auburn wig which, I presume, represented the colour of her previous hair and which was always more or less on one side. She had the deep sonorous voice and the extremely distinct utterance of all her family, and an extraordinary vehemence of gesture quite unlike their quiet dignity and reserve of manner. She would slap her thigh in emphatic enforcement of her statements, which were apt to be on an incredibly large scale, not infrequently exclaiming, 'I declare to God!' or 'I wish I may die!', all of which seemed to us very extraordinary.

Mrs. Whitelock used to tell us stories of the United States which we always received with extreme incredulity. She told us anecdotes of General Washington, to whom she had been presented and often seen (his favourite bespeak was always *The School for Scandal*), and of Talleyrand, whom she also had often met. She was once terrified by being followed at evening, in the streets of Philadelphia, by a red Indian savage, an adventure which has many times recurred to my mind while traversing the streets of that most peaceful Quaker city, distant now by more than a thousand miles from the nearest red Indian savage.

Nothing could be droller than to see her with Mrs. Siddons, of whom she looked like a clumsy, badly finished imitation. Her vehement gestures and violent objurgations contrasted comically with her sister's majestic stillness. Occasionally Mrs. Siddons would interrupt her, saying 'Elizabeth, your wig is on one side'; the other would shove the offending head-gear quite as crooked in the other direction, and even Melpomene would have

DALE H. GRAMLEY LIBRARY.
SALEM COLLEGE
WINSTON-SALEM, N. C.

recourse to her snuff box to hide the dawning smile on her face.

I imagine my education must have made but little progress during the last year of our residence at Craven Hill. I had no masters and my aunt Dall could ill supply the want of teachers. Moreover, I was troublesome and unmanageable, a tragically desperate young person.

CHAPTER 2

Becoming a Dutiful Daughter
1821–1829

Fanny's juvenile desperation manifested itself in a fantasy about poisoning her sister with privet berries and a half-hearted attempt to run away. Both were triggered off by rebukes or punishments considered unjust by the victim. The former, confessed to Aunt Dall, was tactfully ignored; the latter brought her a week of bread and water and solitary confinement in the toolshed where she sang at the top of her voice at every passing footstep to prove how little she cared. The problem child was once more bundled off to school, this time to an establishment in Paris run by a Mrs. Rowden whose previous school in Knightsbridge had included among its pupils Miss Mitford, author of Our Village, *and the eccentric Lady Caroline Lamb.*

Fanny was now nearly twelve years old and the year 1821. Her school-fellows were almost all English, but French was the only language spoken, and Fanny, a natural mimic, was soon not only speaking it like a native but also thinking in it all the time. During holidays she sometimes stayed with a French family in 'just such a residence as Balzac describes in his Scenes of Parisian and Provincial Life'. *She loved the 'sunny freedom' of her visits to these kind, thoroughly bourgeois friends.*

Mrs. Rowden had been an ardent admirer of the stage in general and of my uncle John Kemble in particular; but when I was placed under her charge, theatres and things theatrical had given place in her esteem to churches and things clerical. We were taken every Sunday to two and sometimes three services; we were required to write down from memory the sermons we heard and read them aloud at our evening devotional gathering. Sometimes, upon an appeal that we had paid the utmost attention and *couldn't* remember a single sentence, we were allowed to choose a text and compose an original sermon of our own; and I think a good sized volume might have been made of homilies of my composition, indited for myself and my companions. I have always had rather an inclination for preaching.

13

Whatever want of assiduity I may have betrayed in my other studies, there was no lack of zeal for my dancing lessons. I had a perfect passion for dancing and I am persuaded that my natural vocation was that of an opera dancer. Far into middle life I never saw beautiful dancing without a rapture of enthusiasm, and I remember, during Elssler's[1] visit to America, when I had long left off dancing in society, being so transported with her execution of a Spanish dance that I was detected by my cook in my store-room, in the midst of sugar, rice, tea, coffee, flour, etc., standing on the tips of my toes with my arms above my head in one of the attitudes I had most admired in her striking performance. The woman withdrew in speechless amazement and I alighted on my heels, feeling wonderfully foolish. How I thought I should never be able to leave off dancing! And so I thought of riding! And of singing! and could not imagine what life would be when I could no more do these things. I was not wrong perhaps in thinking it would be difficult to leave them off: I had no conception how easily they would leave me off.

I did not go home during the three years I spent in Paris and my real holidays were the rare and short visits my father paid me. At all other seasons Paris might have been Patagonia for anything I saw or heard or knew of its brilliant gaiety and splendid variety. But during those holidays of his and mine, my enjoyment and his were equal, I verily believe, though probably not, (as I then imagined), perfect. I remember seeing several times with him the inimitable comic actor, Poitier, in a farce called *Les Danaïdes* – a burlesque upon a magnificent mythological ballet. The piece was the broadest and most grotesque quiz of the 'grand genre classique et héroïque'; yet it was the essence of decency and propriety compared with *La Grande Duchesse*, *La belle Hélène*, *Orphée aux Enfers* and all the vile succession of indecencies and immoralities that the female good society of England in these latter days has delighted in witnessing.

But by far the most amusing piece in which I recollect seeing Poitier was *Les Anglaises pour Rire*. The Continent was just then beginning to make acquaintance with the travelling English to whom the downfall of Bonaparte had opened the gates of Europe and who then began to carry amazement and amusement from the shores of the Channel to those of the Mediterranean by their wealth, insolence, ignorance and cleanliness. *Les Anglaises pour*

[1] Fanny Elssler (1810–1844). Celebrated Austrian dancer and daughter of Haydn's valet and copyist.

Rire was a caricature of the English female traveller of that period. Coal-scuttle poke-bonnets, short and scanty skirts, huge splay feet arrayed in indescribable shoes and boots, colours which swore at each other – these were the outward and visible signs of the British fair of that day. To these were added a mode of speech in which the most ludicrous French, in the most barbarous accent, was uttered in alternate bursts of loud abruptness and languishing drawl. Tittering shyness, all giggle-goggle and blush; stony and stolid stupidity; angular postures and gestures; kittenish frolics and friskings – all together made *Les Anglaises pour Rire* one of the most comical pieces of acting I have seen in all my life.

Though Mrs. Rowden had become what in the religious jargon of the day was called serious, she winked at, if she did not deliberately encourage, sundry dramatic representations which her Paris pupils got up.

Our most ambitious essay in acting was Racine's *Andromaque*. We had an imposing audience and were all duly terrified, but at length it was all over and I had electrified the audience, my companions and still more myself; and so to avert any ill effects of this general electrification, Mrs. Rowden thought it wise to say to me, 'Ah, my dear, I don't think your parents need ever anticipate your going on the stage; you would make but a poor actress.' And she was right enough. I did make but a poor actress certainly, though that was not for want of natural talent but for want of cultivating it with due care and industry.

With this performance of *Andromaque*, all taste for acting, if it ever existed, evaporated, and though a few years afterwards the stage became my profession, it was the very reverse of my inclination.

I remained in Paris till I was between fifteen and sixteen years old. My father came to fetch me home, and the only adventure I met with on the way back was losing my bonnet, blown from my head into the sea, which obliged me to purchase one as soon as I reached London, and I so far imposed upon my father's masculine ignorance in such matters as to make him buy for me a full sized Leghorn hat, under which enormous sombrero I seated myself by him on the outside of the Weybridge coach and amazed the gaping population of each successive village with its vast dimensions.

Weybridge was not then reached by train in half an hour from London: it was two or three hours' coach distance – a rural, rather deserted looking and most picturesque village.

My mother's rural yearnings had now carried her beyond her suburban refuge at Craven Hill, and she was infinitely happy in her small cottage on the outskirts of Weybridge and the edge of its picturesque common. She delighted in it and so did we all except my father who had no real taste for the country. He used to come down on Saturday and stay till Monday morning, but the rest of the week he spent at what was then our home in London, no. 5 Soho Square. It was a comfortable, roomy house and has now, I think, been converted into a hospital.[2]

I followed no regular studies whatever during our summers at Weybridge. We lived chiefly in the open air, on the heath, in the beautiful wood above the meadows of Brooklands and along the lovely windings of the river Wey. But from that time began for me an epoch of indiscriminate, omnivorous reading which lasted until I went upon the stage. Besides reading every book that came within my reach, I now commenced scribbling verses without stint or stay – some, I suppose, in very bad Italian and some, I am sure in most indifferent English.

Our three happy Weybridge summers had but one incident of importance for me – catching the small-pox, which I had very severely. I was but little over sixteen, and had returned from school a very pretty girl, with fine eyes, teeth and hair, a clear vivid complexion and rather good features. The small-pox did not affect my three advantages first named, but, beside marking my face very perceptibly, it rendered my complexion thick and muddy and my features heavy and coarse, leaving me so moderate a share of good looks as quite to warrant my mother's satisfaction in saying when I went on the stage, 'Well, my dear, they can't say we have brought you out to exhibit your beauty'. Plain I certainly was, but I by no means always looked so; and so great was the variation in my appearance at different times that my comical old friend, Mrs. Fitzhugh, once exclaimed, 'Fanny Kemble, you are the ugliest and the handsomest woman in London!'

All my French dancing lessons had not given me a good deportment. I stooped, slouched, poked and exhibited an altogether disgracefully ungraceful carriage. In order that I might 'bear my body more seemly', various methods were resorted to; among others a hideous engine of torture of steel covered with

[2] It was still there in 1977, unchanged from Fanny's day except for philistine alterations to the ground floor. It was, however, on offer for sale to property developers.

red morocco which consisted of a flat piece of wood placed on my back, strapped to my waist and secured at the top by two epaulettes over my shoulders. From the middle of this there rose a steel rod or spine, with a steel collar which encircled my throat and fastened behind. The grace and ease which this horrible machine was expected to impart were, however, hardly perceptible and to my ineffable joy it was taken off. I was placed under the tuition of a sergeant of the Royal Foot Guards who undertook to make young ladies carry themselves and walk well, and not exactly like grenadiers either. This warrior, having duly put me through a number of exercises such as we see the awkward squads on parade grounds daily drilled in, took leave of me with the verdict that I was 'fit to march before the Duke of York', then commander of the forces.

At this time Fanny occasionally stayed at Heath Farm in Hertfordshire with the widow of her uncle John Kemble [who had died in Lausanne in 1823]. There she met Harriet St. Leger, who was to become her dearest and lifelong friend. Harriet, of Anglo-Irish descent, lived at Ardgillan Castle, some eighteen miles along the coast north of Dublin. The two were seldom able to meet; instead they corresponded regularly and at length over half a century, not only recounting their day to day news, but often engaging in deep religious and philosophical discussions. It was the return to Fanny of all her letters to Harriet, 'amounting to thousands — a history of my life', that started her writing her Records. *They were to form the backbone of the work.*

Harriet was about thirty years old when I first met her; tall and thin, her figure wanted roundness and grace, but it was as straight as a dart, and the vigorous, elastic movements of her limbs and her firm, springing step gave her whole person and deportment a character like that of the fabled Atalanta. Her forehead and eyes were beautiful. The rest of her features were not handsome, though her mouth was full of sensibility and sweetness and her teeth were the most perfect I ever saw. She was eccentric in many things, but in nothing more than her dress and especially her hats and boots. The latter were made by a man's bootmaker and infinite were the pains she took to procure the cumbrous, misshapen things that as much as possible concealed and disfigured her finely turned ankles and high Norman instep. Black and grey were the only colours I ever saw her in; and her dress, bare of every ornament, was literally only a covering for her body; but it was difficult to find cashmere fine enough for her scanty skirts or lawn exquisite enough for her collars and cuffs of immaculate freshness. Nobility, intelligence and tenderness were my dear Harriet's predominating qualities and her intellect was of a very uncommon order: she delighted in metaphysical subjects of the greatest difficulty and abstract questions of the most laborious solution.

> *The idyllic existence at Weybridge and the visits to Heath Farm were overshadowed by continuous worry about the theatre which, in spite of Charles Kemble's untiring efforts, still did not prosper. Among many other set-backs, the rise of the sensational Edmund Kean at the rival establishment, Drury Lane, attracted audiences away from the staider precincts of Covent Garden. Apart from steadily rising debts, the owners were involved in a chancery suit which dragged on for years, and which 'always seemed to envelop us in an atmosphere of palpitating suspense or stagnant uncertainty'. Yet there were occasional successes and one of these was a production of Weber's* Der Freischütz.

We went to see it until we literally knew it by heart and I contrived to get up a romantic passion for the great composer, of whom I procured a hideous little engraving (very ugly he was, with high cheek-bones, long hooked nose and spectacles) which, folded up in a small square and sewed into a black silk case, I carried like an amulet round my neck until I completely wore it out.

The immense success of the *Freischütz* and the important assistance it brought to the funds of the theatre induced my father to propose to Weber to compose an opera expressly for Covent Garden. This was *Oberon* and he was invited to come to London and himself superintend its production. He took up his abode at the house of Sir George Smart, the leader of the Covent Garden orchestra, and the two men were constantly at our house while rehearsals went forward. The first day they dined at my father's was an event for me, especially as Sir George assured Weber that I and all the young girls in England were over head and ears in love with him. With my guilty satchel round my neck, I felt ready to sink with confusion and stammered something about Herr von Weber's beautiful music, to which, with a comical, melancholy smile he replied, 'Ah, my music! It is always my music, but never myself!'

Oberon was brought out and succeeded; but in a degree far below the sanguine expectations of all concerned. Poor Weber's health, which had been wretched before he came to England and was most unfavourably affected by the climate, sank entirely under the mortification of the comparatively small success of his great work. Very soon after its production he became dangerously ill and died – not as people said, of a broken heart, but of disease of the lungs.

A circumstance which tended to embitter a good deal the close of Weber's life was the arrival in London of Rossini, to whom and to whose works the public immediately transferred its demonstrations of passionate affection. The brilliant, joyous Italian was a far better subject for London lionising than his sickly, sensitive, shrinking and rather soured German competitor for fame and public favour.

About this time I returned to visit Mrs. Kemble at Heath Farm and renew my days of delightful companionship with Harriet St. Leger. My visit was prolonged beyond her stay and my living converse with my friend was exchanged for unrestricted selections from my aunt's book-shelves, from which I made a choice of extreme variety, since Lord Byron and Jeremy Taylor [the seventeenth century moral theologian] were among the authors with whom I then first made acquaintance. I read them on alternate days, sitting on the mossy-cushioned lawn under a beautiful oak tree, with a cabbage leaf of fresh-gathered strawberries and a handful of fresh-blown roses beside me, which accompaniments to my studies appeared to me equally adapted to the wicked poet and the wise divine.

I also came upon Wraxall's *Memoirs of the House of Valois* and, reading it with great avidity, determined to write an historical novel, of which the heroine should be Françoise de Foix, the beautiful Countess de Chateaubriand. I eagerly set to work, my abundant production of doggerel suffering no diminution from this soberer undertaking, to which I added a brisk correspondence with my absent friend.

Eastlands Cottage, Weybridge, 1827

My dear Harriet, I wrote to you immediately upon our arriving here, which is now nearly a month ago, but having received no answer, I conjecture that our charming post office had done as it did last year, and kept my letters to itself. We have taken a house in [St.] James Street, Westminster, which appears to be in every way a desirable and convenient abode; it is comfortable and cheerful and its nearness to Henry's school [for reasons of economy he had been removed from boarding school and entered at Westminster] and comparative nearness to the theatre, together with its view over the park and (though last, not least) its moderate rent make up a mass of combined advantages which few other situations offer that we could afford at present.

I am extremely busy, dearest Harriet, and extremely elated about my play. I know I mentioned it before, but you may have reckoned it as one of the soap bubbles I am so fond of blowing, admiring and forgetting; however, when I tell you that I have finished three acts, and that the proprietors of Covent Garden have offered me, if it succeeds, two hundred pounds (the price Miss Mitford's *Foscari* brought her) you will agree that I have some reason to be proud as well as pleased. As nobody but myself can give you any opinion of it, you must be content to take my own, making all allowances for, etc. etc. I think, irrespective of age or sex, it is not a bad play; perhaps, considering both, a tolerably fair one. There is some good writing in it, and good situations.

> *St. James Street, October 11, 1827*

On Monday evening I sat down at six o'clock to begin my fifth act and by half past eleven had completed my task. On Tuesday evening I read it to my parents and I was so encouraged by the delighted looks they were continually exchanging that I believe I read it with more effect than they either of them had thought me capable of. When it was done I was most richly rewarded for they seemed so pleased with me and so proud of me that the most inordinate author's vanity would have been more than satisfied.

Fanny's projected novel had been abandoned in favour of a play on the same subject. In spite of the speed at which it was written Francis I *is immensely long; it is a blood and thunder melodrama in high-flown blank verse reminiscent of Shakespeare and full of purple passages. Typical, for instance, is the moment when Francis I first sets eye on the heroine, Françoise de Foix:*

> Had a limner's hand
> Traced such a heavenly brow, and such a lip,
> I would have sworn the knave had dreamt it all
> In some fair vision of some fairer world.
> See how she stands, all shrined in loveliness:
> Her white hands clasped; her clustering locks thrown back
> From her high forehead; and in those bright eyes
> Tears! radiant emanations! drops of light!

That fall from those surpassing orbs as though
The starry eyes of Heaven wept silver dew.'

December, 1827

Since you last heard from me I have seen the great West India dock and the Thames Tunnel. I must try to tell you what the tunnel is like. You enter by flights of stairs and find yourself on a circular platform which surrounds the top of a well or shaft of about two hundred feet in circumference and five hundred in depth. This well is an immense iron frame of cylindrical form, filled in with bricks; it was constructed on level ground and then by some wonderful mechanism sunk into the earth. In the midst of this is a steam engine, and above or below, as far as your eye can see, huge arms are working up and down, while the creaking, crashing, whirring noises and the swift whirling of innumerable wheels all round make you feel as if you were going distracted. I followed the party down little wooden stairs and along tottering planks to the bottom of the well. On turning round at the last flight of steps through an immense arch, as far as sight could reach stretched a vaulted passage, smooth earth underfoot, the whole lighted by a line of gas lamps, as bright almost as if it were broad day. Mr. Brunel,[3] who was superintending some of the works, offered to conduct us to where the workmen were employed, so we left our broad smooth path of light and got into dark passages, where we stumbled among coils of ropes and heaps of pipes and piles of planks, where ground springs were welling up and flowing in all directions, all of which was very strange. The appearance of the workmen, all begrimed, with their brawny arms and legs bare, some standing in black water up to the knees, others laboriously shovelling the black earth in their cages while they sturdily sang at their task, with the red, murky light of lanterns flashing and flickering about them, made up the most striking picture you can conceive.

After this we rowed down the river to the docks and lunched on board a splendid East Indiaman. I think it is better for me, however, to look at the trees and the sun, moon and stars than at tunnels and docks: they make me too *humanity proud*.

January 1828

I have no new friends, but I have made one acquaintance which might perhaps grow into a friendship. It is with a married

[3] Isambard Kingdom Brunel (1776–1849). Eminent engineer and builder of the Great Western Railway.

woman: her name is Jameson. She is an Irishwoman and author of the *Diary of an Ennuyée*. I like her very much; she is extremely clever. I have been to one dance and one or two dinners lately, but to tell you the truth, dear Harriet, the old people naturally treat me after my years, as a young person; and the young people seem to me stupid and uninteresting; so, you see, I do not like society. I have lately been seeing my father play Falstaff several times and I think it is an excellent piece of acting; he gives all the humour without too much coarseness. They are in sad want of a woman at both Covent Garden and Drury Lane. I've half a mind to give Covent Garden one. Don't be surprised!

February, 1828

In my last letter want of time and room prevented my enlarging upon my hint about the stage, but as far as my own determination goes, I think it is the course I shall most likely pursue. You know that independence of mind and body seems to me the great desideratum of life; my heart and my head are engrossed with the idea of exercising the literary talent which I think I possess. This is my world in which I live and have my happiness; and moreover, I hope, my means of fame, the prize for which I pray. To a certain degree, it may be my means of procuring benefits of a more substantial nature. I do not think I am fit to marry, to make an obedient wife or affectionate mother. I think I should be unhappy and the cause of unhappiness to others if I were to marry. Now, if I do not marry, what is to become of me in the event of anything happening to my father? His property is almost all gone; I doubt if we shall ever receive one pound from it. Is it likely that, supposing I were willing to undergo the drudgery of writing for my bread, I could live by my wits, or is such an existence desirable? The stage is a profession that people who have a talent for it make lucrative and which honourable conduct may make respectable; one which would place me at once beyond the fear of want, and that is closely allied in its nature to my beloved literary pursuits. And the mere mechanical labour of writing costs me so little that the union of the two occupations does not seem to me a difficulty. I spoke earnestly to my father and mother on this subject lately and they both with some reluctance thought I might succeed.

My father's income is barely eight hundred a year. My brother John's expenses, since he has been at college, have been nearly three. Five hundred a year for such a family as ours is very close and careful work, dear Harriet, and if my going on the stage would nearly double that income, lessen my dear father's anxieties and remove the many privations which my dear mother cheerfully endures, as well as the weight of her uncertainty about our future provision, would not that be a 'consummation devoutly to be wished'?

For the moment, however, there was no more talk of Fanny's becoming an actress. The next year – 'the happiest of my life' – was spent in Edinburgh with Mrs. Henry Siddons, daughter-in-law of Sarah, whose husband, manager of the Edinburgh theatre, had died leaving her with four small children. Herself an actress, she became joint proprietor of the theatre with her brother John Murray.

Fanny had become nervous, irritable and subject to unaccountable aches and pains and minor illnesses. Away from London and the miasma-like threat from Covent Garden, in her aunt's happy, well-regulated household, she gradually regained her equilibrium. She developed a taste for religion, forcing herself to give up reading Byron because she convinced herself that his poems had an 'injurious effect', stirring her whole being to a 'tempest of excitement'. Fanny's life in Edinburgh was not, however, unrelievedly serious. Aunt Siddons, for whom she rapidly developed a teenage crush, had a wide circle of interesting and cheerful friends; and there was a sentimental flirtation with her cousin Henry who went off to serve in the Indian Army with her name engraved on his sword – an inscription which, on his marriage, he spent long hours unsuccessfully trying to efface. The girl also revelled in solitary walks in and around Edinburgh – to Portobello for before-breakfast bathes, to the rocks and sands of Cramond Beach, and to Newhaven.

(*Records*)[4] I went down to the pier at Newhaven one blowy, blustery day and stood watching the waves taking their mad run and leap over the end of the pier till it suddenly occurred to me that it would be delightful to be out among them. I stopped at a cottage on the outskirts of the fishing town (it was not much more than a village then) and knocked. Invited to come in, I did so, and there sat a woman, one of the very handsomest I ever saw, leisurely combing a magnificent curtain of fair hair that almost swept the ground. She was seated on a low stool, but looked tall as well as large, and her foam-fresh complexion and grey-green eyes might have become Venus Anadyomene herself, turned into a Scottish fishwife. 'Can you tell me of anyone who will take me out in a boat for a little while,' quoth I. She looked steadily at

[4] See Introduction, p. xiv.

me for a minute, and then answered laconically, 'Ay, my man and boy shall gang wi' ye.' A few lusty screams brought her husband and son forth and at her bidding they got a boat ready, and with me well covered with tarpaulins and rough dread-naughts of one sort and another, rowed out from the shore into the turmoil of the sea. A very little of the dancing I got now was enough for me, and, deadly sick, I besought to be taken home again, when the matronly Brunhilda received me with open-throated peals of laughter and then made me sit down till I had conquered my qualms and was able to walk back to Edinburgh. Before I went she showed me a heap of her children, too many, it seemed, to be counted; but as they lay in a mass on the floor, there may have seemed more arms and legs forming the radii of which a clump of curly heads was the centre, than there really were.

I often went back to visit my middle-aged Christie Johnstone, and more than once saw her and her fellow fish-women haul up the boats on their return after being out at sea. They all stood on the beach clamouring like a flock of seagulls, and, as a boat's keel rasped the shingles, rushed forward and seized it, while the men in their sea clothes, all dripping like huge Newfoundland dogs, jumped out and took their way to their several houses. Their stalwart partners, hauling all together at the rope, drew the boat up beyond watermark, and seized and sorted its freight of fish, and stalked off each with her own basket full, with which she trudged up to trade and chaffer with the 'gude wives' of the town, and bring back to the men the value of their work. It always seemed to me that these women had about as equal a share of the labour of life as the most zealous champion of the rights of their sex could desire.

I did not indulge in any more boating expeditions, but admired the sea from the pier and became familiar with all the spokes of the fish-wife's family wheel; at any rate enough to distinguish Jamie from Sandie, and Willie from Johnnie, and Maggie from Jeanie, and Ailsie from Lizzie, and was great friends with them all.

My happy year in Edinburgh ended, I returned to London where I found my parents much burdened with care about the affairs of the theatre which were rapidly falling into irretrievable embarrassment.

CHAPTER 3

Another Mrs. Siddons?
1829

It was in the autumn of 1829, my father being then absent on a
professional tour in Ireland, that my mother, coming in from
walking one day, threw herself into a chair and burst into tears.
She had been much depressed for some time and I begged her to
tell me the cause. 'Oh, it has come at last. Our property is to be
sold. I have seen that fine building all covered with placards and
bills of sale; the theatre must be closed and I know not how many
hundred poor people will be turned adrift without employment.'
I believe that the theatre employed regularly seven hundred
persons, without reckoning the great number of supernumeraries
hired by the night for any specially showy spectacle. Seized with
a sort of terror, like the Lady of Shallott, that 'the curse is come
upon me', I comforted my mother and, as soon as I left her, wrote
a most urgent entreaty to my father that he would allow me to act
for myself or seek employment as a governess, so as to relieve
him at once at least of the burden of my maintenance.

The next day my mother asked me whether I seriously thought
I had any talent for the stage. I could only answer that I had not
the slightest idea whether I had or not. She begged me to learn
some part and say it for her, and I chose Shakespeare's Portia –
then as now my ideal of a perfect woman. Having learnt it by
heart, I recited it to my mother whose only comment was, 'There
is hardly enough passion in this part to test any tragic power. I
wish you would study Juliet for me.' Study to me then and
unfortunately long afterward simply meant to learn by heart,
which I did again and repeated my lesson to my mother, who
again heard me without any observation whatever. Meanwhile
my father returned to town, and one morning my mother told me
she wished me to recite Juliet to him; and so in the evening I stood
up before them both and with indescribable trepidation repeated
my first lesson in tragedy.

They neither of them said anything beyond 'Very well – very
nice, my dear', with many kisses and caresses, from which I

25

escaped to sit on the stairs and get rid of my repressed nervous fear in floods of tears. A few days after this my father took me to the theatre to try whether my voice was of sufficient strength to fill the building. That strange looking place, the stage, with its racks of pasteboard and canvas – streets, forests, banqueting halls and dungeons – was empty and silent; not a soul was stirring in its mysterious depths which seemed to stretch indefinitely behind me. In front the great amphitheatre, equally empty and silent, would have been absolutely dark but for a long, thin shaft of light from far above me that alighted in a vivid spot of brightness on the stage. Set down in the midst of twilit space, as it were, with only my father's voice coming to me from where he stood hardly distinguishable in the gloom, my voice resounded through the great vault and, completely carried away by the inspiration of the wonderful play, I acted Juliet as I do not believe I ever acted it again, for I had no Romeo and no visible audience to thwart my imagination.

At least I had no consciousness of any, though in the back of one of the private boxes sat an old friend of my father's – a passionate lover of the stage and a first rate critic. Joining my father at the end of the performance he said, 'Bring her out at once; it will be a great success'. And so, three weeks from that time I was brought out and it was a 'great success'.

Three weeks was not much time for preparation of any sort for such an experiment – to become acquainted with my fellow actors and actresses, not one of whom I had ever spoken with or seen off the stage before; to learn all the technical business of the stage; how to carry myself towards the audience, how to concert my movements with the movements of those I was acting with while giving the greatest effect of which I was capable to my own.

I do not wonder, when I remember this brief apprenticeship to my profession, that Mr. Macready once said that I did not know the elements of it. Three weeks of morning rehearsals at the theatre, and evening consultations at home as to what I should wear as Juliet, how my hair should be dressed, etc. – in all of which I remained absolutely passive, taking no part and not much interest in the matter – ended in my mother's putting aside all suggestions of innovation like the adoption of the real picturesque costume of mediaeval Verona in favour of the traditional stage costume for the part, which was simply a dress of plain white satin with a long train, with short sleeves and a low body. My hair was dressed as I usually wore it. A girdle of fine paste brilliants and a small comb of the same were the only theatrical parts of the dress, which was as perfectly simple and as unlike anything Juliet ever wore as possible.

I have often admired the consummate good sense with which, confronting a whole array of authorities – historical, artistical, aesthetical – my mother stoutly maintained that nothing was to be adopted on the stage that was in itself ugly, ungraceful or even curiously antiquated, however correct it might be with reference to the particular period or even to authoritative portraits of individual characters of the play. The passions, actions and sufferings of human beings, she argued, were the main concern of a fine drama, not the clothes they wore.

It is very true that, as she said, Garrick acted Macbeth in a full court suit of scarlet: knee-breeches, powdered wig, pigtail and all; and Mrs. Siddons acted the *Grecian Daughter* in piles of powdered curls with a forest of feathers on top of them, high-heeled shoes and a portentous hoop, and both made the audiences believe they looked just as they should do. But for all that, actors and actresses who were neither Garrick nor Mrs. Siddons were not less like the parts they represented by being at least dressed as they should be. In later years, after I became the directress of my own stage costumes, I adopted one for Juliet which combined my mother's *sine qua non* of simplicity with a fashion in keeping with the supposed period of the play.

My frame of mind under the preparations for my début appears to me now curious enough. Though I had found out that I could act, my going on the stage was absolutely an act of duty, strengthened by my own conviction that I was bound to help my parents by every means in my power. The theatrical profession was, however, utterly distasteful to me, though *acting* itself was not; and every detail of my future vocation was more or less repugnant to me. Nor did custom ever render this aversion less; and liking my work so little and being so devoid of enthusiasm, respect or love for it, it is wonderful to me that I ever achieved any success in it at all.

This is the reason why, with an unusual gift and many unusual advantages, I really did so little; why my performances were always uneven in themselves, never complete as a whole, however striking in occasional parts, and never at the same level two nights together; depending for their effect upon the state of my nerves and spirits, instead of being the result of deliberate thought and consideration.

My father not acting Romeo with me (there were many objections to that) deprived me of the most poetical and graceful stage lover of his day; but the public, who had long been familiar with his rendering of the part of Romeo, gained as much as I lost by his taking that of Mercutio, which has never since been so admirably represented. It was not an easy matter to find a Romeo for me, but the part was eventually given to Mr. Abbott, an old-established favourite with the public, a very amiable and worthy man, old enough to have been my father, whose performance, not certainly of the highest order, was nevertheless not below inoffensive mediocrity. But the public, who were bent upon doing more than justice to me, were less than just to him, and the abuse showered upon his Romeo might have embittered his stage relations with me to the point of making me an object of detestation to him, all through our theatrical loves.

The report of my approaching appearance on the stage excited a good deal of interest among the acquaintances and friends of my family and occasioned a renewal of cordial relations which had ceased for some time between Sir Thomas Lawrence and my father and mother.

Lawrence's enthusiastic admiration for my Uncle John and Mrs. Siddons, testified by the numerous striking portraits in which he recorded their personal beauty and dramatic picturesqueness, led to a most intimate friendship between the great painter and the eminent actors, and subsequently to very painful circumstances which estranged him for years from all our family.

While frequenting Mrs. Siddons' house he proposed to her eldest daughter Sarah and was accepted by her. Before long, however, he became extremely and unaccountably wretched. Violent scenes of the most painful emotion took place between himself and Mrs. Siddons, to whom he finally confessed that he had mistaken his own feelings and that her younger daughter, not the elder, was the real object of his affection, and ended by imploring permission to transfer his addresses from the one to the other sister. Maria Siddons became engaged to her sister's faithless lover, but to neither of them was he destined to be united; they were both exceedingly delicate young women with a tendency to consumption. Maria extracted on her death-bed a promise from her sister that she would never become Lawrence's wife. The promise was given and she died, and had not long lain in her untimely grave when her sister was laid in it beside her.

It was many years after these events that Lawrence [now aged

60], meeting my father accidentally in the street, begged permission to come and see my mother and become acquainted with me. From then until his death but a few months later, he was unwearied in acts of affectionate kindness towards me. When in town he never omitted one of my performances,[1] invariably sending me the next morning a letter full of the most detailed and delicate criticism. I used to read over the latest of them before going to the theatre, in order to profit by every suggestion they contained; and I was in the act of reperusing the last I ever received from him when my father came in and said, 'Lawrence is dead.'

I had been sitting to him for some time for a pencil sketch: it was his last work and certainly the most beautiful of his drawings. His death, which was quite unexpected, created a very great public sensation, and there was something sufficiently mysterious about its circumstances to give rise to a report that he had committed suicide.

The shock of this event was terrible to me, although I have sometimes since thought that it was fortunate for me rather than otherwise. I was a very romantic girl, with a most excitable imagination, and such was to me the melancholy charm of Lawrence's countenance, the elegant distinction of his person, and exquisite refined gentleness of his voice and manner, that a very dangerous fascination was added to my sense of gratitude for all his personal kindness to me and my admiration for his genius, and I think it not at all unlikely that, had I sat to him for the projected portrait of Juliet, in spite of the forty years' difference in our ages and my knowledge of his disastrous relations with my cousins, I should have become in love with him myself. His sentimentality was of a peculiarly mischievous order, as it not only induced women to fall in love with him, but enabled him to persuade himself that he was in love with them, and apparently with more than one at a time.

All being in preparation for my coming out, my rehearsals were the only interruption to my usual habits of occupation. On the day of my first appearance I had no rehearsal for fear of over-fatigue and spent my morning as usual in practising the piano, walking in St. James' Park opposite our house and reading in

[1] Tom Moore, the Irish poet, saw Fanny play Belvidera on December 23, 1829: 'Fanny Kemble's acting clever but not touching. . . . Sir T. Lawrence in the orchestra, full of anxiety and delight, and I made it a point, whenever he looked my way, that he should see me clapping enthusiastically.' (*Journal*, p. 193.)

Blunt's Scripture Characters the chapters relating to St. Peter and
Jacob. I remember being quite absorbed by it, which I think was
curious because certainly such subjects were hardly allied to the
painful undertaking so immediately pressing upon me.

My mother, who had left the stage for upwards of twenty
years, determined to return to play Lady Capulet on the night of
my first appearance.[2] We drove to the theatre very early, indeed
while the late autumn sunlight yet shone into the carriage upon
me, and as I screened my eyes from it, my mother said, 'Heaven
smiles on you, my child'. She went to her dressing room to get
herself ready and did not return to me for fear of increasing my
agitation by her own. My dear aunt Dall, my maid and the theatre
dresser performed my toilet for me, and at length I was placed in
a chair, with my satin train carefully laid over the back of it; and
there I sat, ready for execution, with the palms of my hands
pressed convulsively together, and the tears I in vain endeavoured to repress brimming down over my rouged cheeks, upon
which my aunt renewed the colour as often as the heavy drops
made unsightly streaks in it.

At last, 'Miss Kemble is called for the stage!' started me upright
on my feet, and I was led round to the side scene opposite the one
from which I saw my mother advance upon the stage; and, while
the uproar of her reception filled me with terror, dear old Mrs.
Davenport, who was playing my Nurse, and dear Mr. Keely, her
Peter, and half the *dramatis personae* of the play – but not my
father, who had retreated, quite unable to endure the scene –
stood around me as I lay all but insensible in my aunt's arms.
'Courage, courage, poor thing, poor thing!' reiterated Mrs.
Davenport. 'Never mind 'em, Miss Kemble!' urged Keely, in that
irresistibly comical, nervous, lachrymose voice of his, 'Never
mind 'em! Don't think of 'em any more than if they were so many
rows of cabbages!'

[2] Marie-Thérèse Kemble's professional career had begun as Cupid at Drury
Lane at the age of six. She became a member of the company there in her teens,
working so hard that she was said almost to live in the theatre, playing Macheath
in *The Beggar's Opera*, Desdemona, Portia and other Shakespearian parts. After
her marriage in 1806 she joined Covent Garden, adding Ophelia and Beatrice to
her repertoire, acting in her own plays, and creating the part of mad Madge
Wildfire in Terry's *Heart of Midlothian*. In the light of so long and varied a career,
Joseph Knight's comment in the *DNB* in 1892 that 'she was an admirable actress of
chambermaids' seems a little unkind. Thackeray, however, thought her 'an
admirable actress . . . she had a beautiful figure, fine, large, dark eyes and
elevated features, fuller of spirit than softness, but still capable of expressing great
tenderness' (*Letters*, p. 135). She was 55 years old when she played Lady Capulet.

'Nurse!' called my mother, and on waddled Mrs. Davenport, and called in her turn, 'Juliet!' My aunt gave me an impulse forward and I ran straight across the stage, stunned by the tremendous shout that greeted me, my eyes covered with mist and the green baize flooring of the stage feeling as if it rose up against my feet, but I got hold of my mother and stood like a terrified creature at bay confronting the huge theatre full of gazing human beings. I do not think a word I uttered during this scene could have been audible; in the next, the ballroom, I began to forget myself; in the following one, the balcony scene, I had done so and, for aught I knew, I was Juliet – the passion I was uttering sending hot waves of blushes all over my neck and shoulders, while the poetry sounded like music to me as I spoke it, with no consciousness of anything before me, utterly transported into the imaginary existence of the play.

After this, I did not return into myself till all was over and, amid a tumultuous storm of applause, congratulations, tears, embraces and a general joyous explosion of unutterable relief at the fortunate termination of my attempt, we went home. I sat me down to supper that night with my poor, rejoicing parents well content with the issue of my trial; and still better pleased with a lovely little Geneva watch, the first I had ever possessed, all encrusted with gold work and jewels, which my father had laid by my plate and I immediately christened Romeo, and went, a blissful girl, to sleep with it under my pillow.

The eleventh-hour attempt to revive Covent Garden's fortunes by putting the twenty-year-old Fanny on the stage was, for a time at least, completely successful. London audiences had been Kemble fans for a generation: they were curious to see the family's latest recruit to the theatre, eager that she should make good and only too ready to applaud her. The battle was half won before she even set foot on the stage. The critics too were flattering: The Times, *for instance, said, 'Upon the whole we do not remember to have seen a more triumphant début'; and the* Athenaeum, *'The illusion that she was Shakespeare's own Juliet came so speedily as to suspend the power of specific criticism . . . in boldness and dignity she unquestionably approaches more nearly to Mrs. Siddons than any other actress of our time excepting Pasta.' Leigh Hunt alone remained sceptical. He was never to be converted from what he called his heresy with regard to Miss Kemble: 'We remember Mrs. Siddons,' he wrote two years later, 'and whenever we see her niece in the characters that she performed, we cannot help thinking her an inferior likeness of her, cut down and artificialised'.*[3]

James Street, December 14, 1829

Dearest Harriet. . . . My trial is over, and thank Heaven! most fortunately. Our most sanguine wishes could have hardly gone beyond the result, and at the same time that I hail my success as a source of great happiness to my dear father and mother, I almost venture to hope that the interest which has been excited in the public may tend to revive once more the decaying dramatic art. You say it is a very fascinating occupation; perhaps it is, though it does not appear to me to be so, and I think it carries with it drawbacks enough to operate as an antidote to the vanity and love of admiration it can hardly fail to foster. As to the mere excitement proceeding from the public applause of a theatre, I am sure you will believe me when I say I do not think I shall ever experience it. But should I reckon too much upon my own steadiness, I have the incessant care and watchfulness of my dear mother to rely on, both to the purity and good taste of all that I may do on the stage and the quiet and soberness of my mind under all this new excitement. She has borne all her anxieties wonderfully well, and I hope she will now reap some repayment for them. My dear father is very happy; indeed we have all cause for heartfelt thankfulness when we think what a light has dawned upon our prospect, lately so dismal and overcast. Dearest Harriet, I assure you that I have not embraced this course without due dread of its dangers, and a firm determination to watch, as far as in me lies, over its effect upon my mind.

(*Records*) I do not know whence I derived the deep impression I expressed in this letter of the moral dangers of the life upon which I was entering; certainly not from my parents, to whom of course the idea that actors and actresses could not be respectable people naturally did not occur; but the vapid vacuity of the last years of my aunt Siddons' life had made a profound impression upon me – her apparent deadness and indifference to everything which I attributed, unjustly perhaps, less to her advanced age and impaired powers than to what I supposed the withering influence of the overstimulating atmosphere of emotion, excitement and admiration in which she had passed her life. Certain it is that I added an earnest petition to my prayers that I might be

[3] *Dramatic Criticism*, p. 287.

defended from the evil influence I feared it might exercise upon me.

As for my success, there was, I believe, a genuine element in it; but there was also a great feeling of personal sympathy for my father and mother, of kindly indulgence for my youth, and of respectful recollection of my uncle and aunt; and a very general desire that the fine theatre where they had exercised their powers should be rescued, if possible, from its difficulties. All this went to make up a result of which I had the credit.

When I saw the shop windows full of Lawrence's sketch of me, and knew myself the subject of almost daily newspaper notices; when plates and saucers were brought to me with small figures of me as Juliet and Belvidera on them; and finally, when gentlemen showed me lovely buff-coloured neck-handkerchiefs which had, I thought, pretty lilac coloured flowers all over them, which proved on nearer inspection to be minute copies of Lawrence's head of me, I not unnaturally, in the fullness of my inexperience, believed in my own success.

I played Juliet upwards of a hundred and twenty times running, with all the unevenness and immature inequality of which I have spoken. My mother would sometimes come down from her box and, folding me in her arms, say only, 'Beautiful, my dear!' Quite as often, if not oftener, the verdict was: 'Your performance was not fit to be seen! You had better give the whole thing up at once than go on doing it so disgracefully ill.' This was awful and made my heart sink into my shoes, whatever might have been the fervour of applause with which the audience had greeted my performance.

My life now settled into its new shape. I acted regularly three times a week. I always dined in the middle of the day, and invariably on a mutton chop, so that I might have been a Harrow boy, for diet; I was taken early to the theatre by my aunt, and there in my dressing-room sat through the entire play, when I was not on the stage, with some piece of tapestry or needlework. When I was called for the stage, my aunt came with me, carrying my train that it might not sweep the dirty floor behind the scenes; she remained till I came off again, then gathering it on her arm and folding a shawl about me, escorted me back to my dressing room and tapestry; and so my theatrical evenings were passed. My parents would not allow me to go into the green room, where they thought my attention would be distracted, and where I might meet with undesirable associates. My salary was fixed at

thirty guineas a week, and the Saturday after I came out I presented myself for the first and last time at the treasury of the
theatre to receive it, and carried it clinking, with great triumph to
my mother, the first money I ever earned.[4]

[4] Equivalent in 1977 terms to something like £470.

CHAPTER 4

A Little Lion in Society
1829–1830

It would be difficult to imagine anything more radical than the change which three weeks had made in my life. From an insignificant school-girl, I had suddenly become an object of general public interest. I was a little lion in society and the town talk of the day. Approbation, admiration, adulation were showered upon me; every condition of my life had been altered as by the wand of a fairy. Instead of the twenty pounds a year which my father had squeezed out of his hard-earned income for my allowance, I now had an assured income of at least a thousand pounds a year; instead of trudging long distances through the London streets, I had an elegant carriage; I was allowed to take riding lessons and before long had a charming horse of my own and was able to afford the delight of giving my father one. The faded, threadbare, turned and dyed frocks were exchanged for fashionable dresses of fresh colours and fine texture in which I appeared to myself transfigured. Our door was besieged by visitors, our evenings bespoken by innumerable invitations, and every night that I did not act I might, if my parents had thought it prudent, have passed in all the gaiety of the fashionable world and the great London season.

Among the persons I used to see at the theatre was the Rev. Adolphus Fitzclarence, the natural son of William IV and Mrs. Jordan, and vicar of Maple Durham, who attended every one of my performances when I first came out. I encountered him one evening at a very gay ball. Almost as soon as I came into the room he rushed at me, exclaiming, 'Oh, do come and dance with me, there's a dear, good girl'. The 'dear, good girl' had not the slightest objection to dancing with anybody, dancing being then my predominant passion, and a chair a perfectly satisfactory partner if none other could be come by. While dancing, I was unpleasantly struck by the decidedly unreverent tone of my partner's remarks. Clergymen at that time danced without reproach, and I hope that, even in those days of dancing clerks, they did not often talk so much to match the tripping of the light

fantastic toe. My amazement reached its climax when Mr. Fitzclarence said, 'Who are you nodding and smiling to? Oh, your
father. You are very fond of him, an't you?' To my enthusiastic
reply in the affirmative, he said, 'Ah yes. Just so. I dare say you
are.' And then followed an expression of his filial disrespect for
the highest personage in the land, of such robust significance as
fairly took away my breath. I could only say, 'Mr. Fitzclarence, if
you do not change your style of conversation, I must sit down
and leave you to finish the dance alone.' He confounded himself
in repeated apologies and went on to tell me that he had not been
bred to the church and had the greatest disinclination to taking
orders; that he had been trained as a sailor, but that in consequence of the death of a brother, had been literally taken from
on board ship and compelled to go into the church. 'Don't you
think it's a hard case?' reiterated he. At length I suggested that,
since he had adopted the sacred calling, perhaps it would be
better if he conformed to it at least by outward decency of language and decorum of behaviour. To this his assented, adding
with a sigh, 'But, you see, some people have a natural turn for
religion. You have, I'm sure, but you see I have not'. Presently he
asked me if I would write a sermon for him, which sent me into
fits of laughter, although I replied, 'Certainly not, you ought to
write your own!' 'Yes,' he said with a rather touching humility,
'but you see I can't, not good ones at least.'

Whenever now the virtues of the established Church system
are under discussion I try to forget this, and one or two similar
instances I have known of its vices in those days. But that was
near fifty years since and such a story as that of my poor sailor-
parson friend could hardly be told now. Nor could one often now
find the fellow of another friend, also the predestined incumbent
of a family living. He was passionately fond of hunting; and,
clinging to his beloved 'pink' even after holy orders had made it
rather indecorous wear, used to huddle on his sacred garments of
office at week-day funerals or marriages, and afterwards divest
himself of his holy robes and bloom forth in unmitigated scarlet
and buckskins, while the temporary cloud of sanctity which had
obscured them was rapidly rolled into the vestry.[1]

[1] Fanny may have considered such behaviour impossible when she wrote this
in the 1870s. Yet, more than a hundred years later, in October 1976, a television
documentary on the Church of England showed an identical scene to the one here
described, with the single exception that the parson's hunting coat was not scarlet
but black.

For some time after my first coming out I lost my sleep entirely and used to lie awake the greater part of the night. With more use of my new profession this nervous wakefulness wore off; but I was subject to frequent and severe pains in the side which any strong emotion invariably brought on, and which were relieved by nothing but exercise on horseback.

My riding master was the best and most popular in London – Captain Fozzard, or, as he was irreverently called among his young Amazons, 'Old Fozzard'. His methods were so good that all the best lady riders in London were his pupils. His training was eminently calculated to make us all but immovable in the saddle – without stirrup, without holding the reins, with our arms behind us, to go through plunging, rearing and kicking lessons and to take our horses over the bar was a considerable test of a firm seat. In all these special feats I became proficient.

One day a little door under the gallery opened and Fozzard appeared, introducing a middle-aged lady and a young girl, who remained standing there while he put me through all my most crucial exercises. I was always delighted to go through these feats, which amused me excessively and in which I took great pride. So I sat through them all until Fozzard with extreme deference escorted the visitors forth. Returning to dismount me, he informed me that I had given a very satisfactory sample of his teaching to the Duchess of Kent and Princess Victoria who was to be placed under his tuition forthwith.

James Street, Saturday, February 20th, 1830
Dearest Harriet. . . . I have been uncommonly gay for me this winter and I dare say shall continue to be so, as it does not disagree with me, and I am so fond of dancing that a quadrille renders palatable what otherwise would be disagreeable enough – the manner in which society is now organised. I was at a very large party the other night, at the poet Campbell's[2] where every material for a delightful evening – good rooms, pretty women, clever men – made what after all appeared to me nothing but a wearisome, hot crowd. The apartments were overfilled; to converse with anybody for five minutes was impossible. If one stood up one was squeezed to death; if one sat down one was stifled. I too (who was the small lioness of the evening) was stared at the whole night from head to foot. Moreover, a lady spilled some

[2] Thomas Campbell (1777–1844), author of *Ye Mariners of England*, *Lord Ullin's Daughter*, etc.

coffee over a beautiful dress I was wearing for the first time. Now I will tell you what consolations I had to support me: first the self-approving consciousness of the smiling fortitude with which I bore my gown's disaster; secondly, a lovely nosegay which was presented to me, and lastly, at about twelve o'clock, when the rooms were a little thinned, a dance which sent me home perfectly satisfied. By the by, I asked Campbell if he knew any method to preserve my flowers, to which he replied, 'Give them to me and I will immortalise them'. I did so, and am expecting some verses in return.

Along with all the unfamiliar excitements of riding, parties and encounters with celebrities, Fanny was taking the leading parts in half a dozen more plays besides Romeo and Juliet. *Learning them was no problem: in three hours she had by heart one of the longest female roles – Belvidera in Otway's* Venice Preserved. *Acting them was a different matter. Only Portia, 'my favouritest of all Shakespeare's women', pleased her. The others – Belvidera, Euphrasia in Murphy's* Grecian Daughter, *Mrs. Beverley in Moore's* Gamester *for instance – she considered artificial, insipid or plain trashy, a judgment seemingly born out by posterity. All these were parts made famous by Sarah Siddons, and Fanny was conscious that she, a young girl, could scarcely bring to such roles as Euphrasia the dramatic genius with which her aunt had 'clothed so meagre a part in such magnificent preparations'.*

There were consolations, not least her invariable delight in her costumes. Harriet was regaled with minute descriptions of them all: for her first scene as Portia she wore a magnificent dress copied from portraits by Titian and Veronese, her head was covered with diamonds ('not real', she hastened to add) and there were jewels in the roses on her shoes. And, though her distaste for the theatre remained as real as ever, she was beginning for the first time to consider the nature of her profession.

March 9th, 1830

It appears to me that the two indispensable elements of acting are a certain amount of poetical imagination and a power of assumption, which is a good deal the rarer gift of the two; in addition to these a sort of vigilant presence of mind is necessary, which constantly looks after and avoids the petty obstacles that are perpetually destroying the imaginary illusion and reminding one that one is not really Juliet or Belvidera. For instance, in the very last scene of Mrs. Beverley, while I was half dead with crying in the midst of *real* grief, created by an entirely *unreal* cause, I perceived that my tears were falling like rain all over my silk dress and spoiling it; and I calculated most accurately the space that my father would require to fall in and moved myself and my train accordingly in the midst of the anguish I was to feign and absolutely did endure. It is this watchful faculty which never deserts me while I am uttering all that exquisite passionate poetry in Juliet's balcony scene, while I feel as if my own soul is on my lips and my colour comes and goes with the intensity of the sentiment I am expressing, which prevents me from falling over my train, from setting fire to myself with the lamps placed close to me, from leaning upon my canvas balcony when I seem to throw myself all but over it.

In May 1830 Charles and Fanny Kemble set out on a provincial tour which took them to Bath, Edinburgh, Glasgow, Dublin, Liverpool, Manchester and Birmingham. Though Fanny did not complain, it must have been exhausting – long, dusty, bumpy travel by stage coach,[3] often mediocre inns and unfamiliar theatres where, as was the custom, they acted with resident local companies of frequently indifferent standard before audiences less disposed to be indulgent than her 'dear' London one. Still, there were many non-theatrical pleasures: visiting Loch Lomond when George IV's death gave them a welcome holiday; sight-seeing at country houses as well as iron foundries and cotton mills; staying once more with the dearly loved Aunt Siddons in Edinburgh and with Lord and Lady Wilton at Heaton Park near Manchester, and slipping away for a few days by the sea with Harriet at Ardgillan Castle. It was a happy and crowded four months.

Bath, May 31st, 1830
I had my first rehearsal here this morning. My fellow labourers amuse me a good deal; their versions of Shakespeare are very droll. My Romeo is one of my cousins [John Mason]; he has the family voice and manner very strongly, and at any rate does not murder the text of Shakespeare. I must tell you of an instance of provincial prudery (delicacy, I suppose I ought to call it) at rehearsal this morning: the Mercutio, on seeing the Nurse and Peter, called out, 'A sail, a sail!' and terminated the speech in a significant whisper which, being literally inaudible, my mother very innocently asked, 'Does the gentleman leave out the shirt

[3] The journey from London to Edinburgh in 1836, for instance, was scheduled to take 45½ hours. (W. T. Jackman, *Development of Public Transport in Modern England*, p. 685.)

and the smock?' upon which we were informed that 'body linen' was not so much as to be hinted at before a truly refined Bath audience. I am much afraid my father will shock them with the speech of that scamp Mercutio in all its pristine purity and precision.

Glasgow, Monday, June 28th, 1830

My dear Mrs. Jameson,[4] You will naturally expect me to say something of my theatrical experience in the modern Athens. Our houses in Edinburgh very fine, our audiences (as is their national nature) very cold; but upon the whole I believe they were well pleased with us, notwithstanding the damping influence of the newspapers which have all been unfavourable to me. The audiences' death-like stillness, as it afforded me neither rest or stimulus, distressed me a good deal, which the newspaper criticisms did not. But I have sufficient consolation in two notes of Sir Walter Scott's written to the editor of one of the papers, which the latter sent to me, and where he bears such testimony to my exertions as I do not care to transcribe, for fear my cheeks should reflect a lasting blush on my paper.

Among the delightful occurrences of last week I must record our breakfasting with Sir Walter Scott. I was wonderfully happy. The party was small: Sir Walter and his daughter Anne, his old friend Sir Adam Fergusson and Lady Fergusson and Miss Ferrier, the authoress of *Marriage* and *Inheritance*.

Sir Walter was most delightful, and I even forgot all awful sense of his celebrity in his kind and almost affectionate manner towards me. He told me several things that interested me very much; among others, his being present when, after much searching, the regalia of Scotland was found locked up in a room in Edinburgh Castle, where, as he said, the dust of centuries had accumulated upon it, and where the ashes of fires lit more than two hundred years before were still lying in the grate. He told me of a poor old lady, upwards of eighty years of age, who belonged to one of the great Jacobite families, sending to him to implore permission to see the Scottish crown but for one instant. I shall never forget his describing her, appearing for a moment petrified at the sight of it, and then tottering forward and falling on her knees, weeping and wailing over these poor remains of the

---

[4] Anna Jameson (1794–1860), the Irishwoman of whom Fanny had said that she hoped their acquaintance might develop into friendship. Her *Characteristics of Women* (1832), studies of Shakespeare's heroines, was dedicated to Fanny. The two corresponded for many years but never became close friends. Yet many years later, when Anna fell on hard times, Fanny sent £100 to help her.

royalty of her country, as if it had been the dead body of her child.

Sir Adam Fergusson is a delightful person, whose quick, bust-ling manner forms a striking contrast to Scott's quiet tone of voice and deliberate enunciation.

I have also made acquaintance with Jeffrey[5] who, I hear, com-plains piteously that I am not prettier. Indeed, I am very sorry for it and heartily wish I were; but I did not think him handsome either, though I don't care so much about his want of beauty as he seems to do about mine. But I am running on at a tremendous rate and quite forget that I have travelled upwards of forty miles today and that I promised my mother to go early to bed whenever I could.

(*Records*) Of the proverbial frigidity of the Edinburgh public I had been forewarned. Mrs. Harry Siddons had often told me of the intolerable sense of depression with which it affected Mrs. Sid-dons, who, she said, after some of her grandest outbursts of passion to which not a single expression of applause or sympathy had responded, would pant out in despair, under her breath, 'Stupid people, stupid people!'

I can never forget the description Sir Adam Fergusson gave me of a morning he had passed with Walter Scott at Abbotsford, which at that time was still unfinished and swarming with workmen. The room in which they sat was in the roughest condition; the raw, new chimney smoked intolerably. Out of doors the whole place was one chaos of bricks, mortar, tiles and slates. A heavy mist shrouded the landscape of lovely Tweedside and distilled in a cold persistent drizzle. Maida, the well-loved staghound, kept fidgeting in and out of the room, Sir Walter every five minutes exclaiming, 'Eh, Adam! the puir brute's just wearying to get out'; or 'Eh, Adam! the puir creature's just crying to come in.' Sir Adam would open the door to the raw air for the wet, muddy hound's exit or entrance; while Scott, with his face swollen with a grievous toothache and one hand pressed hard to his cheek, with the other was writing the inimitably humorous opening chapters of *The Antiquary*, which he passed across the table sheet by sheet to his friend, saying, 'Now Adam, d'ye think that'll do?'

When the Kembles were acting in Liverpool in August, 1830, the city was in the thick of preparations for the opening of the Liverpool and

[5] Francis Jeffrey (1773–1850), founder and editor of the *Edinburgh Review* and later Lord Advocate and judge of the Court of Session.

Manchester Railway the following month. Fanny counted herself fortunate to be invited for a trial run on this, the first inter-city passenger railway in the world; as she was later to write, it was 'the first mesh of that amazing iron net which now covers the whole surface of England and all the civilised portions of the earth'. She rode in the cab of one of the locomotives with George Stephenson himself, the north-country genius who had been the chief engineer of the new railroad.

Liverpool, August 26th.

My dearest Harriet, A common sheet of paper is enough for love, but a foolscap extra can alone contain a railroad and my ecstasies. . . . A party of sixteen persons was issued into a court-yard where stood several carriages one of which was prepared for our reception. It was a long-bodied vehicle with seats placed across it back to back. The wheels were placed upon two iron bands, which formed the road and to which they are fitted, being so constructed as to slide along without danger of becoming displaced. We were introduced to the little engine that was to drag us along the rails. She (for they make these curious little fire horses all mares) consisted of a boiler, a stove, a small platform, a bench, and behind it a barrel containing enough water to prevent her being thirsty for fifteen miles. She goes upon wheels, which are her feet and are moved by bright steel legs called pistons; these are propelled by steam, and in proportion as more steam is applied to the upper extremities (the hip-joints, I suppose) of these pistons, the faster they move the wheels; and when it is desirable to diminish the speed, the steam, which unless suffered to escape would burst the boiler, evaporates through a safety valve into the air. The reins, bit and bridle of this wonderful beast is a small steel handle, which applies or withdraws the steam from its legs or pistons, so that a child might manage it. The coals, which are its oats, are under the bench. This snorting little ani-mal, which I felt rather inclined to pat, was then harnessed to our carriage, and Mr. Stephenson having taken me on the bench of the engine with him, we started at about ten miles an hour.

The steam horse being ill adapted for going up and down hill, the road was kept at a certain level and appeared sometimes to sink below the surface of the earth and sometimes to rise above it. Almost at starting it was cut through the solid rock which formed a wall on either side of it, about sixty feet high. You can't imagine how strange it felt to be journeying thus without any visible cause of progress other than the magical machine, with its flying white breath and rhythmical, unvarying pace. After proceeding through this rocky defile, we presently found ourself raised upon embankments ten or twelve feet high; we then came to a moss, or swamp on which no foot could tread without sinking, and yet it bore the road which bore us.

We had now come fifteen miles and stopped where the road traversed a wide and deep valley. Stephenson made me alight and led me down to the bottom of this ravine, over which he has thrown a magnificent viaduct of nine arches, the middle one of which is seventy feet high. It was lovely and beautiful beyond words. He explained to me the whole construction of the steam-engine, and said he could soon make a famous engineer of me, which, considering the wonderful things he *has* achieved, I dare say is not impossible.

Now for a word or two about the master of these marvels, with whom I am horribly in love. He is a man of from fifty to fifty-five years of age; his face is fine though careworn and bears an expression of deep thoughtfulness; his mode of explaining his ideas is peculiar and very original, striking and forcible; and although his accent indicates strongly his north-country birth, his language has not the slightest touch of vulgarity or coarseness. He has certainly turned my head.

The Kembles were also present at the grand ceremonial opening of the new railway by the Duke of Wellington on September 15th. This, an occasion of lavish festivity, was thrown into disarray when William Huskisson, M.P. for Liverpool, former cabinet minister and staunch supporter of the railways against landowning and canal interests, was run down by Stephenson's 'Rocket' and fatally injured.

Manchester, September 20th, 1830

You will probably by this time have heard and read accounts of the opening of the railroad and the fearful accident which occurred at it, for the papers are full of nothing else. I will tell you something of the events of the 15th, as, though you may be acquainted with the circumstances of poor Mr. Huskisson's death, none but an eye-witness of the whole scene can form a conception of it.

We started to the number of about eight hundred people. The most intense curiosity and excitement prevailed, and though the weather was uncertain, enormous masses of densely packed people lined the road, shouting and waving hats and handkerchiefs as we flew by them. What with the sight and sound of these cheering multitudes and the tremendous velocity with which we were borne past them, my spirits rose to the true champagne height, and I never enjoyed anything so much as the first hour of our progress. My ecstasy was considerably damped by finding that my mother was frightened to death and intent upon nothing but devising means of escaping from a situation which appeared to her to threaten with instant annihilation herself and all her travelling companions. While I was chewing the cud of this disappointment a man flew by us calling out through a speaking trumpet to stop the engine, for that somebody in the directors' carriage had sustained an injury. We were all stopped accordingly and presently a hundred voices were heard exclaiming that Mr. Huskisson was killed.

From Lady Wilton, who was within three yards of the spot where the accident happened, I had the following details, the horror of which we were spared from witnessing. The engine had stopped to take in a supply of water, and several of the gentlemen had jumped out to look about them. Lord Wilton and Mr. Huskisson among the rest were standing talking in the middle of the road, when an engine on the other line, which was parading up and down merely to show its speed, was seen coming down upon them like lightning. The most active of those in peril sprang back into their seats, while poor Mr. Huskisson, less active from the effects of age and ill-health, bewildered too by the frantic cries of 'Stop the engine!' 'Clear the track!', completely lost his head and was instantaneously prostrated by the fatal machine, which dashed down like a thunder-bolt upon him, and passed over his leg, smashing and mangling it in the most horrible way. Lady Wilton said she distinctly heard the crushing of the bone. So terrible was the effect of the appalling accident that, except that ghastly 'crushing' and poor Mrs. Huskisson's piercing shriek, not a sound was heard nor a word uttered. Lord Wilton was the first to raise the poor sufferer and tied up the severed artery, and for a time at least prevented death by loss of blood. Mr. Huskisson was then placed in a carriage with his wife and Lord Wilton, and the engine, having been detached from the directors' carriage, conveyed them to Manchester.

So great was the shock that the Duke of Wellington declared his intention not to proceed, but to return immediately to Liverpool. However, on its being represented to him that the whole population of Manchester had turned out to witness the procession and that a disappointment might give rise to riots and disturbances, he consented to go on, and gloomily enough the rest of the journey was accomplished.

As we neared Manchester, the sky grew cloudy and dark and it began to rain. The vast concourse of people who had assembled to witness the triumphant arrival of the travellers was of the lowest order of mechanics and artisans, among whom great distress and a dangerous spirit of discontent with the Government prevailed. Groans and hisses greeted the carriage, full of influential personages, in which the Duke of Wellington sat. High above the grim and grimy crowd of scowling faces a loom had been erected, at which sat a tattered, starved-looking weaver, evidently set there to protest against this triumph of machinery and the gain and glory which the wealthy Liverpool and Manchester men were likely to derive from it. The contrast between our departure from Liverpool and our arrival at Manchester was one of the most striking things I ever witnessed.

We had intended returning to Liverpool, but Lady Wilton persuaded us to accompany her home, which we gladly did. Lord Wilton did not return till past ten o'clock, at which hour he brought the intelligence of Mr. Huskisson's death.

I need not tell you of the sort of whispering awe which this event threw over our whole circle; and yet, great as was the horror excited by it, I could not help feeling how evanescent the effect of it was after all. By the next day the occurrence became a subject of earnest but free discussion, and after that was alluded to with almost as little apparent feeling as if it had not passed under our eyes, and within the space of a few hours.

CHAPTER 5

Established Actress
1830–1832

A month later, in October 1830, the Kembles were back in London for the start of Fanny's second season, living now in the former home of John Kemble in Great Russell Street, soon to be taken over to make way for extensions to the British Museum.

Twenty-one and brimful of energy, Fanny allowed her social engagements to interfere no more than strictly necessary with rehearsals, fittings and performances. During the following spring, amateur theatricals at the home of Lord and Lady Francis Egerton proved time-consuming but enjoyable: they brought her 'a lasting friendship and an ephemeral love. The whole thing amused me very much and, mixed up with an element of real and serious interest, kept up the atmosphere of nervous excitement in which I was plunged from morning till night.' Fanny's account of her next two years is largely a catalogue of balls and dinner parties and famous names. Yet there were many serious anxieties underlying the constant round of pleasure, and it is these, rather than the socialising, which this chapter aims to reflect.

The love affair that Fanny hinted at came to nothing but made her deeply unhappy.

Both the Kemble boys were at this time causing concern. The younger, Henry, refused to settle down to a job and John, the older, had disappeared to Spain. 'He is a radical, a utilitarian,' Fanny had written to Harriet two years earlier, 'an advocate of vote by ballot, an opponent of hereditary aristocracy, the church establishment, the army and the navy which he deems sources of unnecessary expense.' Now he had become involved, with his Cambridge friends, John Sterling, John Boyd, Richard Trench, Tennyson and Hallam, in an idealistic but abortive plot to help the exiled leader of the Spanish liberals, General Torrijos, to overthrow the despotic King Ferdinand VII. Tennyson and Hallam, however, got no nearer to Spain than the French Pyrenees.

Great Russell Street, November 8th, 1830

Dearest Harriet. . . . I have heard nothing from my brother; *of* him I have heard. He is at the moment in Spain, trying to levy troops for the cause of the constitutionalists. I need not tell you how much I regret this. I might have thought any young man Quixotic who thus mistook a restless, turbulent spirit eager to embrace a quarrel not his own for patriotism and devotion to a sacred cause; but in my brother, who had professed aims and purposes opposed to tumult and war and bloodshed, it seems to me a subject of much more serious regret. Heaven only knows what plans he has for the future! His present situation affords anxiety enough, but even if the present be regarded with the best hope of success in his undertaking, the natural consideration must be, 'What follows?' It is a melancholy consideration that such abilities should be wasted and misapplied.

Our own country is in a perilous state of excitement, and these troubled times make politicians of us all. Of course the papers will have informed you of the risings in Kent and Sussex; London itself is in an unquiet state that suggests the heaving of a volcano before eruption. It is said that Wellington must resign; I am ignorant, but it appears to me that whenever he does it will be a bad day's work for England. The alarm and anxiety of the aristocracy is extreme and exhibits itself, even as I have observed in society, in the half-angry, half-frightened tone of their comments on public events. If one did not sympathise with their apprehensions, their mode of expressing them would sometimes be amusing.

The aspect of public affairs is injurious to the theatre, and these graver interests thin our houses while they crowd the Houses of Parliament. However, when we played the *Provoked Husband* before the King and Queen the other night, the theatre was crammed from floor to ceiling and presented a most beautiful *coup d'oeil*.

January 9th, 1831

Mr. Barton, a friend of John's whose sister has lately married John Sterling, called here the other day and told us of the very begin-ning of this Spanish expedition and of the share Mr. Sterling and Richard Trench[1] had in its launching.

It seems that they were plentifully supplied with funds[2] with which they purchased and manned a vessel destined to carry arms and ammunition to Spain for the revolutionists. This ship they put under the command of an experienced smuggler, and it

---

[1] Richard Chenevix Trench (1807–1886), later Archbishop of Dublin.

[2] £5,000 was provided by Sterling's cousin, John Boyd, who had recently thrown up a commission in the Indian Army. Torrijos had promised him a colonelcy in the Spanish army if the insurrection was successful.

was actually leaving the Thames with Sterling and Mr. Trench on board, bound for Spain, when by order of Lord Aberdeen it was stopped. Our two young gentlemen jumped into a boat and made their escape, but Mr. Sterling, hearing that government threatened to proceed against the captain, came forward and owned it as his property and exonerated the man as far as he could from any share of the blame. Matters were in this state, with a prosecution pending, when the ministry was changed, and nothing further has been done or said by government since.

My brother had gone off to Gibraltar previously to take measures for facilitating their landing; he is now quietly and I hope comfortably wintering there. Torrijos, it seems, is not at all disheartened, but is waiting for the propitious moment, which however, from the appearance of things, I should not consider to be at hand just yet.

February 7th, 1831

I have heard from my brother John and now expect almost hourly to see him. The Spanish revolution, as he now sees and as many foresaw, is a mere vision. The people are unready, unripe, unfit and therefore unwilling; it is as impossible to urge on the completion of such a change before the time as to oppose it when the time is come. John now writes that, all hope of rousing the Spaniards being over and their party consequently dispersing, he is thinking of bending his steps homewards.

Since I began this letter I have heard a report that John is a prisoner, that he has been arrested and sent to Madrid. Luckily I do not believe a word of this; if he has rendered himself obnoxious to the British authorities in Gibraltar, they may have locked him up for a week or two there, and I see no great harm in that; but that he should have been delivered to the Spaniards and sent to Madrid I do not believe, because I know that the whole revolutionary party is going to pieces and that they have neither the power nor the means to render themselves liable to such a disagreeable distinction.

At this worrying moment Charles Kemble was facing yet another threat to his theatre. Since the Restoration the two main London playhouses, Covent Garden and Drury Lane, had operated under Royal Patent, and their companies, known as 'His Majesty's Servants', were still the only ones permitted to perform the 'legitimate' drama. For some time the other theatres, hitherto limited to pre-

senting melodrama, pantomime, spectacle, burlesque and so on, had been increasingly vociferous in demanding an end to the monopoly. This was not to come about until 1843, but meanwhile the renewed agitation involved Kemble in yet another law suit and in giving evidence before a House of Commons Select Committee.

(*Records*) My father showed forth the evils likely, in his opinion, to result to the dramatic art and public taste by throwing open to unlimited speculation the right to establish theatres and give theatrical representations. The great companies of good, sterling actors would be broken up and dispersed; the best plays would no longer find adequate representatives in any but a few of the principal parts, the school of fine and careful acting would be lost, no play of Shakespeare's would be decorously put on the stage, and the profession and the public would alike fare the worse for the change. But he was one of the patented proprietors, one of the monopolists, a party most deeply interested in the issue, and therefore perhaps an incompetent judge in the matter. The cause went against us, and every item of his prophecy has undoubtedly come to pass. The profession was decidedly the worse for the change; I am not aware, however, that the general public have suffered much by it.

March 9th, 1831

Why are you not here to kiss and congratulate me? I am so proud and happy! Mr. Murray[3] has given me four hundred and fifty pounds for my play! Only think of it – was there ever such publishing munificence? My father has the face to say *it is not enough!* but looks so proud and pleased that his face alone shows it is *too much* by a great deal; my mother is enchanted and I am so happy, so surprised and charmed to think that what gave me nothing but pleasure in the doing has given me such profit; it is too good almost to be true. And yet it is true.

But I am happy and have been much excited for another reason today. Richard Trench, John's dear friend and companion, is just returned from Spain and came to see us. John is well and in good spirits. Mr. Trench, before leaving Gibraltar, had used every persuasion to induce my brother to return with him and had even got him on board the vessel in which they were to sail, but John's heart failed him at the thought of forsaking Torrijos and he went

[3] John Murray (1778–1843), Byron's friend and publisher. *Francis I* ran to ten editions in London and six in New York.

back. They had hired a house where they passed their time smoking and drinking ale, John holding forth upon German metaphysics, which grew dense in proportion as the tobacco fumes grew thick and his glass grew empty.[4]

Sunday, March 20th, 1831

I am sorry to say I shall not have a good benefit; unluckily the second reading of the Reform Bill comes on tomorrow and there will be as many people in the House of Commons as in *my* house and many more in Parliament Street than either; it is unfortunate for me, but it cannot be helped. The publication of my play is not to take place till after this Reform fever has a little abated.

Wednesday, April 27th.[5] The town is one blaze of rejoicing for the Reform Bill triumph; the streets are thronged with people and choked up with carriages and the air is flashing and crashing with rockets and squibs and crackers, to the great discomfort of the horses. So many *R's* everywhere that they may stand for reform, revolution, ruin according to the interpretation of every individual's politics; the most general acceptation in which they will be taken by the popular understanding will assuredly be *row*.

May 29th

The Reform Bill, modified as it now is, has my best prayers and wishes, for to say that the removal of certain abuses will not give the people the bread they expect is nothing against it; but at the same time as I sincerely hope this measure will be carried, I cannot conceive what government will do *next*, for though trade is prosperous, great poverty and discontent exist among large classes of the people, and as soon as these needy people find out that Reform is not really immediate, they will seek something else which it may be difficult to give them. Party spirit here has reached a tremendous pitch; old friendships are broken up and

[4] John Kemble and his friends were members of the élitist Cambridge society known as the 'Apostles', which met behind locked doors on Saturday evenings to discuss such subjects as the origins of evil and the derivation of moral sentiments. Tennyson would say little, Hallam a great deal, and 'Jack Kemble would announce that the world was one great thought "and he was thinking it".' (Harold Nicolson, *Tennyson*, p. 74).

General Torrijos and 52 of his fellow revolutionaries including John Boyd (who had put up the money for the boat) were executed by firing squad in Malaga on March 21, 1831. John Kemble returned to England in May of that year. He was to become a noted Anglo-Saxon scholar.

[5] This and subsequent passages preceded by the day and date of the month are taken from the diary Fanny had started keeping a couple of months previously.

old intimacies cease; former cordial acquaintances refuse to meet
and the dearest relations are disturbed, if not destroyed. Society
is become a sort of battlefield, for every man (and woman too) is
nothing if not political.

Tuesday, June 2nd. My mother had a visit from a lady who
interested me immensely by her account of Mrs. Fry's[6] visits to
Newgate Prison. What a blessed, happy woman to do so much
good; to be the means of comfort and consolation, perhaps of
salvation, to such desolate souls! How I did honour and love
what I heard of her.

(*Records*) I had the great honour of accompanying Mrs.
Fry on one of her visits to Newgate, but received a rather painful
impression instead of the very different one I had anticipated.
Her divine labour of love had become famous and fine ladies of
fashion pressed eagerly to be present at the Newgate exhortations. The unfortunate women she addressed were ranged
opposite their less excusable sisters of the better class, and I
hardly dared to look at them, so entirely did I feel out of place at
the side of Mrs. Fry and so sick for their degraded attitude and
position. If I had been alone with them and their noble teacher I
would assuredly have sat down among them. On the day I was
there a poor creature sat in the midst of the congregation attired
differently from all the others, who was pointed out to me as
being under sentence of transportation. Altogether I felt broken
hearted for *them* and ashamed for *us*.

Wednesday, June 8th. While I was writing to Harriet my mother
came and told me Mrs. Siddons is dead. I was not surprised; she
had been ill and gradually failing for so long. I could not be much
grieved, for of course I had but little intercourse with her, though
she was always very kind to me. She died at eight o'clock this
morning, peaceable and without suffering, and in full consciousness.

*The Kembles' summer provincial tour in 1831 took in Bristol, Exeter,
Plymouth, Weymouth, Portsmouth and Southampton. It formed a
pleasantly peaceful and reasonably lucrative interlude, with no greater
excitements than one or two excessively hot and dusty stage coach
journeys, a boat trip to the Plymouth breakwater ruined by rough seas*

[6] Elizabeth Fry (1780–1845), Quaker and prison reformer. Her association for
the improvement of women prisoners at Newgate was formed in 1817.

*and torrential rain, the manager of one theatre being briefly impris-
oned for debt, and one local company producing* Romeo and Juliet *in
an 'improved version; sundry wicked words were decorously dispensed
with, many fine passages received judicious additions and not a few
others were equally judiciously omitted altogether. What a shocking
hash!' Back in London, the dark clouds settled closer over Covent
Garden, and Charles Kemble, 'worried to death with anxiety, vexation and hard work', fell dangerously ill.*

Monday, November 30th. I went to rehearsal. It seems that the
managers and proprietors (of course not my poor father) had
summoned a meeting of all the actors to try and induce them to
accept for the present a reduced rate of of salary until the theatre
can in some measure be relieved of its most pressing difficulties. I
knew nothing of this and, finding them all very solemnly assembled in the green room, asked them cheerfully why they were all
there, which must have struck them strangely enough. I dare say
they do not know how little I know, or wish to know, about this
disastrous concern.

On my return home I heard that Dr. Watson had seen my
father and requested that Dr. Wilson be sent for. They fear
inflammation of the lungs. He has gone to the very limit of his
tether, for had he continued fagging a night or two longer, the
effects might have been fatal. Poor, poor father! In the evening I
helped my mother to move all the furniture, which I think is
nothing in the world but a restless indication of her anxiety; it is
the fourth time since she came back from the country.

Tuesday, December 1st. It seems that in the arrangement, whatever
it may be, between the actors and the management, Mr. Harley
and Mr. Egerton are the only ones who declined the accommodation. Young has behaved like an angel, offering to play for
nothing till Christmas. All the others have been as considerate
and generous as possible. But the thing is doomed and will go to
the ground, in spite of every effort that can be made to stave the
ruin off.

Tuesday, 6th. My father is much worse. Dall met me on the stairs
this morning and gave a miserable account of him; he had just
been bled and that had somewhat relieved him. I sat with him
while my mother drove out in the carriage and he seemed a little
better.

Saturday, 10th. My poor mother is in the deepest distress about my father. It seems he is spitting blood. I felt as if I were turning to stone when I heard it. I came up to my room and cried most bitterly for a long time.

Great Russell Street, December 18th, 1831
Dear Harriet. . . . My father, thank God, is once more recovering, but we have twice been alarmed at such sudden relapses that we hardly dare venture to hope he is really convalescent. He has not yet left his bed, to which he has been confined for nearly a month. The exertion I have been obliged to make when leaving him to go and act was so full of misery and dread lest I should find him worse, perhaps dead, on my return, that no words can describe what I have suffered at that dreadful theatre.

Wednesday, 28th. My dear, dear father came down to breakfast, looking most miserably thin. Monday week he talks of resuming his work again as Mercutio. It is now determined that Henry should go into the army.

In the evening, not having to be anybody tragical or heroical, I indulged in my own character and had a regular game of romps with the boys [her brothers John and Henry]; my pensive public would not have believed its eyes if it could have seen me with my hair all dishevelled, not because of my woes, but because of riotous fun, jumping over chairs and sofas and dodging behind curtains and under tables to escape from my pursuers.

December 29th, 1831
I have some hope of obtaining a commission for Henry. Sir John Macdonald, at whose house you dined in the summer with my mother, is now Adjutant General, and I know not what besides; and after my mother and I had expended all our eloquence in winding up my father's mind to resolve upon the army as Henry's profession, she thought the next best thing I could do would be to attack Lady Macdonald and secure the General's interest. She is extremely kind and good natured and I am sure will exert herself to serve us, and if this can be accomplished I shall be haunted by one anxiety the less.

Henry is too young and too handsome to be doing nothing but lounging about the streets of London, and even if he should be ordered to the Indies, it is something to feel that he is no longer objectless in life – a mere squanderer of time, without interest, stake or duty in this existence.

(*Records*) Henry had had a passionate desire to be a sailor, and on one occasion Admiral Lake, a friend of my parents, offered to have him trained for his profession under his own supervision. Such, however, was my mother's horror of the sea and dread of losing her darling, that she induced my father to decline this most advantageous offer. Henry never after that exhibited the slightest preference for any other profession and always said, 'They may put me at a plough-tail if they like.' Finally, it was decided that he should go into the army, and my mother, unable to refuse her consent to this second favourable opportunity, was well content to see her boy-ensign sent over with his troops to Ireland. But from Ireland his regiment was ordered to the West Indies, and she never saw him again in her life.

Saturday, 4th January, 1832. My play *Francis I* is to be brought out at Covent Garden. I received official notice that it was to be read in the green room today. I felt very uncomfortable and awkward; but after all, writing a play is not a sin, so I plucked up my courage and sat down with the rest of the actors. My father read it beautifully, but even cut as it is, it is of an *endurable* length. They were all very kind and civil and applauded it very much. Driving to the theatre at half past five, my father told me that they had entirely altered the cast from what I had appointed and determined to finish the play with the fourth act. I felt myself get very red, but I didn't speak, though I cannot but think an author has the right to say whether he or she will have certain alterations made in their work. My position is a difficult one, for did I not feel bound to comply with my father's wishes, I would have no hand in this experiment. I would forfeit fifty – nay, a hundred – pounds willingly rather than act in this play which I am convinced ought not to be acted at all.

February 24th, 1832
Dearest Harriet. . . . I am greatly worried and annoyed about my play. The more I see and hear of it the stronger my perception grows of its defects which, I think, are rendered even more glaring by the curtailments and alterations necessary for its representation, and the whole thing distresses me as much as a thing can.

Saturday 25th. Finished Fenimore Cooper's interesting and pathetic novel, *The Borderers*. I came down into the drawing room with a headache, a sideache and swollen red eyes, and my mother greeted me with the news that the theatre was finally ruined, that at Easter it must close, that we must all go different ways, and I probably to America. I was sobered from my imaginary sorrow directly; I could not answer my mother, but I went to the window and looked up and down the streets that were getting empty and dark and silent, and my heart sank as I thought of leaving my home, my England.

It is very hard and sad to be come so far into age as my father is, without any hope of support for himself and my mother but toil and that of the severest kind; but God is merciful. He has hitherto cared for us as He cares for all His creatures, and He will not forsake us if we do not forsake Him or ourselves. My father and I need scarcely remain without engagements either in London or the provinces. If our salaries are smaller, so must our expenses be. The house must go, the carriage must go, the horse must go, and yet we may be sufficiently comfortable and very happy, unless indeed we have to go to America, and that will be dreadful. We are all stout and strong and we are yet together. It is pitiful to see how my father still clings to that theatre. Even today, after summing up all the sorrow and care and toil, the waste of life and fortune which that concern has cost his brother, himself and all of us, he exclaimed, 'Oh, if I had but £10,000 I could set it all right again, even now!' My mother and I actually stared at this infatuation. If I had twenty, or a hundred thousand pounds, not one farthing would I give to redeeming that fatal millstone which will infallibly drag everything tied to it down to the level of its own destruction.

Saturday, 3rd March. Henry has obtained his commission, one great piece of good fortune amid all the bad.[7]

(*Records*) The liberal price given me by Mr. Murray for *Francis I* enabled me to purchase my brother's commission, which however the money would not have obtained without the extremely kind interest exerted in his favour by Lord Hill, then Commander, and Sir John Macdonald.

[7] The commission did not cure Henry's fecklessness. In 1880 Fanny told Henry James how, as a young, penniless, luxury loving ensign, he had become engaged to a 'dull, plain, commonplace heiress'. Though threatened with disinheritance,

Tuesday, 6th. After breakfast went with Henry and my father to Cox and Greenwood's, the great army agents, to pay for his commission. Oh, what a good job, to be sure! Then to the Horse Guards, to thank dear Sir John Macdonald, and then home, much happier than I have been for a long time.

> *In the spring of 1832, with the Kembles' future still undecided and rehearsals under way for two new productions at Covent Garden, Fanny became too busy and preoccupied to continue her Journal; nor were there any letters to Harriet.*

(*Records*) My friend Miss St. Leger came and paid me a long visit, during which my play, *Francis I*, and Knowles' *Hunchback* were produced, and it was finally settled that Covent Garden should be let to the French manager and entrepreneur, Laporte, and that my father and myself should go for two years to America.

The success of *Francis I* was one of entirely indulgent forbearance on the part of the public. An historical play, written by a girl of seventeen, and acted in it by the authoress at one-and-twenty was, not unnaturally, a subject of some curiosity, and as such it filled the house for a few nights. Its entire want of real merit made it impossible that it should do anything more; and after a few representations it made way for Knowles' delightful play which had a success as great and genuine as it was well deserved.

Thursday, 14th June. A long break in my journal, and what a dismal beginning to it again! At five o'clock Harriet started for Ireland. When I returned after seeing her off, I went disconsolately to my own room. As I could not sleep, I took up the first book at hand, but it was *Tristram Shandy* and too horribly discordant with my frame of mind; besides I don't like it at any time; it seems to me much more coarse even than witty and humorous.

Saturday 16th. Alfred Tennyson dined with us. I am always a little disappointed with the exterior of our poet in spite of his eyes,

she remained determined to marry him in spite of Fanny's firm advice to the contrary. He, on the other hand, realising that the threat was in earnest, walked out on the young lady. In due course she came into her fortune, and after some ten years abroad, Henry returned to find her still unmarried, proposed again and was refused, although she still cared for him. The story gave James the idea for *Washington Square*. (Matthiessen and Murdock, *Notebooks of Henry James*, p. 12.)

which are very fine; but his head and face, striking and dignified as they are, are almost too ponderous and massive for beauty in so young a man, and every now and then there is a sarcastic expression about his mouth that almost frightens me, in spite of his shy manner and habitual silence. But after all, it is delightful to see and be with any one that one admires and loves for what he has done, as I do him.

Thursday, 21st. At the theatre in the evening, the house was good and I played very well. How sorry I shall be to go away! The actors too all seem so sorry to have us go, and it will be hard to see none of the accustomed faces, to hear none of the familiar voices, while discharging the tasks that are often so irksome to me.

Friday, 22nd. At the end of the play Mr. Bartley [the stage manager] made the audience a speech, mentioning our departure and bespeaking their goodwill for the new management. The audience called for Knowles and then clamoured for us till we were obliged to go out. They rose to receive us, and waved their hats and handkerchiefs and shouted farewell to us. It made my heart ache to leave my kind, good, indulgent audience; my friends, as I feel them to be, my countrymen, English folk; and as I thought of the strangers for whom I am now to work in that distant strange country to which we are going, the tears rushed into my eyes. I scarcely think I made even the conventional courtesy of leave-taking to them, but I snatched my little nosegay of flowers from my sash and threw it into the pit with handfuls of kisses, as a farewell token of my affection and gratitude. And so my father, who was very much affected, led me off, while the house rang with cheering. I took an affectionate farewell of poor dear Rye, the property man, and his boy Louis gave me two beautiful nosegays. It was all wretched, and yet it was a pleasure to feel that those who were dependent on us cared for us. I know all the servants and workpeople of the theatre were fond of me; and it was sad to say goodbye to all these kind, civil, cordial, humble friends – from my good, pretty little maid, who stood sobbing by my dressing room door, to the grim wrinkled visage of honest old Rye.

(*Records*) That was the last time I ever acted in the Covent Garden my uncle John built; where he and my aunt Mrs. Siddons took leave of the stage and I made my first entrance upon it. It was soon after altered and enlarged and turned into an opera house; eventually it was burnt down, and so nothing remains of it.

August 1st. Sailed for America.

CHAPTER 6

First View of New York
1832

S.S. Pacific, Off Sandy Hook, Monday September 3rd, 1832
My dearest Harriet, . . . Here we are within three hours sail of
New York, but we are becalmed and the sun shines so bright and
the air is so warm and breathless that we seem to have every
chance of lying here for the next – Heaven knows how long! In
point of time our voyage has been very prosperous, though the
weather has been squally, with constant head winds. I do not
think we have had in all six days of fair wind, so that we have no
reason whatever to complain of our advance, having come thus
far in thirty-two days.

I have been called away from this letter by one of those little
incidents which Heaven in its mercy sends to break the monotony of a sea voyage. Ever since day-break this morning an
English brig has been standing at a considerable distance behind
us. About an hour ago we went up to watch a boat which they
were sending off in our direction. The distance was about five
miles, and the men had a hard pull in the broiling heat. The ship
was a merchantman from Bristol, bound to New York; she had
been out eleven weeks and provisions were beginning to run
short. Our captain furnished them with flour, tea, sugar, porter,
cold tongue, ham, eggs, etc. As the men were remanning their
boat, we saw a whole cargo of eatables carried to it from our
steerage passengers. You know that these are always poor people
who are often barely supplied themselves with necessaries for
their voyage. The poor are almost invariably kind and com-
passionate to one another.

The men from the brig gave us news from Halifax, where they
had put in. The cholera has been in Boston, Philadelphia, Baltimore and New York; the latter town was almost deserted, and
the people flying in numbers from the others.

My father, though a bad sailor and suffering occasionally a
good deal, has, upon the whole, borne the voyage well. Poor dear
Dall has been the greatest wretch on board; she has been perfectly

miserable the whole time. It made me very unhappy, for she has come away from those she loves dearly on my account and I cannot but help feeling sad to see that excellent creature now, in what should be the quiet time of life, leaving home and all its accustomed ways and habits.

We have seen an American sun and an American moon and American stars, and we think 'they get these things up better than we do'. We have had several fresh squalls and one heavy gale; we have shipped sundry seas; we have had rat-hunting and harpooning of porpoises; we have caught several hake and dog-fish.

New York, America, September 5th, 1832

Here we really are, dear Harriet. We made New York harbour Monday night at sunset and cast anchor at twelve o'clock off Staten Island, where we lay till yesterday morning, when a steamboat came alongside to take the passengers to the shore. A thick fog covered the shores and the rain poured in torrents. The town, as we drove through it, struck me as foreign in its appearance – continental, I mean; trees are mixed with the houses which are painted various colours and have green blinds on the outside, giving an idea of coolness and shade. Our hotel is pleasantly situated and our rooms gay and large. The cholera has been very bad, but it is subsiding and the people are returning to town. We shall begin our work in about ten days.

For the whole of the American tour which was to – and in fact did – restore the Kemble family fortunes, Fanny wrote her journal more assiduously than ever. Fascinated by the new world, she daily recorded each and every novel sight and experience, some pleasing, others distasteful. Her record of these two years, which ended with the death of aunt Dall, her marriage and her father's return to England, was the only part of her journal to be published until her old age; and when it appeared in 1835 it caused some offence among those who had welcomed her and her father with open arms, even though the manuscript had been heavily edited and all proper names replaced by dashes. Moreover the general public, always sensitive to any criticism from the British, had been incensed by Frances Trollope's recently published disparaging Domestic Manners of the Americans, *and was not inclined to take kindly to further animadversions from yet another foreign Fanny. In fact, most of Fanny Kemble's strictures were no more than the brash and superficial reactions of a homesick young woman unused to the more free and easy manners of Americans and*

*convinced that they ordered these matters better in England.
Nevertheless she found much that delighted her in this unfamiliar
society and 'this lovely land'.*

Wednesday, September 5th 1832. I have been in a sulky fit half the
day because people will keep walking in and out of our room,
without leave or licence. When I made my appearance in my
dressing gown (my clothes not being come, and the day too hot
for a silk pelisse), great was my amazement to find our whole
ship's company at the table. At half past two we walked down to
the quay to convey them to their steamboat for Boston. We bade
them good-bye and walked briskly on to the battery, which is a
beautiful marine parade, commanding the harbour and entrance
to the bay. A sort of public promenade, formed of grass plots
planted with a variety of trees, it affords a very agreeable position
from whence to enjoy the lovely view. My companion informed
me that this was a fashionable resort some time ago; but owing to
its being frequented by the lowest and dirtiest of the rabble, who
in this land of liberty roll themselves on the grass and otherwise
annoy the more respectable portion of the promenaders, it has
been much deserted lately. The trees and grass were vividly
green, but the latter grew rank and long. 'Oh', I thought, 'for a
pair of English shears, to make these carpets as smooth and thick
as close-piled Genoa velvet.' Came home up Broadway, which is
a long street of tolerable width, full of shops, where all people go
to exhibit themselves and examine others. The women that I have
seen hitherto have all been very gaily dressed, with a pretension
to French style, and a more than English exaggeration of it. They
all appear to me to walk with a French shuffle, which I can only
account for by their wearing shoes made in the French fashion,
which are enough in themselves to make a waddler of the best
walker that ever set foot on earth.

After tea my father and I crossed the Park (a small bit of grass
enclosed in white palings, in plain English, a green) to the
theatre. The house is pretty though rather gloomy, well formed,
with plenty of gold carving and red silk about it, looking rich and
warm. The audience was considerable, but all men; scarce twenty
women in the dress circle, where, by the way, I saw men sitting
with their hats on.

Thursday, 6th. My father has been introduced to half the town and
tells me that far from the democratic *Mister* which he expected to

be every man's title here, he has made the acquaintance of a score of municipal dignitaries and some sixty colonels and major-generals – of militia. Their omnibuses too are vehicles of rank, and the *Ladies* Washington, Clinton and Van Rensalaer rattle their crazy bones up and down Broadway all the day long like any other old women of quality.

This hotel reminds me most extremely of our 'iligant' and untidy appartment in dear, nasty Dublin, at the Shelbourne. The paper in our bed-room is half peeling from the walls, our beds are without curtains; then to be sure there are pier looking-glasses and one or two pieces of showy French furniture in it.

Friday, 7th. After dinner we walked to the end of Broadway, a distance of two miles I should think, and then back again. After walking nearly a mile we came to Canal Street; it is broader and finer than any I have yet seen in New York; at one end of it a Christian church, copied from some Pagan temple, looked exceedingly well in the full flood of the silver moonlight. The street was very much thronged and I thought the crowd a more civil and orderly one than an English crowd. The men did not jostle or push one another, or tread upon one's feet, or crush one's bonnet into one's face, or turn it round upon one's head, all of which I have seen done in London streets. This crowd was abroad merely for pleasure, sauntering along, which is a thing never seen in London. I observed that the young men tonight invariably made room for women to pass, and many of them, as they drew near us, took the segar from their mouth, which I thought especially courteous. Came in rather tired, took tea, sang an immensity, wrote journal, looked at the peerless moon and will now go to bed.

Sunday, 9th. Went to Church with my father. 'Tis long since I have heard the church service so well read, with so few vices of pronunciation or vulgarisms of emphasis. Our own clergy are shamefully negligent on this point. There was no clerk to assist in the service, and the congregation were as neglectful of the directions in the prayer book and as indolent and remiss in uttering the responses as they are in our own churches. The organ and chanting were very good; infinitely superior to the performances of those blessed little parish cherubim who monopolise the praises of God in our churches, so much to the suffering of all good Christians not favoured with deafness.

I did nothing but look out of the window all the blessed day long: I did not think in my old age to acquire so Jezebel a trick; but the park is so very pretty and the streets so gay with their throngs of smartly dressed women that I find my window the most entertaining station in the world.

After dinner, sat looking at the blacks parading up and down; most of them in the height of fashion, with every colour in the rainbow about them. At seven o'clock Dall and I walked out together. During the promenade two fire engines passed us, attended by the usual retinue of shouting children; this is about the sixth fire since yesterday evening. They are so frequent here that the cry 'Fire, Fire' seems to excite neither alarm nor curiosity, and except for the above mentioned juveniles, none of the inhabitants seem in the least disturbed by it.

Tuesday, 11th. At four o'clock I sent for a hairdresser, that I might in good time see that I am not made an object on my first night. He was a Frenchman, and after listening profoundly to my description of the head-dress I wanted, replied, 'Madame, la difficulté n'est pas d'exécuter votre coiffure, mais de la bien concevoir'. However, he conceived and executed sundry very smooth-looking bows, and upon the whole dressed my hair very nicely but charged a dollar for so doing: O nefarious!

My father came home at about half past six from an expedition to Hoboken, a place across the water, famous once for duelling but now the favourite resort of a turtle-eating club, who go there every Tuesday to cook and swallow turtle. The wording of the card of invitation was as follows: 'Sir, the Hoboken Turtle Club will meet at the grove for *spoon exercise* on Tuesday, 11th inst. by order of the President'. My father's account of his dinner was anything but delightful, and his feeling description of the damp trees, damp clothes and damp atmosphere gave me the rheumatiz, letting alone they had nothing to eat but turtle, and that out of iron spoons.

Thursday, 13th. Visited the fish and fruit markets: the latter reminded me of Aladdin's treasure: the heaps of peaches, filling with their rich, downy balls high baskets ranged in endless rows and painted a bright vermilion which threw a ruddy ripeness over the fruit. The enormous baskets, such as are used in England to carry linen, piled with melons, wild grapes, pears and apples – all so fragrant, so plenteous, so beautiful in form and colour, leading the mind to the wondrous bounteousness which has dowered this land – the whole enchanted me. The fish of these waters may be excellent in the water; but, owing to the want of care with which they are kept after being caught, they are seldom worth eating when brought to table. The lobsters, crabs and oysters are all gigantic, frightful to behold, and not particularly well-flavoured: their size makes them tough and coarse.

The day was beautiful and my father proposed crossing the river to Hoboken, scene of the turtle-eating expedition. Steamers cross every five minutes, conveying passengers on foot and on horseback, gigs, carriages, carts, anything and everything. The broad, bright river was gemmed with a thousand sails. We reached the opposite coast and walked through a beautiful wood which crowns the high bank of the river; through the trellis work of the varied foliage we caught exquisite glimpses of the glorious waters and the glittering city, decked out in all the loveliest contrast of sun and shade.

Mr. —— began expatiating on the happiness of the original possessors of these fair lands and waters, the Indians – Red Children of the soil, who followed the chase through these lovely wildernesses and drove their light canoes over these broad streams till the predestined curse came upon them, till the white sails of the invaders threw their shadow over these seas and the work of extermination began. No one, beholding the prosperous and promising state of this fine country could wish it again untenanted of its enterprising possessors; yet even while admiring all they have achieved, and looking with expectation amounting to certainty to all they will yet accomplish, 'tis difficult to refrain from bestowing some thoughts of pity and sadness upon those whose homes have been overturned, whose language has passed away and whose feet are daily driven further from those territories of which they were once sole and sovereign lords.

Saturday, 15th. At five dressed and went to the Hones, where we were to dine. Mr. Philip Hone is one of *the* men of New York in point of wealth, influence and consideration. He has retired from business, having, among his other honours, filled the office of Mayor of New York. His is one of the first houses here, so I conclude that I am to consider what I see as a tolerable sample of the ways and manners of the *best* society in New York. There were about twenty people; the women were in a sort of French demi-toilette, with bare necks and long sleeves, heads frizzed out after the very last petit courier, and thread net handkerchiefs and capes; the whole of which, to my English eye, appeared a strange marrying of incongruities. The younger daughter of our host is beautiful, with a smile that was, not to say a ray, but a whole focus of sun-rays, a perfect blaze of light.

The dinner was plenteous and tolerably well dressed, but ill served; there were not half servants enough and we had neither water glasses nor finger glasses. Now, though I don't eat with my fingers (except peaches, whereat I think the aborigines, who were peeling theirs like so many potatoes, seemed rather amazed) yet do I hold a finger glass at the conclusion of my dinner requisite to comfort. After dinner we had coffee, but no tea, whereat my English taste was in high dudgeon.

I was very glad to come home. I sang to them two or three things, but the piano was pitched too high for my voice – by the way, in that large, lofty fine room they had a tiny old fashioned becurtained cabinet piano stuck right against the wall, unto which the singer's face was turned and into which his voice was absorbed.

Had Fanny but known it, Philip Hone for his part was not unduly impressed by his young guest. He wrote on the same day in his diary: 'Miss Kemble, like all young persons who have become celebrated, has many and strong admirers. Her manners are somewhat singular. Allowance must be made for her, just arrived among strangers, with a consciousness that she is one of the lions of the day and as such the object more of curiosity than affection. She talks well, but will only talk when and to whom she chooses, and she has an air of nonchalance not calculated to make her a favourite with the beaux. . . . She has astonishing requisites for the stage. Her features separately are not good, but combined they make a face of great power and expression. I am of the opinion she does not like her profession. It is not her favourite theme of conversation. Her father is a gentleman of fine manners and dignified deportment, somewhat stiff — he is a Kemble — but evidently accustomed to good society.'[1]

New York, September 16th, 1832
My dearest Harriet . . . My father, thank God, is wonderfully improved in health, looks and spirits; the fine, clear, warm (hot, it should be called) atmosphere agrees with him and the release from the cares of that troublesome estate of his will be of the

[1] *The Diary of Philip Hone*, Vol. I, p. 61.

greatest service to him. He begins work tomorrow night with
Hamlet, and on Tuesday I act Bianca. The heat seems to me almost
intolerable, though it is here considered mild autumn weather. I
do nothing but drink iced lemonade and eat peaches and melons,
in spite of the cholera.

Baths are a much cheaper and commoner luxury (necessary) in
the hotels here than with us. What a blessing! There are no water
pipes or cisterns in this city such as we have, but men go about as
they do in Paris, with huge water-butts, supplying each house
daily. There are fine springs and a full fresh-water stream at a
distance of some miles; but the municipality is not very rich and is
economical of the public money, leaving New York ill-paved,
ill-lighted and indifferently supplied with a good many necessaries and luxuries of modern civilisation.

Monday, 17th. At twelve went to rehearsal. Mr. Keppel, the
washed-out man who failed in London when he acted Romeo
with me is to be my Fazio; let us hope he will know some of his
words tomorrow night, for he is at present most innocent of any
such knowledge. At seven went to the theatre. It was my dear
father's first appearance in this new world, and my heart ached
with anxiety. The weather was intensely hot, yet the theatre was
crowded: they gave him what everybody here calls an immense
reception; but they should see our London audience get up and
wave hats and handkerchiefs and shout welcome. My father
looked well and acted beyond all praise.

> *New York audiences were well accustomed to visiting English 'stars' of
> Charles Kemble's magnitude. Twelve years earlier the brilliant
> Edmund Kean had taken the city by storm, followed by John Junius
> Booth, Macready and others. This was the first time, however, that
> they had seen an actress as eminent as Fanny and they rose to her with
> immense enthusiasm. According to George C. D. Odell, historian of
> the New York stage, she was 'something of a divine manifestation' to
> that city, and the Kembles' season there 'one of the most glorious in
> our annals'.* [2]

Tuesday, 18th. At half-past six went to the theatre. They acted the
farce of *Popping the Question* first, in order, I suppose, to get the
people to their places before the play began. Poor Mr. Keppel was
gasping for breath: I comforted him all I could, gave him some of
my lemonade, for he was choking with fright. In the second

[2] *Annals of the New York Stage*, Vol. III, p. 598.

speech he was quite out; it was in vain that I prompted him; he was too nervous to take the word and made a complete mess of it. I thought the whole thing must necessarily go to pieces. However, once rid of my encumbrance, I gathered up my strength and set to work comfortably by myself; whereupon the people applauded, I warmed (warmed? the air was steam) and got through satisfactorily, or so it seems. My dresses were very beautiful, but oh, but, oh, the musquitoes had made dreadful havoc with my arms, which were covered with hills as large and red as Vesuvius. Came to bed at half-past twelve, weary and half melted away. The ants swarm on the floors, on tables, in beds, about one's clothes; the plagues of Egypt were a joke to them.

Wednesday, 19th. Mr. Keppel has been dismissed, poor man! What a funny passion he had for going down upon his knees. In *Fazio* at the end of the judgment scene, when I was down upon mine down he went upon his, and there we were, looking for all the world like one of those conjugal vis-à-vis that adorn antique tombs in our cathedrals. It really was exceedingly absurd. Poor fellow, he bothered me a good deal, yet I'm sincerely sorry for him.

The steward of our ship, a black – a very intelligent and obliging servant – called this morning to ask my father for an order [complimentary ticket] adding with some hesitation, 'It must be for the gallery, if you please, sir, for people of colour are not allowed to go to the pit or any other part of the house'. I believe I must have turned black myself, I was so indignant. The prejudice against these unfortunate people is of course incomprehensible to us. On board ship, after giving that same man some trouble, Dall poured him out a glass of wine when we were having dinner, whereupon the captain looked at her with utter amazement and I thought some little contempt and said, 'Ah, one can tell by that that you are not an American'; which sort of thing makes one rather glad that one is not.

Friday, 21st. Mr. Simpson sent me a letter from Mr. Keppel soliciting another trial and urging the hardness of his case in being condemned upon a part which he had had no time to study. My own opinion is that no power on earth or in heaven can make him act decently; however of course I did not object to his trying again; he did not swamp me the first night and so I don't suppose he will the fifth. We have been told that he has been writing to the papers to convince them and the public that he is a good actor, at the same time throwing out hints, which seem aimed our way, of injustice, oppression, hard usage and the rest on't.

The few critiques I have seen on our acting have been, upon the whole, laudatory. One was sent me from a paper called *The Mirror* which pleased me very much;[3] not because the praise in it was far beyond my deserts, but that it was written with great taste and feeling and evidently not the produce of a common press hack. There appeared to me in all the others the true provincial dread of praising too much and of being *led* into approbation by previous opinions; a sort of jealousy of critical freedom which, together with the established *nil admirari* of the press, seems to keep them in a constant dread of being thought enthusiastic.

Saturday, 22nd. Got into a hackney coach with Dall and returned all manner of cards. The hackney coaches here are very different from those perilous receptacles of dust and dirty straw which disgrace the London stands. They are comfortable within and clean without; and the horses never exhibit those shocking specimens of cruelty which the poor hack horses in London present.

Went into a shop to order a pair of shoes. The shopkeepers in this place are either condescendingly familiar or insolently indifferent. Your washerwoman sits down before you, while you are *standing* speaking to her; a shop boy bringing things for your inspection not only sits down, but keeps his hat on in your drawing room. The worthy man to whom I went for my shoes was so amazingly ungracious that at first I thought I would go out of the shop. All this has its origin in a vulgar misapprehension which confounds ill-breeding with independence, and leads

---

[3] A week later the *Mirror* gave its considered verdict on Fanny's first four weeks in New York: '. . . firstly her faults. Of these the most prominent is a monotonous delivery of elaborate passages. . . . She flings herself into a stateliness of manner, when making only an ordinary remark, delivering her words with a lengthened and too deliberate attempt at stage effect, an error, we suspect, of the school of which she is such a rich ornament. . . . The great peculiarity of her acting is mind. . . . Only the highest intellect and the most warmly affectionate nature could conceive the illustrations of thought and feeling which consititute the charm and glory of this young girl's acting . . . her hate is sardonic, *Kean-like*, and almost intolerable; her love, deeply impassioned and tender, all bashful girl-ishness and full of exquisitely graceful touches – *full* of them. Her fixed look of despair hushes every sound, till her silent glance of scorn shakes the house with a sudden peak of thunder. This is, indeed, *acting*.' (Odell, *op. cit.*, p. 608.)

people to fancy that they elevate themselves above their condition by discharging its duties and obligations discourteously.

Monday, 24th. At six went to the theatre. My gown was horribly ill-plaited and I looked like a blue-bag. The play was *Venice Preserved*, with Mr. Keppel. The house was very full and they received him with acclamations and shouts of applause. The first scene passed well; but oh, the next, and the next, and the next to that. He did nothing but seize my hand and grapple it so hard that unless I had knocked him down (which I felt much inclined to try) I could not disengage myself. In the senate scene, when I was entreating for mercy and struggling, as Otway has it, for my life, he was prancing round the stage, flourishing his dagger in the air. Once, after struggling in vain to free myself, I was obliged, in the middle of my part to exclaim, 'You hurt me dreadfully, Mr. Keppel'. Come what may, *I* will not be subject to this experiment again. At the end, the clever New Yorkers actually called for Mr. Keppel. This most worthless clapping of hands, most worthlessly bestowed upon a worthless object, is what by the nature of my craft I am bound to care for; I spit upon it from the bottom of my soul!

We came home tired and thoroughly disgusted and found no supper. The cooks, who do not live in the house but come and do their work and depart whenever it suits their convenience, had not thought proper to stay to prepare any supper for us: so we had to wait for the readiest things that could be prepared out of doors for us. At last appeared a cold boiled fowl and some monstrous oysters. Six mouthfuls each: they were well-flavoured, but their size displeased me. I swallowed but one and came to bed.

CHAPTER 7

Introduction to Philadelphia
1832

After their first month-long engagement in New York, the Kembles and aunt Dall set off for Philadelphia, travelling part of the way by stage coach and part in the large paddle steamers which looked, Fanny remarked, like 'castles on the main'. An exclusively American phenomenon, they were the most practical and comfortable means of transport in the United States before the widespread deployment of the railroads.

Monday, October 8th. Just as the night was folding its soft black wings we took our departure from that mansion of little ease, the American Hotel, and our fellow lodgers the ants. We were recommended it as the best and most comfortable in New York; and truly the charges were as high as one could have paid at the Clarendon, in the land of comfort and taxation. The wine was exorbitantly dear: champagne and claret about eleven shillings a bottle; sherry, port and madeira from nine to thirteen. The living was by no means good, the whole house being conducted on a close scraping system of inferior accommodations and extravagant charges. The number of servants was totally inadequate, and they had no bedrooms, but slept about anywhere, in the public rooms or on sofas in drawing rooms let to private families. And so we departed therefrom nothing loath.

The Philadelphia steam boat was large and commodious, as all these conveyances are. They have three stories. The upper one is a terrace on the leads of the second, and a very desirable situation when the weather is neither too foul or too fair. The second floor or deck has the advantage of the ceiling above, and yet, its sides being open, it is airy and allows free sight of the shores. The deck below is a spacious room completely roofed and walled in, and at the end of it is a smaller cabin for the use of the ladies, with beds and a sofa and all the conveniences necessary if they should like to be sick; whither I came and slept till breakfast time.

The breakfast was good, and served and eaten with decency

70

enough. Walked on the deck with my father. The width of the river struck me as remarkable; but the shores were flat and uninteresting, except for the rich and varied tints which the thickets of the woods presented, and which are as superior in brilliancy and intenseness to our autumnal colouring as their gorgeous skies are to ours.

At about half past ten we reached the place where we left the river to proceed across a part of the State of New Jersey to the Delaware. The landing was beyond measure wretched: the marshy soil, rendered doubly soft and squashy by the damp weather, was strewn with broken potsherds, stones and bricks by way of pathway; these presently failed and some slippery planks half immersed in mud were the only roads to the coaches that stood ready. Oh, those coaches! They are shaped something like boats, their sides being merely leathern pieces removable at pleasure but which in bad weather are buttoned down to protect the inmates from the wet. Two of the three seats were filled, each with three people, and there should by rights have been a third on the seat which Dall and I occupied, for this nefarious black hole on wheels is intended to carry nine. Away walloped the four horses, and away we went after them, bumping, thumping, jumping, tossing and tumbling over the wickedest road, I do think the cruellest, hard-heartedest road that ever wheel rumbled upon, through bog and marsh, and ruts wider and deeper than any Christian ruts I ever saw, with the roots of trees protruding across our path, their boughs now and then giving us an affectionate scratch through the windows. Even my father's solid proportions were jerked up to the roof and down again every three minutes. Our companions laughed and talked incessantly – the young ladies at the top of their voices. We had not been long in the coach before one of them complained of being dreadfully sick. This, in such a space, with seven near neighbours! Fortunately she was near the window, and during our whole fourteen miles of purgatory she alternately leaned from it overcome with sickness, then reclined languishingly in the arms of her neighbour, and then, starting up with amazing vivacity, joined her voice to the duet of her two pretty companions with a superiority of shrillness that might have been the pride and envy of Billingsgate.

The few cottages and farm houses we passed reminded me of similar dwellings in France and Ireland; yet the peasantry here have not the same excuse for disorder and dilapidation as either the Irish or French. The farms had the same desolate, untidy look; the gates broken, the fences carelessly put up, the farming utensils sluttishly scattered about a littered yard, where the pigs seemed to preside by undisputed right; dishevelled women and barefooted, anomalous looking human young things – none of the stirring life and activity which such places present in England and Scotland.

At the end of fourteen miles we turned into a swampy field, the whole fourteen coachloads of us, and were packed into the coaches which stood on the railway ready to receive us. The carriages were not drawn by steam, like those of the Liverpool railway, but by horses, with the mere advantage in speed afforded by the iron ledges which, compared to our previous progress through the ruts, was considerable.

In about half an hour we reached the end of our railroad part of the journey and found another steamboat awaiting us, when we all embarked on the Delaware. One improvement they have adopted on board these boats is to forbid smoking except in the fore part of the vessel. I wish they would suggest that gentlemen should refrain from spitting too. The universal practice here of this disgusting trick makes me absolutely sick: every place is made a perfect piggery of – today on board it was a perfect shower of saliva all the time.

At about four o'clock we reached Philadelphia, having performed the journey of a hundred miles in less than ten hours. We were presently stowed into a coach which conveyed us to the Mansion House, the best reputed inn in Philadelphia. They showed Dall and myself into a double-bedded room. On my remonstrating, the chamber maid replied that they were not accustomed to allow lodgers so much room as a room apiece. However, they gave me a little nest just big enough to turn about in, but where at least I can be by myself.

Tuesday, 9th. Went and took a bath. The ladies' baths were closed, but as I was not particular, they gave me one in the part of the house usually allotted to the men's use. I was much surprised to find two baths in one room, but it seems to me that the people of this country have an aversion to solitude, whether eating, sleeping or under any other circumstance.

After breakfast, took a walk through some of the principal streets. The town is perfect silence and solitude compared with New York; there is a greater air of age about it too, which pleases

me. The red houses are not so fiercely red, nor the white facings
so glaringly white; in short, it has not so new and flaunting a look.
We passed one or two pretty buildings in pure white marble, and
the bank in Chestnut Street, which is a beautiful little copy of the
Parthenon. The shops here are much better looking than those at
New York: the windows are larger and more advantageously
conducted for the display of goods. The streets were very full of
men hurrying to the town house to give their votes. It is election
time and much excitement subsists with regard to the choice of
the future President.

The democrats or radicals are for the re-election of General
Jackson, but the aristocratic party, which here at all events is the
strongest, are in favour of Henry Clay. Here is the usual quantity
of shouting and breaking windows that we are accustomed to on
these occasions. I saw a caricature of Jackson and Van Buren, his
chief supporter, entitled, 'The King and his Minister'. Van Buren
held a crown in his hand, and the devil was approaching Jackson
with a sceptre.[1]

Wednesday, 10th. The streets were in an uproar all night, people
shouting and bonfires blazing; in short, electioneering fun,
which seems pretty much the same the world over.

> *That evening, Fanny watched her father's performance with unusu-*
> *ally close attention and later set down in her journal a careful and*
> *perceptive analysis of his style of acting, comparing it with the fiery*
> *passion of Edmund Kean who in 1814 had electrified London audi-*
> *ences long accustomed to the classical, considered, slow and meticu-*
> *lously spoken Kembles. On first seeing him as a girl, Fanny had*
> *promptly become 'a violent Keanite' and, though she later modified her*
> *enthusiasm, she steadfastly maintained his genius in frequent argu-*
> *ments with those in her family 'whose theatrical code would not*
> *permit them to acknowledge him as a great actor'.*

The great beauty of all my father's performances, but particularly of Hamlet, is a wonderful accuracy in the detail of the
character; an accuracy which modulates the emphasis of every
word, the nature of every gesture, the expression of every look;
and which renders the whole a most laborious and minute study,
toilsome of conception and acquirement, and most toilsome in
the execution. But the result, though a natural one, is not such as

[1] Andrew Jackson – 'Old Hickory' – with Martin van Buren as running mate
won a decisive second-term victory in the 1832 Presidential election.

he expects as the result of so much labour. Few are able to follow such a performance with the necessary attention, and it is almost as great an exertion to see it understandingly as to act it. I think that style of acting the best which skilfully husbands the actor's and spectator's powers and puts forth the whole of one to call forth the whole of the other occasionally only; leaving the intermediate parts sufficiently level to allow him and them to recover the capability of again producing and again receiving such impressions. At the same time I am far from advocating that most imperfect conception and embodying of a part which Kean allows himself: literally acting detached passages alone and leaving all the others, and indeed the entire character, utterly destitute of unity or the semblance of any consistency whatever.

But Kean and my father are immediately each other's antipodes, and in adopting their different styles of acting it is evident that each has been guided as much by his own physical and intellectual ability as by any fixed principle of art. The one, Kean, possesses particular physical qualifications – an eye like an orb of light, a voice exquisitely melodious in its tenderness, and in the harsh dissonance of vehement passion terribly true. To these he adds the intellectual one of vigour, intensity, amazing powers of concentrating effect: these give him an entire mastery over his audience in all striking, sudden, impassioned passages, in fulfilling which he has contented himself; leaving unheeded what he probably could not compass – the unity of conception, refinement of detail and evenness of execution.

My father possesses certain physical defects – a faintness of colouring in the face and eye, a weakness of voice; and the corresponding intellectual deficiencies – a want of intensity, vigour and concentrating power. These circumstances have led him (probably unconsciously) to study the finer and more fleeting shades of character, the more delicate manifestations of feeling, the exquisite variety of all minor parts, the classic keeping of a highly wrought whole. To all these polished and refined tastes, a native grace, gentleness and refinement have been his prompters; but they cannot inspire those startling and tremendous bursts of passion which belong to the highest walks of tragedy, and to which he never gave their fullest expression. I fancy my aunt Siddons united the excellences of both these styles.

There is one thing in which I do not believe my father has ever been or ever will be excelled: his high and noble bearing; his gallant, courteous deportment; his perfect good breeding on the stage. He appears to me the beau ideal of the courtly, thorough-bred, chivalrous gentleman.

Thursday, 11th. After rehearsal came home, habited and went to the riding school to try some horses. *Merci de moi!* What quad-rupeds! How they did wallop and shamble about, poor half-broken dumb brutes! I found something I think my father can ride with tolerable comfort, but must go again tomorrow and see after something for myself. Came home in high delight with this Quaker city, which is indeed very pretty and pleasant.

Friday, 12th. Went to the theatre: the house was full and Dall and my father say that I was extremely ungracious in my ack-nowledgment of their greeting. I did not mean to be so; I made them three courtesies and what woman could do more? Of course I can neither feel nor look so glad to see them as my own dear London people. This audience is the most unapplausive I ever acted to, not excepting my *excitable* friends north of the Tweed. They were attentive, certainly, but how they did make me work. 'Tis amazing how much an audience loses by this species of hanging back. Excitement is reciprocal between the performer and the audience: he creates it in them and receives it back from them again. I know that my aunt Siddons has frequently said the same thing.

Saturday, 13th. Came down to tea and found a young gentleman sitting with my father; one Mr. ——. He was a pretty spoken, genteel youth enough: he drank tea with us and offered to ride with me. He has, it seems, a great fortune; consequently, I sup-pose (in spite of his inches), a great man. Now I'll go to bed: my cough's enough to kill a horse.

> *The young man of short stature here so summarily dismissed by Fanny was Pierce Butler, whom she was to marry less than two years later. In Philadelphia he was constantly at her side, finding her good mounts and taking her riding — a sure way to her heart. He followed the party back to New York and later on to Boston; and since he was a good flautist, often contrived to get a place in the orchestra so as to be near her when she was on stage.*

Monday, 15th. So we are to act *The Gamester* here. Went and ordered a dress for Mrs Beverley, my own being in New York.

Chose a beautiful claret coloured velvet which will cost Miss Kemble eleven guineas, by this living light.

Came home, put things out for the theatre, practised an hour; dined at three. After dinner read a canto in Dante: he is my admiration! – great, great master! A philosopher profound, as all poets should be; a glorious poet, as I wish all philosophers should be.

At six, went to the theatre. I never beheld anything more gorgeous than the sky at sunset. Autumn is emperor here, clothed in crimson and gold, and canopied with ruddy, glowing skies. Yet I like the sad russet cloak of our own autumnal woods.

Tuesday, 16th. Just as I had finished dinner, a most beautiful, fragrant nosegay was brought to me, with a very laconic note from a Philadelphia *'friend'*, dashed under, as though from a Quaker. Whoever 'tis, Jew or Gentile, Puritan or Pagan, he, she or it hath my most unbounded gratitude. Spent an ecstatic half hour arranging my flowers in glasses.

Thursday, 18th. Found another beautiful nosegay from my unknown furnisher of sweets. This is almost as tantalizing as it is civil; and I would give half my lovely flowers to find out who sends them to me.

Tuesday, 23rd. While writing a letter, was interrupted by a strange woman, apparently in much confusion. She told me a story of great distress and claimed my assistance as a fellow country-woman. I had not a farthing of money; Dall and my father were out; so I took the reference she gave me and promised to enquire into her condition.

The greatest evil arising from the many claims of this sort which are made upon us wherever we go, is the feeling of sus-picion which they engender, and the sort of excuse which they teach us to apply plausibly to our unwillingness to answer such demands. 'Oh, ten to one an imposter', is soon said, and instances enough may unfortunately be found to prove the prob-ability of such a conclusion. Yet in this sweeping condemnation, one real case of misery may be included, and that possibility should make us pause.

Wednesday, 24th. Went with Dall to find out about my yesterday's poor woman. The references were sufficiently satisfactory – that is to say, they proved that she was poor and in distress, and willing to work. I gave her what I could, and the man by whom she is employed seems anxious to afford her work; so I hope she will get on a little.

Friday, 26th. We sallied forth to see the giantess of a ship the Americans have been building, to thrash us all. This lady of the seas was propped up on a hundred stays, surrounded by scaffolding. We went on deck: in fact the *Pennsylvania* has been boarded by the English in our persons before she ever sets foot upon the sea. How I should like to see that ship launched! She is larger than any East Indiaman; the largest ship in the world. When my wonderment had a little subsided, it occurred to me that she would not perhaps be so available a battleship as one of a smaller size: it must be impossible to manoeuvre her with any promptitude.

Sunday, 28th. Had only time to swallow a mouthful of breakfast and off to church. I must say it requires a deal of fortitude to go into an American church: there are no pew openers and the people seem to rush indifferently into any seats that are vacant. This congregation, by frequenting an Episcopalian temple, evidently professed the form of faith of the English church; yet they neither uttered the responses, nor observed any one of the directions in the Common Prayerbook. Thus, during those portions of the worship where kneeling is enjoined, they sat or stood; and while the creed was being read, half the auditors were reclining comfortably in the pews: the same thing with the Psalms and all parts of the service. I suppose their love of freedom will not suffer them to be amenable to forms, or wear the exterior of humbleness and homage even in the house of the Most High God.

Friday, November 2nd. The day was so hot that I could scarcely endure my boa. The election was going on; the streets full of rabblement, the air full of huzzaing, and the sky obscured with star-spangled banners, and villainous transparencies of 'Old Hickory' hung out in all directions. We went round the Town House and looked at the window out of which Jefferson read the Act of Independence that proclaimed the separation between England and America. We were obliged to go all manner of roundabouts to the play-house in order to avoid the rabble that choked up the principal streets. I, by way of striking salutary awe into the hearts of all rioters who might cross our path, brandished my father's sword out of the coach window the whole way along.

On our return home, found a most exquisite nosegay waiting for me – so sweet, so brilliant, so fragrant and fresh.

Monday, 5th November. Dressed myself by candlelight, started from the Mansion House (which is a very nice inn) at six, and reached the quay just in time to meet the first rosy breaking of the clouds over the Delaware. I am sorry to leave Philadelphia. I like the town and the little I have seen of its inhabitants very much.

The Kembles' second spell in New York proved as rewarding as their first. As well as appearing at the Park Theatre four or five times a week, there were endless callers, parties, dances, outings on horseback, picnics with champagne, cake and cherry bounce. For Fanny the highspot was an excursion to West Point. She filled page after page of her journal with a moment by moment account of the expedition. Far too long to quote in full, the chief interest of the entry for this red letter day is her description of the steamboat trip up the Hudson River.

Saturday, 10th. Nobody who has not seen it can conceive the strange aspect of the long room of one of these fine boats at meal time. The crowd, the hurry, the confusion of tongues like the sound of many waters, the enormous consumption of eatables, the cloud of black waiters hovering down the sides of the immense tables, the hungry, eager faces seated at them, form altogether a most amusing subject of contemplation; and a caricaturist would find ample matter in almost every other devouring countenance.

The way in which the boats are conducted deserves the highest commendation. Nothing can exceed the comfort with which they are managed, and the order and alacrity with which passengers are taken up from or landed at the various points along the river. The steamer goes at fifteen miles an hour; and in less than two minutes, when approaching any place of landing, the engine stops, the boat is lowered – the captain always convoys his passengers himself from the steamer to the shore – and away darts the tiny skiff. As soon as it grazes the land, its freight, animate and inanimate, is bundled out; the boat hauls itself back in an instant, and immediately the machine is in motion and the vessel again bounding over the water like a race-horse.

Doubtless all this has many and great advantages, but to an

English person the mere circumstance of being the whole day in a crowd is a nuisance. As to privacy at any time or under any circumstances, 'tis a thing that enters not the imagination of an American. They live all the days of their lives in a throng, eat at ordinaries of two or three hundred, sleep five or six in a room, take pleasure in droves and travel by swarms. This mode of journeying has its drawbacks; and the greatest of all, to me, is being companioned by so many strangers, who crowd about you, pursue their conversation in your very ears, or, if they like it better, listen to yours, stare you out of all countenance and squeeze you out of all comfort.

After several thousand words of lyrical description of the 'noble waters' of the Hudson and the riverside hills and woods, clad in all the splendour of the American fall, Fanny concluded her account of a memorable day with a characteristic outburst.

Where are the poets of this land? Is there none to come here and worship among these hills and waters till the hymn of inspiration flows from his lips and rises to the sky? O surely, surely, there will come a time when this lovely land will be vocal with the sound of song; when every close-locked valley and waving wood, rifted rock and flowing stream shall have their praise. Yet 'tis strange how marvellously unpoetical these people are! How swallowed up in life and its daily realities, wants and cares! How full of toil and thrift and money-getting labour! Perhaps some hundred years hence, when the face of society begins to grow checkered, as in the old lands of Europe, when inequalities of rank shall exist and the rich man shall be able to pay for the luxury of poetry – perhaps when all this comes to pass, America will have poets.

Yet at that very moment Fanny was herself helping in some strange, small indirect way to form one American poet. One of her most devoted fans at that time was thirteen year old Walt Whitman, who again and again crossed by ferry from Brooklyn to see her act. Fifty years later he recalled boyhood escapades which 'undoubtedly enter'd into the gestation of Leaves of Grass . . . *And certain actors and singers had a great deal to do with the business . . . Fanny Kemble – name to conjure up great mimic scenes withal – perhaps the greatest. . . . Nothing finer did ever stage exhibit – the veterans of all nations said so, and my boyish heart and head felt it in every minute cell'.*[2]

[2] *Specimen Days*, p. 19.

Wednesday, 21st. At nine we adjourned to a 'small party, my dear'. After a little time dancing was proposed. When I stood up to waltz, my partner observed that Dr. Wainwright [minister at Grace Church which the Kembles attended] was gone, as he never chose to be present while waltzing was going on. I felt shocked to death that unconsciously I should have been instrumental in driving him away, and much surprised that those who knew his disapprobation of waltzing should have proposed it. However, he was gone and did not return. Therefore I waltzed myself out of my conscientious remorse.

Thursday, 22nd. Dr. Wainwright called and gave me a sermon about waltzing. As it was perfectly good sense, to which I could reply nothing whatever in the shape of objection, I promised him never to waltz again, except with a woman or my brother. After all, 'tis not fitting that a man should put his arm round one's waist. 'Tis much against what I have always thought most sacred – the dignity of a woman in her own eyes and those of others. I like Dr. Wainwright most exceedingly. After saying he felt convinced, from conversations which he had heard amongst men, that waltzing was immoral in its tendency, he added, 'I am married and have been in love, and cannot imagine anything more destructive of the deep and devoted respect which love is calculated to excite in every honourable man's heart, not only for the individual object of his affections but for her whole sex, than to see any and every impertinent coxcomb in a ballroom come up to her and clasp her waist, imprison her hand and absolutely whirl her round in his arms'. So spake the Doctor; and my sense of propriety and conviction of right bore testimony to the truth of his saying. So farewell, sweet German waltz! I shall never keep time to your pleasant measure again! – no matter; after all, anything is better than to be lightly spoken of and to deserve such mention.

Monday, 26th. Yesterday was the anniversary of the evacuation of the island [Manhattan] by the British troops, but as yesterday was the Lord's day also, the American militia army postponed their yearly exhibition and quietly went to church and praised God for that same. Today, however, we had firing of pop-guns, waving of star-spangled banners, infantry marching through the streets, cavalry and artillery prancing along them, to the infinite ecstasy and peril of a dense mob. They were certainly not quite so bad as

Falstaff's men of ragged memory; for, for aught I know to the contrary, they perhaps *all* had shirts to their backs. But some had gloves and some had none; some carried their guns one way and some another; some had caps of one fashion and some of another; some had no caps at all but 'shocking bad hats' with feathers in them. The infantry were, however, comparatively respectable troops. They did not march many degrees out of the straight line, or stoop *too much*, or turn their heads *too often*. But the cavalry! what gems without price they were! apparently frightened at the shambling, *tituppy* charges upon whose backs they clung, straggling in all directions, putting the admiring crowd in fear of their lives. Some wore boots and some wore shoes, and one independent hero had on grey stockings and *slippers*! The bands of these worthies were worthy of them – half a dozen fifers and drummers playing old English jig tunes. The parade terminated with a full half-hour's *feux de joie*.

Dined at three. My father went to Tammany Hall (a place devoted to political meetings, chiefly I believe those termed here democratic), where there was a grand democratic dinner in honour of the triumph of the Jackson party, the mob men here.

The play was *Isabella*; the house crammed; a regular holy day audience, shrieking, shouting and laughing like one of our Christmas audiences. I acted like a wretch. My dresses looked very handsome, but those *animaux bêtes* who dragged me off tore a beautiful point lace veil I had on to tatters, a thing that cost three guineas, if a farthing.

Friday, 7th December. I was horrified at Dr. ——'s account of the state of the negroes in the south. To teach a slave to read or write is to incur a penalty either of fine or imprisonment. They form the larger proportion of the population by far; and so great is the dread of insurrection on the part of the white inhabitants that they are kept in the most brutish ignorance and too often treated with the most brutal barbarity in order to ensure their subjection. Oh what a breaking asunder of old manacles there will be some of these fine days; what a fearful rising of the black flood; what a sweeping away, as by a torrent, of oppressions and tyrannies; what a fierce and horrible retaliation for wrong too long endured – so wickedly inflicted.

CHAPTER 8

American Tour
1833

For the next seven months the Kembles, and Aunt Dall with them, were constantly on the move. The last day of 1832 found them setting out for Baltimore after a second engagement in Philadelphia.

Monday, 31st December. We arose at half past four. Dall and I were bundled into a coach and rumbled and tumbled over the stones, through the blackness of darkness down to the steam boat. 'Tis curious; there was a man on board whom I have now seen every time I have been going to or from New York to Philadelphia. He was a man of about from thirty to thirty-five, *I guess*, with a great appearance of strength and activity. His face was that of a foreigner, and the piercing black eyes, dark hair and brown complexion gave a Spanish character to his countenance. There was a sort of familiar would-be gentlemanly manner in his deportment and address, and a species of slang gentility in his carriage and conversation, that gave me a curiosity to ascertain what on earth he could be. After about an hour's steaming, we disembarked to cross the narrow neck of land which divides the Delaware from the Chesapeake. Here we got into a coach holding some twelve of us, to be conveyed over the rail-road by one of Stevenson's [*sic*] engines. Neither the road nor the conveyances are comparable to those of the Liverpool and Manchester Railway; and instead of those luxurious, roomy coaches we were squeezy and uncomfortable to a degree. The distance from the Delaware to Frenchtown on the Elk, where we were again to take to the water, is about sixteen miles, which we did in an hour. The Elk, which in this world of huge waters is considered but a paltry ditch but which in our country would be thought a very decent sized river, was a few days ago frozen up, thereby putting a stop to steamboat travelling. But fortunately for us, it was open today, and presently we beheld the steamer coming puffing up to take us from the pier.

At dinner the strange dark man was sitting opposite us and

discoursing in a strain and tone in which shrewdness and swagger and vulgarity and a sort of braggart gallantry were curiously jumbled. When dinner was over, I asked my father if he had any idea who this strange man was. 'I am told', was his reply, 'that he is but just returned from New York, where he has been tried for piracy.'

Touching pirates, Baltimore, I was told, is famous for them. They have small schooners there of a particularly light build, and raking masts, which are the prettiest things in the world to look at and the swiftest that sail sea. The Baltimore clippers are proverbial for their elegance and fleetness: they are like greyhounds on the water. These, I was told, were frequently owned by gentlemen of a rather ambiguous character, something between pirate, smuggler and wrecker, perhaps a judicious mixture of all three. Their trade is chiefly, I believe, with the West India islands. I looked at my Spanish-faced friend with redoubled curiosity. He was the very man for a pirate.

My spirits always sink when I come to a strange place; and as we came along the wharf sides at Baltimore, under the red dingy-looking warehouses, between which the water ran in narrow dark-looking canals, I felt terribly gloomy. We drove up to Barnhams's, the best house in the town; and having found out where to lay my head, I had my fill of crying.

Baltimore, January 2nd, 1833

My dearest Harriet, . . . We arrived in this place on Monday at half-past four. Baltimore, as far as I have seen it, strikes me as a large, rambling, red-brick village on the outskirts of one of our manufacturing towns, Birmingham or Manchester. It covers an immense extent of ground, but there are great gaps of gravelly ground, meadow land and large vacant spaces – which will all no doubt be covered with buildings in good time, for it is growing daily and hourly.

While my father and I were exploring about together yesterday, we came to a print shop whose window exhibited an engraving of Reynolds' Mrs. Siddons as the Tragic Muse and Lawrence's picture of my uncle John in *Hamlet*. My father looked with a good deal of emotion at these beautiful representations of his beautiful kindred, and it was a sort of sad surprise to meet them in this other world where we are wandering, aliens and strangers.

In a week's time we are going to Washington, where we shall

find dear Washington Irving,[1] whom I think I shall embrace for England's sake as well as his own.

We are earning money very fast and though I think we work too incessantly and too hard, yet, as every night we do not act is a certain loss of so much out of my father's pocket, I do not like to make many objections to it, although I think it is really not unlikely to be detrimental to his own health and strength.

(*Records*) Washington Irving was intimately acquainted with my parents and a most kind and condescending friend to me. It was when he was an obscure young man of business in London that he was introduced to my mother, whose cordial kindness to him made a profound impression. Unaffected, unconstrained, kindly and good, he seemed so entirely to forget his own celebrity that one almost forgot it too in talking to him. I remember his coming the day after my first appearance at Covent Garden, and I ran to show him the pretty new watch I had received from my father the night before. He took it and slowly turned it about, commending its fine workmanship; then, putting it to his ear with a most mischievous look of affected surprise, exclaimed, as one does of a child's watch, 'Why, it goes, I declare!'

Sunday, 6th. We walked up to the cathedral, which is a large, unfinished stone building standing on the brow of a hill. The interior is large and handsome, and has more the look of a church than anything I have been inside of in this country yet. I have not been in a Catholic place of worship since I was at school. They sang that exquisitely mournful and beautiful *Et incarnatus est* of Haydn's, which made my blood all run backwards. One thing disgusted me dreadfully; though the priests who were officiating never passed or approached the altar without bending the knee to it, they kept spitting all over the carpet that surrounded and covered the steps to it, interrupting themselves in the middle of the service to do so, without the slightest hesitation. We had a very indifferent sermon: the service of course was in Latin.

Monday, 7th. The play was *Romeo and Juliet*; the house was extremely full. They are a delightful audience. My Romeo had gotten on a pair of breeches that looked as if he had borrowed them from some worthy Dutchman of a hundred years ago. He looked like a magical figure growing out of a monstrous strange-

[1] 1783–1859. American author and diplomat.

coloured melon, beneath which descended his unfortunate legs, thrust into a pair of red slippers. The play went off pretty well, except that they broke one man's collar-bone and nearly dislocated a woman's shoulder by flinging the scenery about. My bed was not made in time, and when the scene drew, half a dozen carpenters in patched trowsers and tattered shirt sleeves were discovered smoothing down my pillows and adjusting my draperies. The last scene is too good not to be given verbatim:

Romeo	Tear not our heart strings thus! They crack! They break! – Juliet! Juliet! (*dies*)
Juliet (*to corpse*)	Am I smothering you?
Corpse (*to Juliet*)	Not at all; could you be so kind, do you think, as to put my wig on again for me? – it has fallen off.
Juliet (*to corpse*)	I'm afraid I can't, but I'll throw my muslin veil over it. You've broken the phial, haven't you?
(*corpse nodded*)	
Juliet	Where's your dagger?
Corpse	'Pon my soul, I don't know.

Sunday, 13th. By half past ten we were packed in what in this country is termed an exclusive extra – i.e. a stage coach to ourselves – and progressing towards Washington. The coach was comfortable enough; as for the road, I can't think of it without aching, but at last we arrived, with no bones broken, at the capital and seat of government of the United States. Upon the height immediately above the city is situated the Capitol, a very handsome building, of which the Americans are not a little proud; but it seems placed there by mistake, so little do the miserable untidy hovels above, and the scattered, unfinished red-brick town below accord with its patrician marble and high-sounding title. We drove to Gadsby's, which is an inn like a little town, with more wooden galleries, flights of steps, passages, doorways, exits and entrances than any building I ever saw.

Monday, 14th. We walked up to the Capitol and went first into the Senate because Webster[2] was speaking, whom I especially wished to hear. The room itself is neither large nor lofty; the senators sit in two semi-circular rows in comfortable armchairs.

[2] Daniel Webster (1772–1852). Lawyer, Senator and famous orator.

Literally sitting among them were a whole regiment of ladies, whispering, laughing and fidgeting. A gallery, divided by a low partition from the main room, ran round the apartment: this too was filled with pink and blue and yellow bonnets; and every now and then, while Webster was speaking, a tremendous bustle and waving of feathers and rustling of silks would be heard and in came streaming a reinforcement of political beauties, and then would commence a jumping up, a sitting down, a squeezing through and a how-d'ye-doing. The senators would turn round, even Webster would hesitate. Webster's face is very remarkable, particularly the forehead and eyes. The subject upon which he was speaking was not one of particular interest – an estimate of the amount of French spoliations, by cruizers and privateers, upon American commerce.

The heat of the room was intolerable, and we adjourned to the House of Representatives. On the way thither we turned off to the Library, which is a comfortable, well-sized room, where we looked over Audubon's Ornithology, a beautiful work, and saw a man sitting with his feet upon the table, reading, which is an American fashion.

The House of Representatives is lofty and large and very handsome, but extremely ill-constructed for the voice which is completely lost among the columns and only reaches the gallery, where listeners are admitted, in indistinct and very unedifying murmurs. The members not infrequently sit with their feet up on their desks.

Tuesday, 15th. Went to see the original of the Declaration of Independence and afterwards to the War Office, where we saw sundry Indian properties – bows and arrows, and what interested me much more, the pictures of a great many savage chiefs and one or two Indian women. One of the women's names amused me a great deal – *The Woman that Spoke first*; which title occasioned infinite surmise as to the occasion on which she first earned it.

Afterwards we went on to the President's house, which is a comfortless, handsome-looking building, with a withered grass plot in wooden palings in front and a desolate reach of uncultivated ground down to the river behind.

We heard a most entertaining account of the levées, or rather the public days, at the President's House. Every human being has a right to present himself there: the consequence is that great numbers of the very commonest sort of people used to rush in and follow about the servants who carried refreshments, seizing upon whatever they could get, and staring and pushing about to the infinite discomfiture of the more respectable and better behaved part of the assembly. Indeed the nuisance became so great that they discontinued the eatables and in great measure got rid of the crowd.

Thursday, 17th. Proceeded to the Presidency to be presented in due form. His Excellency Andrew Jackson is very tall and thin, but erect and dignified in his carriage – a good specimen of a fine old well-battered soldier. His hair is very thick and grey; his manners are perfectly simple and quiet, therefore very good.

Saturday, 19th. Washington is the strangest thing by way of a town that can be fancied. It is laid out to cover, I should think, some ten miles square, but the houses are here, there and no where: the streets are roads, crooked or straight, where buildings are *intended* to be. Every now and then an interesting gap of a quarter of a mile occurs between those houses that *are* built: in the midst of the town you can't help fancying you are in the country. Washington altogether struck me as a rambling, red-brick image of futurity, where nothing *is*, but all things *are* to be.

New York, Monday, 18th February. The play was *Macbeth* for my benefit: the house was very full, and I played very ill. I had an interesting discussion about the costume and acting of the witches in this awful play. It has always been customary to make some low comedians act the witches and to dress them like old fisherwomen. Instead of the wild, unearthly appearance which Banquo describes, we have three jolly-faced fellows with as due a proportion of petticoats as any woman, letting alone a witch, might desire, jocose red faces, peaked hats and broomsticks. If I had the casting of *Macbeth*, I would give the witches to the first melodramatic actors on the stage and give them such dresses as would accord a little better with the blasted heath, the dark fungus-grown wood, the desolate, misty hill-side and the flickering light of the caldron cave.

In April 1833 the Kembles proceeded to Boston, with Pierce Butler in assiduous attendance. Almost every day he took Fanny riding, and so enchanted was she with the beauties of the spring-time countryside

*and the exhilaration of gallops along the seashore at Chelsea beach that
there is scarcely a mention of the theatre in her journal during the
whole of their five-week season there. And yet her success was pheno-
menal. 'Every young girl who could sported Fanny Kemble curls — to
be thought to look like her was their aspiration. I remember making a
long pilgrimage on horseback to gaze upon a young lady whose attraction was a fancied resemblance to Fanny Kemble. As for us Harvard
students, we all went mad. As long as funds held out there was a
procession of us, hastening breathless over the road to Boston as the
evening shade came on.'*[3]

Monday, 15th. We rode out to *Cambridge*, the University of Massachusetts, about three miles distant from Boston. The village
round it, with its white cottages and the green lawns and trees
round the college, reminded me of England. We rode on to a
place called Mount Auburn, a burial place which the Bostonians
take great pride in. The entrance is a fine, solid, granite gateway
in a species of Egyptian style. The whole place is at present in an
unfinished state, but its capabilities are very great. The enclosure
– of about one hundred acres – contains several high hills and
deep ravines, at the bottom of which are dark, still, melancholy-
looking meres. The whole is cut, with much skill and good taste,
by roads for carriages and narrow footpaths. Already two or three
white monuments are seen palely glimmering through the
woods, reminding one of the solemn use to which this ground is
consecrated, which for its beauty might seem a pleasure garden
instead of a place of graves. My astonishment was unfeigned
when, upon an after-inspection, I found this very lofty gateway
was constructed of *painted wood*! What! a cheat, a sham thing at
the threshold of the grave! – surely thereabouts pretences should
have an end. Anything would be better than an imitation gateway.

Wednesday, 27th. It is quite comical to see the people in the
morning at the box office: our window is opposite to it and 'tis a
matter of the greatest amusement to me to watch them. They
collect in crowds for upwards of an hour before the doors open,
and then there is a yelling and shouting as if the town were on
fire. In they rush, thumping and pummelling one another and
not one comes out without rubbing his head or back or showing a
piteous rent in his clothes. I was surprised to see men of a very

[3] Henry Lee: *Atlantic Monthly*, May 1893, p. 664.

low order pressing forward to obtain boxes, but I find that they sell them again at an enormous increase; and, the better to carry on their traffic, they smear their clothes with molasses, in order to prevent any person of more decent appearance from coming near the box office: this is ingenious and deserves a reward. Our other window looks out upon a large churchyard, in the midst of which stands a cenotaph erected by Franklin in honour of his father. Between the view of the playhouse and the view of the burial ground, my contemplations are curiously tinged.

Thursday, 2nd May. After breakfast, went over to rehearsal; at half past eleven went out to ride: the day was heavenly, bright and mild, with a full, soft sweet spring breeze blowing life and health over one. The golden willow trees were all in flower, and the air rich with their fragrance. The whole world was full of loveliness, and my spirits were in most harmonious tune with all its beauty. We rode along the chiming beach, talking gravely of many matters, temporal and spiritual: and when we reached the pines, I dismounted, entreated for a scrap of paper and scribbled down some miserable doggerel to ease my heart.

My ride did me ten thousand goods. As we were riding through a farm, a little boy came running to meet me with his hand full of beautiful flowers, which he stood upon tiptoe to thrust into my hand, and without waiting to be thanked rushed back into the house. I was delighted: the flowers were exquisite and the manner of the gift very enchanting. Altogether, I do not know when I have been so completely filled with pleasurable emotions as during this ride.

LINES

To the smooth beach, the silver sea
Comes rippling in a thousand smiles,
And back again runs murmuringly,
To break around yon distant isles.
The sunshine, through a floating veil
Of golden clouds, looks o'er the wave,
And gilds, far off, the outline pale,
Of many a rocky cape and cave.
The breath of spring comes balmily
Over the newly blossom'd earth;
The smile of spring, on sea, and sky,
Is shedding light, and love, and mirth.

I would that thou wert by my side,
To feel this soft air on thy brow,
And listen to the chiming tide
Along that smooth shore breaking now;
I would that thou wert here to bless,
As I do now, the love and care,
That with such wealth of loveliness,
Have made life's journeying-land so fair.

CHAPTER 9

Romance and Tragedy
1833–1834

During the Boston spring Fanny was clearly falling in love with Pierce Butler. As ever reticent about her deeper emotions, she makes no mention of the attachment in her published writings, though in the Journal frequent lines of asterisks almost certainly indicate the excision of more intimate material.

It seems likely that the engagement took place during a long holiday tour up the Hudson and Mohawk rivers to the Niagara Falls. That she was already considering the possibility before she set out is apparent from an oblique reference in one of her letters home: 'Though England will always be home to my heart, it may be that this country will become my abiding-place'. At any event by September the affair was common gossip in New York, when Philip Hone noted a report that 'she is married already, or about to be, to Mr. Pierce Butler of Philadelphia'. In the diary of the journey, however, it is Edward Trelawny, who joined the party after their first stop, who on the surface at least appears to claim more of Fanny's attention than Pierce Butler. Years later she recalled her first impressions of the man who had been a friend of Shelley and Byron.

(*Records*) Trelawny's wild career of sea adventure with de Ruyter, who was supposed to have left him at his death all his share of the results of their semi-buccaneering exploits, his friendship with Byron and Shelley, the funeral obsequies he bestowed on the latter on the shore of the Gulf of Spezzia, his companionship in the mountains of Greece with the patriot chief Odysseus and his marriage to that chief's sister, are all circumstances given with more or less detail in his book *The Adventures of a Younger Son*, which was Englished for him by Mary Shelley, Trelawny himself being quite incapable of any literary effort which required a knowledge of common spelling. He was strikingly handsome when I first knew him, with a countenance habitually serene and occasionally sweet in its expression, but sometimes savage with the fierceness of a wild beast. His speech and movement were

91

slow and indolently gentle, his voice very low and musical; he was very tall and powerfully made, and altogether looked like the hero of a wild life of adventure such as his has been. I hear he is still alive, a very wonderful looking old man, who sat to Millais for his picture, exhibited in 1874, of his 'Old Sea Captain'.

Tuesday, 2nd July. Packed up my bag; bade a very unwilling farewell to the pretty place, and rowed over to West Point, where Mr. Trelawny was waiting for us. When the boat came up, the rush was without exception the most frightful thing I ever saw. Safely on board, I took out my work and Mr. Trelawny sat down by us. As a nuisance, which all unsought-for companionship is, he is quite the most endurable possible, for he has seen such things, and known such people that it is greatly worth while to listen to him. Everything he says of Byron and Shelley confirms my impresssion of them.

At about half-past three the angry-looking clouds lay heaped like chalk upon a leaden sky and every preparation was made for a storm. We scuttled down to the lower deck as fast as ever we could, but the storm met us at the bottom of the stairs, and in an instant I was drenched. Chairs, tables, everything, was over-turned by the gust; and the boat was running with water in every direction. I stood by the door of the furnace and dried leisurely, talking the while to Mr. Trelawny, who is sun-burnt enough to warm one through with a look. During our progress, one of the wheels (or paddles as they are properly called) took it into its head to knock its case to pieces, and banged the boards in a strange way. Accident the second: – one of the men, a black who was employed in tending the fire, got so dreadfully heated that he rushed out of the engine room and swallowed two or three draughts of cold water. The effect was instantaneous: he fell down in violent internal spasms and died, poor wretch! before we arrived at Albany.

Saturday, 6th. We reached Troy (Troy! and that Troy has a Mount Ida! The names of places in this country are truly astonishing) and walked up into the town. A man very civilly invited us to come into his shop and sit down. The shop we were in was a china store; and the nice cold crockery ware made one cool to look at it; the weather was roasting. Mr. Trelawny left us to gather infor-mation, and kindly brought me back word that the population of Troy was five hundred, *or* five thousand, I really forget which;

and that the store-keeper assured him the Trojans were an exceedingly refined and literary set of folks; and that the society was no whit behind Boston: there's for Boston!

Mr. Trelawny dined with us: what a savage he is, in some respects! He is a curious being: a man with the proportions of a giant for strength and agility; yet with the most listless, indolent carelessness of gait; and an uncertain, wandering way of dropping his feet to the ground, as if he didn't know where he was going, and didn't much wish to go anywhere. His face is as dark as a Moor's; with a wild, strange look about the eyes and a mark like a scar upon his cheek: his whole appearance giving one an idea of toil, hardship, peril and wild adventure. His hands are as brown as a labourer's: he never profanes them with gloves, but wears two strange magical-looking rings: one of them, which he showed me, is made of elephant's hair.

Wednesday, 10th. We started at two from Schenectady and proceeded by canal to Utica, a distance we performed in a day and a night. I like travelling by the canal boats very much. Ours was not crowded; and the country through which we passed being delightful, the placid, moderate gliding through it at about four miles and a half an hour seemed to me infinitely preferable to the noise of wheels, the rumble of a coach and the jerking of bad roads, for the gain of a mile an hour. The only nuisances are the bridges over the canal, which are so very low that one is obliged to prostrate oneself on the deck of the boat to avoid being scraped off it; and this humiliation occurs, upon an average, once every quarter of an hour. Mr. Trelawny read Don Quixote to us.

Thursday, 11th. At Utica we dined, and after dinner I slept profoundly. The gentlemen went out to view the town, which twenty years ago *was not* and is now a flourishing place, with fine-looking shops, two or three hotels, good broad streets and a body of lawyers who had a supper at the house where we were staying and kept the night awake with champagne, shouting, toasts and the clapping of hands: so much for the strides of civilisation through the savage lands of this new world.

Friday, 12th. We all breakfasted together early, and immediately set off for Trenton. At last, after about fifteen miles, we reached the house at which visitors put up: a large comfortable enough dwelling kept by a couple of nice young people who maintain themselves and a beautiful big baby by the profits they derive from the pilgrims to Trenton. We ordered dinner and set forth. Presently we arrived at the first fall. I can't describe it: I don't know either its height or width; I only know that it was extremely beautiful and came pouring down like a great rolling heap of amber. After standing before the tumbling mass of water for a length of time, we climbed to the brink above and went on to the beautiful circular fall. Pierce and I loitered by the rapid waters, flinging light branches and flowers upon the blood coloured torrent. We sat with our feet hanging over the black caldron, just opposite a vivid rainbow that was clasping the waterfall. We sat here till I began to grow dizzy with the sound and motion of the churning darkness beneath us, and begged to move, which we did very cautiously. When I was tired with walking, and Pierce was lifting me up to seat me on a fallen tree by another fall, we saw Mr. Trelawny coming towards us. He stopped and spoke to us and presently passed on; we remained behind, talking and dipping our hands into the fresh water.

Saturday, 13th. Left Utica at six o'clock: we were to go as far as Auburn, a distance of seventy-six miles. Mr. Trelawny began talking about Greece, and getting a good deal excited, presently burst forth into 'The isles of Greece! the isles of Greece!' which he recited with amazing vehemence and earnestness. He reminded me of Kean several times: while he was declaiming he looked like a tiger. 'Tis strange how, in spite of the contempt and even hatred which he often expresses for England and everything connected with it, his thoughts and plans, and all the energies of his mind, seem for ever bent upon the changes to be wrought in England – freer government, purer laws, more equal rights.

Thursday, 16th. At six, started from Rochester for Murray, where we proposed breakfasting. As we were nearing the inn and we were all earnestly engaged in a discussion, I suddenly felt a tremendous sort of stunning blow and as soon as I opened my eyes found that the coach was overturned, lying completely on its side. I was very comfortably curled up under my father who, by Heaven's mercy, did not suffocate me; opposite sat Dall, white as a ghost, with her forehead cut open and an awful looking stream of blood falling from it; by her stood Mr. Trelawny, also pale as ashes: Pierce was perched like a bird above us all, on the edge of the doorway which was open. The first thing I did was to cry, 'I'm not hurt, I'm not hurt!' The next thing was to get my father up: in accomplishing which he trampled upon me most cruelly. As soon as I was relieved from his mountainous pressure, I got up and saw, to my dismay, two men carrying Mr. Trelawny into the house. We were all convinced that some of his limbs were broken: I ran after as quickly as I could and presently the house was like a hospital. They carried him into an upper room, here too they brought Dall, all white and bleeding. Our hand-baskets and bags were ransacked for salts and eau de cologne. Cold water, hot water, towels and pocket handkerchiefs were called into requisition; and I, with my clothes all torn and one shoulder all bruised and cut, went from the one to the other in dismay. Presently Mr. Trelawny revived and gave ample testimony of having the use of his limbs by getting up and in the most skilful manner plastering poor Dall's broken brow. Pierce went in quest of my father, who had received a violent blow on his leg and was halting about, looking after the baggage and the driver, who had escaped unhurt. While the coach was being repaired and the horses changed, we – bound up, bruised and aching, but still very merry – sat down to breakfast. Mr. Trelawny, who had been merely stunned, seized on the milk and honey and stuffed away with great zeal; poor Dall was the most deplorable of the party, with a bloody handkerchief bound over one half of her face; I only ached a little and I believe Pierce escaped with a scratch on his finger. Seeing it was no worse, we thanked God and devoured. After breakfast, we packed ourselves in again and progressed.

Wednesday, 17th. An uneasy, rickety cart without springs was the sole conveyance we could obtain to the Niagara Falls. As we squeaked and creaked up the hill, I felt absolutely nervous with expectation. The sound of the cataract is, they say, heard within fifteen miles when the wind sets favourably; today, however, there was no wind; the whole air was breathless with the heat of midsummer and, though we stopped our waggon once or twice to listen, all was profoundest silence. When we were within about three miles of the Falls Pierce stopped the waggon, and then we heard distinctly the voice of the mighty cataract. Looking over the woods we beheld one silver cloud rising into the sky – the everlasting incense of the waters. A perfect frenzy of impatience seized me; and when at length the carriage stopped at the Niagara House, waiting neither for my father, Dall nor Pierce, I rushed through the garden and down the steep footpath cut in the rocks. I heard steps behind me; Trelawny was following. Down, down I sprang, and along the narrow footpath and saw through the boughs the white glimmer of that sea of foam. 'Go on, go on; don't stop,' shouted Trelawny, and in another minute I stood upon Table Rock. Trelawny seized me by the arm and dragged me to the edge of the rapids, to the brink of the abyss. I saw Niagara – Oh, God! Who can describe that sight?

So ends Fanny's 'purely egotistical record' as she described her Journal in her preface to the London Edition. From Niagara, the Kembles proceeded across Lake Ontario and down the St. Lawrence to Montreal and Quebec, having put behind them some thousand miles of travel by road and water since leaving New York. The injuries sustained by Dall in the coach accident proved more serious than anyone realised at the time: she had gravely injured her spine. During the winter of 1833–4 she became increasingly ill and incapacitated.

Boston, April 16th, 1834
Dear Mrs. Jameson, . . . You will be sorry when I tell you that our good, dear friend Dall is dangerously ill. I am writing at the moment by her bed. This is the only trial of the kind I have ever undergone: God has hitherto been pleased to spare all those whom I love and to grant them strength and health. This is my first lonely watching by a sick bed, and I feel deeply the sadness and awfulness of the office. My poor dear aunt's illness is giving us a professional respite, for which my faculties, physical and mental, are very grateful. They needed it sorely; I was almost worn out with work and latterly with anxiety and bitter distress.

We terminated our last engagement here on Friday last, when the phlegmatic Bostonians seemed almost beside themselves with excitement and enthusiasm: they shouted at us, they cheered us, they crowned me with roses. Conceive, if you can, the shocking contrast between all this and the silent sick-room, to which I went straight from the stage.

New York, Thursday April 24th, 1834
My dear Harriet, This will be but a short letter, the first short one you will have received from me since we parted. Dear Dall has gone from us. She is dead; she died in my arms and I closed her eyes. It has been a dreadful shock though it was not unexpected; but there is no preparation for the sense of desolation which oppresses me, and which is beyond words. We shall probably be

in England on the 10th of July. The sole care of my father, who is deeply afflicted, and charge of everything devolves entirely on me now.

We left Boston on Tuesday. I act here tonight for the first time since I lost that dear and devoted friend who was ever near at hand to think of everything for me, to care for me in every way. I have cried my eyes out daily for the last three months: but that is over now. I am working again, and go about my work feeling stunned and bewildered.

God bless you, dear Harriet. We shall meet ere long, and in the midst of great sorrow that will be a great joy to

Yours affectionately,

F.A.K.

We have buried dear Dall in a lonely, lovely place in Mount Auburn cemetery, where Pierce and I used to go and sit together last spring, in the early time of our intimacy. I wished her to lie there, for life and love and youth and death have their trysting place at the grave.

Fanny did not return to England. She ends her Record of a Girlhood *with a bald statement:*

I was married in Philadelphia on the 7th of June, 1834, to Mr. Pierce Butler of that city.

Part Two

Part Two

CHAPTER 10

Mr. Butler's Bride
1834–1836

Philadelphia, October 26th, 1834
Dear Mrs. Jameson, However stoutly your incredulity may have
held out hitherto against the various 'authentic' reports of my
marriage, I beg you will, upon receipt of this, immediately believe
that I was married on the 7th June last and have now been a wife
for nearly five mortal months. You know that in leaving the stage
I left nothing that I regretted, but the utter separation from my
family is a serious source of pain for me.

With regard to what you say about the first year of marriage not
being as happy as the second, I know not how that may be. I had
pictured to myself no fairyland of enchantments within the mysterious precincts of matrimony; I expected from it rest, quiet,
leisure to study, to think and to work, and legitimate channels for
the affections of my nature.

In the closest and dearest friendship, shades of character and
the precise depth and power of the various qualities of mind and
heart never approximate to such a degree as to preclude all
possibility of occasional misunderstandings. No two human
beings were ever fashioned absolutely alike, even in their outward bodily form, and how should the fine and infinite spirit
admit of such similarity with another? But the firm principles
upon which all honourable and enduring sympathy is founded –
the love of truth, the reverence for right, the abhorrence of all that
is base and unworthy – admit of no difference or mis-
understanding; and where these exist in the relations of two
people united for life, it seems to me that love and happiness as
perfect as this imperfect existence affords may be realised.

What can I tell you of myself? My life and all its occupations are
of a sober, neutral tint. I am busy preparing my journal for the
press. I read but little. I have never read much and am disgracefully ignorant; I am looking forward with delight to hours of
quiet study and the mental hoards in store for me. I am at present,
and have been ever since my marriage, staying in the house of my

101

brother-in-law [John Butler] and feel not a little anxious to be in a home of my own. But painters, and carpenters, and upholsterers are dirty divinities of a lower order, not to be moved or hastened by human invocations (or even imprecations) and we must e'en bide their time.

I please myself much in the fancying of furniture and fitting up the house; and I look forward to a garden, greenhouse and dairy among my future interests, to each of which I intend to addict myself zealously.

My pets are a horse, a bird and a black squirrel, and I do not see exactly what more a reasonable woman could desire. Human companionship, indeed, at present I have not much of; but like will to like and I do not despair of attracting towards me, by and by, some of my own kind. But you can form no idea – none – none – of the intellectual dearth and drought in which I am existing at present.

Fanny had been Mrs. Butler for only five months when she wrote this letter, hardly what might be expected from one so recently married.[1] *Although the couple were undoubtedly much in love, they very soon woke up to the reality of their totally different temperaments and diametrically opposite views on the relationship between husband and wife. Fanny could not and would not 'subject her will to his' as Pierce demanded from the first: he, never expecting otherwise, was baffled and angry. The first clash arose over the indiscreet American journal which Fanny had sold to a publisher months before her marriage. Pierce, as of right, blue-pencilled long passages and she was furious. A month after writing to Mrs. Jameson and while they were still living with their in-laws in Philadelphia, she packed her bags and left, intending to go home to England, but within a few hours she was back, not having been able to find the hotel she was looking for. It was the first of many such gestures of defiance and subsequent reconciliations.*

Philadelphia, November 27th, 1834

My dear Harriet, I think it must be near on three weeks since I wrote to you, which is a sin and a shame. To say I have not had time to write is nonsense, yet it almost seemed as if I had not. I have been constantly driving out to the farm to watch the prog-

---

[1] The seventeen year old Fanny Appleton, who later married the poet Longfellow, stayed in the same hotel as the Butlers at Newport, Rhode Island, two months previously: 'Mrs. Pierce Butler is here. . . . She is so engaged in writing her book of travels that she only appears in the evening, when she is very gay, waltzing and gallopading most gracefully. Her manners have become much more

ress of the painting, whitewashing, etc. etc. In town I have been engaging servants, ordering china, glass and furniture, choosing carpets, curtains and house-linen, and devoutly studying all the time *Dr. Kitchener's Housekeeper's Manual and Cook's Oracle.*

The other day, for the first time, I explored my future domain. It is bounded on the right by the high-road; on the left by a not unromantic little mill-stream. I think the extent of our *estate* is about 300 acres. Except a kitchen garden, there is none that deserves the name; no flower-beds, no shrubberies, no gravel walks. There is nothing that can call itself a lawn, though coarse grass grows all around the house. There are four pretty meadows and a very pretty piece of woodland which will, I foresee, become a favourite haunt of mine. There is a farmyard, a cider press, a pond, a dairy and outhouses and adjuncts innumerable.

Miss Martineau is just now in Philadelphia: I have seen and conversed with her, and I think, were her stay long enough to admit of so agreeable a conclusion, we might become good friends. Her deafness is a serious bar to her enjoyment of society, and some drawback to the pleasure of conversing with her, for, as a man observed to me last night, 'One feels so like a fool saying "How do you do?" through a speaking trumpet in the middle of a drawing room'; and unshoutable commonplaces form the staple of all drawing room conversation. They are giving literary parties to her; and balls to one of their own townswomen just returned from abroad, which makes Philadelphia rather gayer than usual; and I have had so long a fast from dissipation that I find myself quite excited at the idea of going to a dance again. I have succeeded in engaging an apparently tolerably decent staff of servants; the house is freshly painted and clean, the furniture finished and the carpets ready to lay down. Next week I hope to send our household out and the week after I sincerely hope I shall be in a home of my own.

I toil on, copying my journal, and one volume of it is already printed, but now that the object of publication is gone, I feel rather disgusted at the idea of publishing it at all. Now that I have become careless of its money value it seems to me a mere mass of trivial detail. When I sold it, it was an excellent good book

affable, and I must say she is capable of being truly fascinating. . . . Her flashing glances are still beautiful though she is frightfully coarse to examine. By exposure to the sun she is burned to a bright mahogany color and yet wears every evening a white muslin with bare neck and gloveless arms! She dresses in shocking taste.' (*Mrs. Longfellow*, p. 14.)

for I thought it would help to make a small independence for my dear Dall; now she is gone, and it is mere trash, but I have sold it.[2]

My country life will, I hope, be one of study and quiet happiness. I have one very great pleasure almost in contemplation. I think it probable that my friend Miss Sedgwick will visit Philadelphia this winter and remain a short time here, which will be a great delight to me.[3]

(*Records*) My long experience of life in America presents the ideas and expectations with which I first entered upon it in an aspect at once ludicrous and melancholy to me now. The Englishwoman's notions of country interests, duties and occupations – the village, the school, the poor, one's relations with one's employees and one's own especial hobbies of garden, dairy, etc. – had all been contemplated by me from a point of view taken from rural life in my own country, which had not the slightest resemblance to anything in any American existence.

Butler Place – or, as I called it, 'The Farm' – was in no way superior to a second-rate farmhouse in England. It was amply sufficient, however, for my desires; but, since we inhabited it by kind allowance of an old relation to whom it belonged, all my busy visions of gardening and greenhouse improvement, etc.

[2] Many Americans were incensed by Fanny's picture of their country. She was accused of bad taste, lack of delicacy and downright rudeness to those who had offered her friendship and hospitality; and indeed it was not the most tactful of books to come from one who had so recently become an American. 'There is all the light gossip, the childish prejudice, the hasty conclusions from erroneous first impressions in which the diary of an imaginative youthful traveller in a country in which all things are new and untried may be supposed to abound', wrote Philip Hone when he read it, and went on to comment indignantly on her description of the dinner at which he had introduced her into American society, 'written . . . with all the flippancy and want of reflection that one might expect to find in the commonplace book of a giddy girl who has just returned from a dinner party in which herself was the principal object of notice and attention, and from which, I can tell her, she went away leaving no very favourable impressions behind her'. (*Diary*, Vol. I, p. 126.) Opinions were little more complimentary when the book appeared on the English side of the Atlantic. Princess Victoria concluded that 'the authoress must be very pert and ill-bred' and that a book so full of 'trash and nonsense' could only do Fanny harm. Victoria read on, however, admitting later that it much amused her and that there were 'some very fine feelings in it' (*Girlhood*, pp. 128 and 132) – a reaction similar to many others, including Macready's: 'Despite the general disgusting character of her book, you can see evidence of thought and superior intellect.' (*Reminiscences*, ed. Toynbee, vol. I, p. 231.)

[3] Catherine Maria Sedgwick (1789–1867), New England novelist. She and her many relations were to become Fanny's closest friends in America and to give her constant love and support in difficult times.

had to be indefinitely postponed. Subsequently I made flower beds and laid out gravel walks and left an abiding mark of my sojourn there in a double row of two hundred trees. Many of them, from my and my assistants' combined ignorance, died or came to no good growth. But those which survived form a screen of shade to the grounds and protect them in some measure from the dust and glare of the highway.

Cultivating my garden was not possible. My first attempt at cultivating my neighbours' goodwill was a ludicrous and lamentable failure. I offered to teach the little children of my gardener and farmer, and as many of the village children as liked to join them, to read and write; but found my benevolent proposal excited nothing but a sort of contemptuous amazement. There was the village school, where they received instruction for which they were obliged and willing to pay, which answered all their purposes and where the small students made their exits and their entrances without pulling of forelock or any other superstitious observance of civilised courtesy. My gratuitous education was sniffed at alike by parents and progeny. Of course the whole idea upon which I had proferred it was mistaken and misplaced and may have appeared to them to imply an impertinent under-valuing of a system with which they were perfectly satisfied. These people and their children wanted nothing I could give them. The 'ladies' liked the make of my gowns and would have borrowed them for patterns with pleasure, but this was all they desired or required from me.

On the first 4th July I spent there, being alone, I organised (British fashion) a feast and rejoicing such as I thought should mark the birthday of American independence and the expulsion of the tyrannical English from the land. I had a table set under the trees and a dinner spread. Beer and wine were liberally provided, and fireworks for due honouring of the evening. I did my best to give my visitors a good time, but succeeded only in imposing upon them a dinner and afternoon of uncomfortable restraint, from which the juniors alone seemed happily free. Neither the wine nor the beer were touched; my Quaker farmer and his family were all absolute temperance people; indeed, he objected to me repeatedly that it was 'a shame and a pity to waste such a fine day for work in doing nothing'.

Of any charitable interest to be derived from the poverty of my village neighbours, I very soon found my expectation equally vain. Our village had no *poor* in the deplorable English acceptation of that word. Comparatively poor people it undoubtedly had – hard workers, toiling for their daily bread, but none who could not get well-paid work or find sufficient bread. The abject element of ignorant, helpless, hopeless pauperism, looking for its existence to charity and substituting alms-taking for independent labour, was unknown there. As for 'visiting' among them, as technically understood and practised by Englishwomen among their poorer neighbours, such a civility would have struck mine as simply incomprehensible.

(*Records*) The country between the Wissihiccon and the Pennipack – two small picturesque streams flowing, the one into the Schuylkill, the other into the Delaware – was a prosperous farming region with stretches of pretty, wild woodland, and divided by the main high road, once the chief channel of communication between New York and Philadelphia.

Six miles from the latter, at a village called Branchtown and only a few yards from the road, stood my home. It would be difficult for those who do not remember 'the old York road', as it was called, to imagine the change which nearly fifty years has produced in the whole region. No one who now sees the pretty, populous villadom which has grown up round the home of my early married years – the neat cottages and cheerful country houses, the trim lawns and bright flower gardens – could easily conceive the sort of abomination of desolation which its aspect formerly presented to eyes accustomed to the rural English landscape.[4]

Between five and six miles of hideous and execrable turnpike road, aridly detestable in the glare, heat and dust of summer and almost dangerously impassable in winter, made driving into Philadelphia an undertaking which neither love, friendship or pleasure – nothing but inexorable business or duty – reconciled one to.

Per contra, it was then country and now is suburb. There were woods and lanes where now there are stations and railroads, and the solitude of rural walks and rides instead of the 'continuation of the city', which will presently convert that whole neighbourhood into a mere appendage of Philadelphia, wildly driven over by city rowdies with fast trotting teams or mad gigantic daddy-long-legs-looking sulkies, and perambulated by tramps pretending poverty and practising theft.

[4] Butler Place was demolished in the late nineteen twenties.

[Early] 1835

Dear Mrs. Jameson, . . . I am well and happy; my whole state of life and being has assumed a placid and even course which, after the violent excitements of my last few years, is both agreeable and wholesome. I should think, ever since my coming out on the stage, I must have lived pretty much at the rate of three years in every one. It seems difficult to imagine that the remainder of my years is lying stretched before me, like a level, peaceful landscape through which I shall saunter leisurely towards my grave. This is the pleasant probable future: God knows what changes and chances may sweep across the smiling prospect, but at the present none is likely to arise. As I write these words, I *do* bethink me of one quarter from which our present existence might receive a shock – the South.

The family into which I have married are large slave-holders; our present and future fortune depends greatly upon extensive plantations in Georgia. But the experience of every day, besides our faith in the great justice of God, forbids dependence on the duration of the mighty abuse by which one man is held in abject physical and mental slavery by another. As for me, though the toilsome earning of my daily bread were to be my lot again tomorrow, I should rejoice with unspeakable thankfulness that we had not to answer for what I consider so grievous a sin against humanity.

June 27th, 1835

My dearest Harriet, Since my baby has made her entrance into the world [Sarah, (Sally) born May 28th] I neither read, write nor cast up accounts, but am as idle, though not nearly so well dressed, as the lilies of the field.

I have just finished writing a long and vehement treatise against negro slavery which I wanted to publish with my Journal, but was obliged to refrain from doing so, lest our fellow citizens should tear our house down – a favourite mode of remonstrance in these parts with those who advocate the rights of the unhappy blacks.

I read; I enter in a large book all the passages I meet with in my readings tending to elucidate obscure parts of the Bible. I read my Bible diligently every day, and every day wish more and more earnestly that I understood what I was reading. I mean this with regard to the Old Testament only, however. The life of Christ is that portion of the New alone vitally important to me, and that, thank God, is comparatively comprehensible.

Then I do a little housekeeping; then I do a little music; then I waste a great deal of time in feeding and cleaning a large cageful of canary birds, of which, as the pleasure is mine, I do not choose to give the rather disgusting trouble to anyone else. I stroll round my garden, watching my bee-hives – every chink and cranny between all this desultoriness is filled with 'the baby'.

October 31st, 1835

I cannot believe that women were intended to suffer as much as they do, and be as helpless as they are, in child-bearing. In spite of the third chapter of Genesis, I cannot believe that all the agony and debility attendant upon the entrance of a new creature into the world was ordained; but rather that both are the consequence of our many and various abuses of our constitutions and infractions of God's natural laws. Tight stays, tight garters, tight waistbands and tight bodices must have a tendency to injure irreparably the compressed parts, to impede the circulation and respiration in many ways we are not aware of. Many women here, when they become mothers, seem to lose looks, health and strength and are mere wrecks. One is tempted to wish that the legislature would interfere and prevent the desperate injury which is thus done to the race.

I attend a Unitarian church. I did so first by accident, being taken there by the people to whom I now belong, and where I hear admirable instruction and exhortation, and eloquent, excellent preaching. I am acquainted with several clergymen of that profession who are among the most enlightened and cultivated men I have met with in this country.

I have for the last two days been discharging a most vexatious duty – vexatious to be sure chiefly from my own fault. We have a household of six servants, a very abundant vegetable garden, dairy and poultry yard; but I have been very neglectful lately of all domestic details and the consequences have been manifold abuse, disorder and waste in the kitchen, pantry and store room. I have been reproaching myself and reproving others, and heartily regretting that, instead of Italian and music, I had not learned a little domestic economy, and how much bread, butter, flour, eggs, milk, sugar and meat ought to be consumed per week in a family of eight persons, not ogres.

I am sorry to find that my physical courage has been very much shaken by my confinement. Whereas formerly I scarcely knew the sensation of fear, I have grown almost cowardly on horseback or in a carriage. Our horses ran away with the carriage the other day; I had the child with me, and though I did not lose my wits at all, after getting her safely out of the carriage and alighting myself, I shook from head to foot, for the first time in my life, with fear.

Dear Mrs. Jameson, . . . Our summer has been detestable: such wintry squalls! such torrents of rain! The autumn however has been fine, and we spent part of it in one of the most charming regions imaginable.[5] A 'Happy Valley' indeed! – the valley of the Housatonic, locked in by walls of every shape and size, from grassy knolls to bold, basaltic cliffs. A beautiful little river wanders singing from side to side in this secluded paradise: it looks only fit for people to be baptised in.

In one part of this romantic hill region exists the strangest worship. I do not know whether you have ever heard of a religious sect called the Shakers. Seven hundred men and women whose religion has for one of its principal objects the extinguishing of the human race and the end of the world, by devoting themselves and persuading others to celibacy and the strictest chastity. They live all together in one community and own a village and considerable tract of land in the beautiful hill country of Berkshire. They are perfectly moral and exemplary in their lives and conduct, wonderfully industrious, miraculously clean and neat, and incredibly shrewd, thrifty and money-making.

Their dress is hideous and their worship consists of a fearful species of dancing, going round and round, shaking their hands like the paws of a dog sitting up to beg, and singing a deplorable psalm-tune in brisk jig time. The men, in shirt sleeves with their lank hair hanging on their shoulders, and wearing a sort of loose knee-breeches, have a grotesque air of stage Swiss peasantry. The women, without a single hair escaping from beneath their hideous caps, are mounted upon very high-heeled shoes, and every one of them with a white handkerchief folded napkin-fashion and hanging over her arm. In summer they all dress in white, and what with their pale immoveable countenances, their ghost-like figures, the whole exhibition was at once so frightful and so ludicrous that I very nearly went off into hysterics when I first saw them.

[5] At Lenox, the home of the Sedgwicks in the Berkshire Hills in Massachusetts where, much later, Fanny bought herself a small house.

December 2nd, 1835

Dearest Dorothy [Harriet St. Leger's friend and companion] . . . I was at first a little disappointed that my baby was not a man-child, for the lot of woman is seldom happy, owing principally, I think, to the many serious mistakes which have universal sway in female education. I do not believe that the just Creator intended one part of His creatures to lead the sort of lives that many women do. In this country the difficulty of giving a girl a good education is even greater than with us. I do not think that even the accomplishments are well taught here; they seem to me for the most part flimsy, frivolous and superficial. More solid acquirements do not abound among my female acquaintance either; and the species of ignorance one encounters occasionally is so absolute and profound as to be almost amusing and quite curious.

March 1st, 1836

Dearest Harriet, . . . You ask of my society. I have none whatever. Though people occasionally drive out from Philadelphia to visit me, and I occasionally drive in to return their calls, and though we occasionally go in to the theatre or a dance, I have no friends, no intimates and no society.

No one that I belong to takes the slightest interest in literary pursuits. I feel most seriously how desirable it is that I should study, because I positively languish for intellectual activity; and yet what would under other circumstances be a natural pleasure is apt to become an effort when those with whom one lives do not sympathise with one's pursuits. However on Monday I am going to read Latin with a master. Any pursuit to which I am compelled will be welcome to me, and I have chosen that in preference to German as mentally more bracing and therefore healthier.

I am expecting a visit from Dr. Channing [6] whom I love and revere. After reading a sermon of his before going to bed the other night, I dreamt that I was in Heaven, from whence I was literally pulled down and awakened to get up and go to church – which, you will allow, was a ridiculous instance of bathos and work of supererogation. But dear me, that dream was very pleasant!

[6] William Ellery Channing (1780–1842) Minister of Federal Street Church in Boston and leader of the Unitarian movement, champion of change and liberal reform. His treatise on slavery (1835) profoundly influenced Fanny's thinking on the subject.

[undated]

There is one interest and occupation of an essentially practical nature in which I am becoming passionately interested – I mean the cause of the Southern negroes.

We live by their labour, and though the estate is not yet ours (an elderly member of the family having a life interest in it), it will be our property one day, and a large portion of our income is now derived from it.

I was told the other day that the cotton lands in Georgia, where our plantation is situated, were exhausted, but that in Alabama there now exist wild lands along the Mississippi where anyone possessing the negroes necessary to cultivate them might, in a few years, realise an enormous fortune. I was asked, jestingly, if I should be willing to go thither. I replied, in most solemn earnest, that I would go with delight, if we might take that opportunity of at once placing our slaves on a more humane and Christian footing. O Harriet! I cannot tell you with what joy it would fill me, if we could only have the energy and courage, the humanity and justice to do this. What would I not give to be able to awaken in others my own feeling of this heavy responsibility.

I have just done reading Dr. Channing's book on slavery; it is like everything else of his, written in the pure spirit of Christianity, with judgment, temper and moderation, yet with abundant warmth and energy.

(*Records*) The ideas and expectations with which I entered upon my life near Philadelphia were impossible of fulfillment and simply ridiculous, under the circumstances. Those with which I contemplated an existence on our Southern estate were not only impossible, but would speedily have found their only result in the ruin and very probably death of all concerned.

I am now able to understand what, when I wrote this letter, I had not the remotest idea of – the amazement and dismay, the terror and disgust, with which my theories must have filled every member of the American family in which my American marriage had connected me. I must have appeared to them nothing but a mischievous madwoman.

March 28th, 1836

My dearest Harriet, . . . The death of an elderly lady puts us in possession of our property [the slave plantation and Butler Place] which she had held in trust during her life. Increase of fortune

brings necessarily increased responsibility and occupation, and
for that I am not sorry, though the death of this relation, of whom
I knew and had seen but little, has been fruitful of disappointments to me. I have been obliged to forego a visit from my
delightful friend, Miss Sedgwick – this, in my lonely life, is a real
privation. And our proposed voyage to England is indefinitely
postponed, and from a thing so near as to be reckoned a certainty,
has withdrawn itself into the misty regions of a remote futurity.
Goodbye, dearest Harriet – oh! I should like to see you once
again!

Apart from the boredom of her life at Butler Place, Fanny was des-
perately homesick and constantly begged Pierce to take her to England.
She even on one occasion contemplated going by herself and leaving
her husband and her baby at Branchtown. 'I am weary of my useless
existence'; she wrote to him, 'you have never allowed it to be other-
wise; you will suffer no inconvenience from its cessation. . . . If you
procure a healthy nurse for the baby she will not suffer; and provided
she is fed, she will not fret after me. . . . I must beg you will take
measures for my going away; and have only to regret that I am not
other than I am, perhaps I might have been happier than I am, and
possessed qualities more acceptable to you than those with which
nature and education have endowed me.'[7]

July 31st, 1836

You ask me if I take no pleasure in gardening; and suggest the
cutting of carnations and raising of lettuce as wholesome employ-
ments for me. The kitchen garden is the only well-attended-to
horticulture of this place. The gardener raises early lettuces and
cauliflowers in frames which remunerate him either by their sale
in market or by prizes that he may obtain for them. His zeal in
floriculture is less.

I spend generally about three hours a day pottering in my
garden, but, alas! my gardening consists chiefly of slaughter. The
heat of the climate generates the most enormous quantity of
insects for the effectual prevention of destruction of which the
gardeners in these parts have yet discovered no means. I have
a few flower beds that I have had made and keep under my own
especial care; also some pretty baskets which I have had expressly
manufactured; these, filled with earth and planted with roses, I

[7] Bobbé: *Fanny Kemble*, p. 103.

have placed on the stumps of some large trees; and thus I contrive to produce something of an English garden effect. But the climate is against me.

I have almost an avenue of fine lemon trees; humming birds which are a marvel and enchantment to me; fire-flies which are exquisite in the summer evenings. I have too a fine hive of bees which has produced already this spring two strong young swarms, whose departure from the parent hive formed a very interesting event in my novel experiences.

August 20th, 1836

I do not keep a diary any more; I do not find chronicling my days helps me to live them. Perhaps I may resume it when we set out for our plantation in the South. We are now altogether proprietors of this place, and I really think, as I am often told, that it is getting to be prettier and better kept than any other in this neighbourhood. It is certainly much improved, but there are yet a thousand things to be done with it.

Wednesday, October 5th

It is a great disappointment to me that I am not after all going to the South this winter. There is no house for me, my baby and her nurse. So it is determined to leave me and the baby behind, and the owner will go with his brother [Pierce and John Butler], but without us, on his expedition to Negroland. As far as the child is concerned I am well satisfied, but I would undergo much myself to be able to go among these people.

You do not know how profoundly the subject of slavery engrosses my thoughts. In every point of view I feel that we ought to embrace the cause of these poor people. They will be free, assuredly – and that before many years; why not make friends of them instead of deadly enemies? Why not give them at once the wages of their labour? Is it to be supposed that a man will work more for fear of the lash than for the sake of an adequate reward? As a matter of policy and to escape personal violence or the destruction of one's property, it were well not to urge them – ignorant, savage and slavish as they are – into rebellion. As a mere matter of worldly interest, it would be wise to make it worth their while to work with zeal and energy for hire, instead of listlessly dragging their reluctant limbs under a driver's whip.

Oh, how I wish I was a man! How I wish I owned these slaves!

instead of being supported (disgracefully, it seems to me) by their unpaid labour.

If I am not allowed to go South this winter, it is just possible that I may spend three months in England.

CHAPTER 11

Changes of Scene
1836–1838

(*Records*) I sailed at the beginning of November [1836] and reached England after a frightfully stormy passage of eight and twenty days. I and my child's nurse were the only women on board. We had violently contrary winds and one gale that lasted nearly four days, during which time I and my poor little child and her nurse were prisoners in the cabin, where we had not even the consolation of daylight, the skylights being all closely covered to protect us from the sea.

The tempest was more formidable than any I have since encountered in eighteen passages across the Atlantic. The vessel sprang its mainmast – a very serious injury to a sailing ship; and for three days we were unable to carry any sail whatever.

At the height of the storm, in the middle of a night which my faithful friend and servant, Margery O'Brien, passed in prayer without once rising from her knees, the frightful uproar of the elements and the delirious plunging of the ship convinced me that we should inevitably be lost. As the vessel reeled under a tremendous shock, the conviction of our impending destruction became so intense that my imagination suddenly presented to me the death vision, so to speak, of my whole life. My life presented itself, not as a procession of events, but as a total – suddenly held up to me as in a mirror, indescribably awful, combined with a simultaneous acute and almost despairing sense of *loss*, of *waste*. This was followed by a rapid survey of the religious belief in which I had been trained, and which then seemed to me my only important concern.

The tension, physical and mental, gave way to complete exhaustion, in which, strangely enough, I found the sort of satisfaction a child does in crooning itself to sleep, in singing every song I could call to memory – English, Scotch, Irish, Welsh, French, German, Spanish – which I chanted sitting on the floor through most of the night.

A curious instance of the mistaken inferences frequently

115

drawn from our actions by others happened when the storm had sufficiently subsided to allow the captain to come and enquire after his poor imprisoned female passengers. He congratulated me on my courage, for, said he, 'at the very height of the storm I was told that you were heard singing away like a bird.'

I returned to my home and my family and stayed with them in London all the time of my visit to England. I returned to the intercourse of all my former friends and acquaintance, and to the London society of the day which was full of delightful interest for me after the solitary and completely unsocial life I had been leading for the two previous years.

My friend, Harriet St. Leger, was abroad, and her absence was the only drawback to the pleasure and happiness of my return to my own country.

My return to London society gave me the privilege of an acquaintance with some of its most remarkable members, many of whom became and remained intimate friends for many years. Lord and Lady Lansdowne, Lord and Lady Ellesmere, Lord and Lady Dacre, Sydney Smith, Samuel Rogers were among the persons with whom I then most frequently associated, and in naming them I mention only a small portion of a brilliant society, full of every element of wit, wisdom, experience, refined taste, high culture and good sense that can make human intercourse valuable and delightful.

I was indebted to Lord Lansdowne for the memorable pleasure of being present at the first meeting between Queen Victoria and her Houses of Parliament. No one who was there will ever forget the impression made upon them. The Queen was not handsome, but very pretty, and the singularity of her great position lent a sentimental and poetical charm to her youthful face and figure. The serene, serious sweetness of her candid brow and clear, soft eyes gave dignity to the girlish countenance, while the want of height only added to the effect of extreme youth of the round but slender person and the gracefully moulded hands and arms. The Queen's voice was exquisite; nor have I ever heard any spoken words more musical in their gentle distinctness than the 'My Lords and Gentlemen' which broke the breathless silence of the illustrious assembly. The enunciation was as perfect as the intonation was melodious, and I think it impossible to hear a more excellent utterance than that of the Queen's English by the English Queen.

I became acquainted with the Rev. Sydney Smith[1] at a dinner at Mr. Rogers'[2] to which I had been asked to meet Lord and Lady Holland[3], by special desire, as I was afterwards informed, of the latter; who, during dinner drank out of Sydney Smith's glass and otherwise behaved herself with the fantastic despotic impropriety in which she frequently indulged, and which might have been tolerated in a spoilt beauty of eighteen, but was hardly becoming in a woman of her age. The impression she made upon me was so disagreeable that, for a time, it involved every member of that dinner party in a halo of undistinguishing dislike in my mind.

Altogether the evening was unsuccessful, if its purpose had been an acquaintance between Lady Holland and myself. I remember a grotesque climax to my dissatisfaction in the destruction of a lovely nosegay of exquisite flowers which my sister had brought with her. Towards the middle of the evening it mysteriously disappeared and was looked for in vain until poor Lord Holland, who was then dependent upon the assistance of two servants to move from his seat, was raised from the sofa on which he had been deposited, and the flowers were discovered, pressed as flat as if for preservation in a book of botanical specimens. On seeing my sister's face of ludicrous dismay Sydney Smith exclaimed, 'I see! Oh dear, oh dear, what a pity! Hot bed! Hot bed!'

It has always been a matter of amazement to me that Lady Holland should have been allowed to ride roughshod over society as she did for so long with such complete immunity. To be sure, people gave way to Lady Holland's domineering rudeness for the sake of their host and fellow guests and spared her out of consideration for them. Another reason was the universal esteem and affectionate respect felt for her husband, whose friends accepted her and her peculiarities for his sake.

The most powerful inducement to patience, however, to the London society on which Lady Holland habitually trampled was

[1] Sydney Smith (1771–1845).Church of England clergyman; author of the 'Plymley Letters' in defence of Catholic emancipation, Canon of St. Paul's Cathedral. Noted for his exuberant drollery and wit.

[2] Samuel Rogers (1763–1855). Poet and friend of Sydney Smith. Offered but declined the Poet Laureateship in 1850.

[3] Henry Richard Vassall Fox, 3rd Baron Holland (1773–1840). Whig statesman, Chancellor of the Duchy of Lancaster in the first reform ministry and under Lord Melbourne. His London home, Holland House, was a great political, literary and artistic centre, frequented by Smith, Rogers and many other eminent writers including Sheridan, Macaulay and Dickens.

the immense attraction of her house and the people who frequented it. Holland House was for years the most brilliant,
charming and altogether delightful social resort. Beautiful, comfortable, elegant – an ideal house, full of exquisite objects and
interesting associations, where persons the most distinguished
for birth, position and intellectual gifts met in an atmosphere of
the highest cultivation. The most perfect civilisation could produce nothing more perfect in the way of enjoyment than that
delightful mansion.

Sydney Smith, with whom I became well acquainted, used to
amuse himself by teasing me on the subject of what he called my
hallucination with regard to having married in America. He
never allowed any allusion to the circumstance without the most
comical expressions of regret for this, as he called it, curious form
of megalomania. 'Now, my dear child, do be persuaded to give
up this extraordinary delusion', he would exclaim.

The special and reportable sallies of Sydney Smith have been of
course often repeated, but the fanciful fun and inexhaustible
humorous drollery of his conversation can never be adequately
reproduced. He bubbled over with mirth, of which his own
enjoyment formed an irresistible element; he shook, his eyes
glistened at his own ludicrous ideas; and it would be impossible
to convey the faintest idea of the genial humour of his habitual
talk by merely repeating separate witticisms and repartees.

Not unnaturally he preferred conversation to music; and at a
musical party one evening, as he was stealing on tip-toe from the
concert room I held up my finger at him, when he whispered,
'My dear, it's all right. You keep with the dillettanti; I go with the
talkettanti'. Once when he was so ill that all his friends were full
of anxiety about him, one of them asked him what sort of night he
had passed. Syndey Smith replied, 'Hòrrid, horrid, my dear
fellow! I dreamt I was chained to a rock and being talked to death
by Harriet Martineau and Macaulay.'

Rogers' helpful benevolence and noble generosity to poor
artists, poor authors and all distressed whom he could serve or
succour was unbounded. He had the kindest heart and the
unkindest tongue of anyone I ever knew. His inveterate tongue
gall was like an irresistible impulse, and he certainly bestowed it
occasionally, without the least provocation, upon persons whom
he professed to like.

He was habitually kind to me and declared he was fond of me.
Walking one day in Green Park, I met Mr. Rogers and Words-

worth, who took me between them and I continued my walk in great exultation of spirit, listening to Rogers and hearing Wordsworth – the gentle rill of the one speech interrupted by sudden loud splashes of the other. Presently, Wordsworth having left us, Rogers told me that, during a visit he (Wordsworth) had lately been paying at Althorpe, he was found daily in the magnificent library, never without a volume of his own poetry in his hand. Years after this, when I used to go and sit with Mr. Rogers, I never asked him what I should read to him without his putting into my hands his own poems which always lay by him on his table.

This visit to England, Fanny's first since her marriage, lasted nine months. Much as she had enjoyed seeing her family and plunging into the London social whirl, she soon began to feel that the 'uninterrupted monotony' at Butler Place was after all no bad thing: 'the turmoil and dissipation of a London life, amusing as they are for a time, soon pall; and I already feel, in my diminished relish for them, that I am growing old', she wrote, aged not yet twenty-eight.

Pierce came over to fetch his family home in August 1837 but stayed in England for a bare three weeks. His boat having been becalmed, he arrived a fortnight later than expected, and he had to be back in America by the middle of October for the reopening of the Pennsylvania Constitutional Convention to which he was a delegate.

Philadelphia, October 29th, 1837
My dearest Harriet, We landed in New York ten days ago. Our passage was of thirty-seven days, stormy as well as tedious, and I was so ill that I did not leave my bed six times during the crossing; the consequence was that on landing I looked more like a ghost than a living creature and was hardly able to stand, so we remained in New York a few days, till I was able to travel. On Monday, when I was a little better, we came on here. I am now every day expecting to be fetched to Harrisburg [where the Convention was being held].

A woman should be her husband's friend, his best and dearest friend, as he should be hers: but friendship is a relation of equality, in which the same perfect respect for each other's liberty is exercised on both sides; and that sort of marriage, if it exists at all anywhere, is, I suspect, very uncommon everywhere. Moreover I am not sure that marriage ever is, can be, or ought to be, such an equality; for even 'when two men ride on one horse,' you know, etc. In the relation of friendship there is perfect freedom, and an undoubted claim on each side to be neither dependent on, nor controlled by, each other's will. In the relation of marriage this is impossible, and therefore certainly marriage is not friendship. A woman should, I think, love her husband better than anything on earth except her own soul: which, I think, a man should respect above everything on earth but his own soul: and there, my dear, is a very pretty puzzle for you, which a good many people have failed to solve. Perhaps you have chosen, if not the wiser and better, at any rate the easier and safer part.

Harrisburg, November 14th, 1837

We are established here during the rest of the Convention, which is a gain for me as here I get companionship. There is a recess in the middle of the day which we employ in riding about the neighbouring country which is beautifully situated in a valley locked round by purple highlands through which runs the Susquehana. The river is beautifully provided too, with a most admirable species of trout weighing from two to four pounds, silvery white without and pale pink within and very excellent to eat as well as lovely to behold.

Many members of the Convention have been to see me and I have attended one of their debates. They are for the most part uncultivated men, unlettered and ungrammared; and among those who are the best educated, or rather the least ignorant, carry their small lore much as a schoolboy carries his, stiffly, awkwardly and ostentatiously. But the shrewdness, the sound sense, the original observations and experience of life of some of these men are striking and remarkable. Though not one of them can speak grammatically they all speak fluently, boldly and without effort or hesitation.

At home again at Butler Place in the winter Fanny resumed her previous uneventful existence. 'I live alone – much alone mentally, and I give myself up to musing and speculation', she told Harriet who, always inclined to religious and philosophical cogitation, had urged her to study Natural Philosophy and had sent her an epitome of the New Testament. With time on her hands – she was expecting her second child – Fanny replied by expounding at considerable length her own religious beliefs.

To reproduce these letters in toto would be tedious, for they are not only long but often prosy and sometimes sententious; to edit them would be unfair to the writer, whose convictions were profoundly held and closely argued. Yet Fanny's remained basically an uncomplicated faith, perhaps best summed up in three short words: 'God is good.'

Philadelphia, February 6th, 1838

The medical mode of treatment in this country appears to me frightfully severe. Sally's scarlet fever has been followed by the enlargement of one of the tonsils which grew to such a size as to threaten suffocation and the physician decided that it must be removed. [The child was not yet three years old.] This was done by means of a small double-barrelled silver tube, through the two pipes of which a wire is passed, coming out in a loop at the other end of the instrument. This wire being passed round the tonsil, is tightened so as to destroy its vitality in the course of four-and-twenty hours, during which the tube remains projecting from the patient's mouth, causing some pain and extreme inconvenience. At the end of the twenty-four hours the instrument is removed, the diseased part being effectively killed by the tightening of the wire. It is then left to rot off in the mouth which it does in the course of a few days, infecting the breath most horribly, and I should think injuring the health by that means. At the same time, I was attacked with violent sore throat which seized upon all our household, and for which I had a hundred leeches at once applied to my throat, which, without reducing me very much, enraged me beyond all expression. No less than seven of us were ill in the house. We are all, however, thank God, now well.

May 7th, 1838

Do you hear that the steamships have accomplished their crossing from England to America in perfect safety, the one in seventeen, the other in fifteen days! just half the time, thirty days being the average of the finest passages this way. Oh, if you knew what joy this intelligence gave me! It seemed at once to bring me again within reach of England and all those whom I love there.

And even though I should not therefore return thither the oftener, the speed and certainty with which letters will now pass between these two worlds is a thing to rejoice at exceedingly. Besides all personal considerations, the wonder and delight of seeing this great enterprise of man's ingenuity and courage thus successful is immense. Thus to see space annihilated, and the furthest corners of the earth drawn together, fills one with admiration for this amazing human nature, more potent than the whole of material creation by which it is surrounded, even than the three thousand miles of that Atlantic abyss.

I am at present sitting in a species of verandah (or piazza, as they call it here) which runs along the front of the house. It has a low balustrade and columns of white painted wood, supporting a similar verandah on the second or bedroom story of the house. Sally, in a buff coat, is zigzagging like a yellow butterfly about the lawn and Margery is mounting guard over her, with such success as you may fancy a person taking care of a straw in a high wind likely to have.

I have just been enjoying a visit from one of the members of the Sedgwick family. They are all my friends and I do think all and each in their peculiar way good and admirable.

Sunday May 27th, 1838

My dear Mrs. Jameson, I have received within the last few days your second letter from London. I hasten, while I am yet able, to send you word of R.S. . . .'s almost complete recovery. . . .

It is now exactly a fortnight since I wrote the above lines, and here I am at my writing table, in my drawing room, having in the interim *perpetrated* another girl baby. My new child was born on the same day of the same month that her sister was, and within an hour of the same time, which I think shows an orderly, systematic and methodical mode of proceeding in such matters which is really creditable to me.

During the summer the older child, Sally, had measles. When she recovered the Butlers went for a sea-side holiday on Long Island which Fanny did not greatly enjoy.

Rockaway, August 10th, 1838

Dearest Harriet, . . . You cannot conceive of anything more strange, and to me more distasteful, than the life which one leads here. The whole watering place consists of a few cottages, the property of some individuals who are singular enough to comprehend the pleasure of privacy; and one enormous hotel, a huge wooden building. How many *can* sleep under this mammoth roof I know not; but upwards of four hundred have sat down to feed at one time in the boundless dining hall. The number of persons now in the house does not, I believe, exceed eighty, and everyone is lamenting the smallness of the company and the consequent dullness of the place,[4] and I am perpetually called upon to sym-

---

[4] There was, however, at least one 'very pleasant ball' not mentioned by Fanny. One of her fellow guests at Rockaway was the Philip Hone whose dinner party she had ridiculed in her *Journal*. Hone, who now maintained that he had never been 'seriously offended' by her remarks, was affable; she was embarrassed. 'She said, "Mr. Hone, I cannot express to you how happy you have made me by the

pathise with regrets that I am so far from sharing that I wish, instead of eighty, we had only eight fellow lodgers.

The general way of life is disagreeable to me. I cannot, do what I will, find anything but constraint and discomfort in the perpetual presence of a crowd of strangers. The bedrooms are small and furnished barely as well as a common servant's room in England. They are certainly not calculated for comfortable occupation or sitting alone in; but sitting alone any part of the day is a proceeding contemplated by no one here.

From this place we go up to Massachussetts – a delightful expedition to me – to our friends the Sedgwicks who are very dear to me and almost the only people among whom I have found mental companionship since I have been in this country.

August 23rd

Dear Mrs. Jameson, . . . The beach here is magnificent – ten good miles of sparkling sand and the broad, open Atlantic rolling its long waves and breaking in one white thunderous cloud along the level expanse. The bathing would be delightful but for the discomfort and positive indecency of the non-accommodation.

There are two small stationary dressing huts on the beach, where one is compelled to disrobe and attire oneself in the closest proximity to any other woman who may wish to go into the water or come out of it at the same time as oneself. Moreover, the beach at bathing time is thronged with spectators, before whose admiring gaze one has to emerge all dripping, like Venus from the waves, and nearly as naked, for one's bathing dress clings to one's figure and makes a perfect wet drapery study of one's various members, and so one has to wade slowly and in much confusion of face under the public gaze through heavy sand about a quarter of a mile to the dressing rooms where, if one can find only three or four persons stript, or stripping, nude or semi-nude, one may consider oneself fortunate.

Lenox, Monday September 3rd, 1838

I am sitting 'on top', as the Americans say, of the hill of Lenox and making common cause in the eating and living way of life with Mary and Fanny Appleton [the future wife of the poet Long-

notice you have taken of me on this occasion. Believe me, I am extremely grateful". During our conversation the tear which stood in her flashing, expressive eye convinced me that this gifted woman . . . possesses the warmth of heart which I thought I had formerly the sagacity to discover and for which I have never failed to give her credit'. (*Diary*, Vol. I, p. 319.)

fellow]. Never was village hostelry so graced before, surely! It strikes me that the old Red Inn is having a sort of blossoming season with all these sweet, handsome young faces shining about in every direction. You know the sort of life that is lived here: the absence of all form, ceremony or inconvenient conventionality whatever. We laugh, talk, sing, play, dance and discuss; we ride, drive, walk, run, scramble and saunter, and amuse ourselves extremely.[5]

Begun at Lenox, ended at Philadelphia, October 29th, 1838
Dearest Harriet, Since the receipt of your last letter, one from Emily has reached me, bringing me the intelligence of my mother's death.[6] . . .

I have just finished the play of which you read the beginning in England – my *English Tragedy* – and I am, as usual, in high delight just now with my own performance. I wish that agreeable sentiment would last; it is so pleasant while it does. I think I will send it to Macready to try if he will bring it out at Covent Garden. I think it might succeed, unless indeed the story is too objectionable for anything – but *reality*.

An English Tragedy was based on a true story Fanny had heard while in London concerning Henry, 22nd Baron de Ros, a profligate whose seduction of his friend's wife was condoned but who was ostracised for gambling with loaded dice. Fanny could not accept such values: her play showed the seduction to be immeasurably more culpable than cheating at the gaming tables. Macready received the manuscript just before Christmas. 'Finished reading Mrs. Butler's play,

[5] A letter from Fanny Appleton, 5.9.1838, fills out the picture: [Mrs Butler] 'arrays herself in her riding costume – white pants (*tout à fait à la mode des messieurs*) and habit, with a black velvet jacket and cap, very picturesque and when mounted on her own fine steed a picture that puts Miss Sedgwick into raptures. She bends to every motion with such grace and perfect control of a sufficiently fiery quadruped. . . . The evening usually is passed at Mrs. Sedgwicks, Mrs. Butler always in white muslin, bare arms and neck if it be cold as November, charming us with singing old ballads with a thrilling pathos, and such nervous excitement herself that she often turns cold as marble for a few moments after dancing the *cachucha* with castanets, and great spirit of discoursing on deep topics with an earnestness and far-reaching intelligence which kindles her face to wonderful shiftings beyond any countenance I ever saw. Her soul seems always boiling at fever point'. *Mrs. Longfellow*, p. 53.
[6] Marie-Thérèse Kemble, always highly strung, had become increasingly neurotic and had chosen to live on her own in a cottage in Surrey. 'My parting with my mother was calmer than I had ventured to anticipate', Fanny had written on the day she sailed for America, 'I thank heaven I was not obliged to leave without seeing her once more.'

which is one of the most powerful of modern plays I have seen — most painful, most shocking, but full of power, poetry and pathos', he wrote in his Journal. 'She is one of the most remarkable women of the day'.[7] He seriously considered putting it on at Covent Garden but, after consultation with friends and colleagues, decided not to do so on account of its 'grossness'.

Philadelphia, November 13th, 1838

My dear Mrs. Jameson, . . . The winter in Georgia, whither we are going immediately, may be beneficial to the invalid member of our party [Pierce had had a serious illness] and that is the only pleasant anticipation with which I set my face towards a part of the country where the whole manner of existence is repugnant to my feelings and where the common comforts of life are so little known that we are obliged to ship a freight of necessary articles of food for our use while we are on the Plantation. Wheaten bread is unknown, meal made out of Indian corn being alone used there and, though game abounds, the only meat, properly so called, which can be procured there is shipped in barrels (salted of course) from the North.

Society, or the shadow of it, is not to be dreamt of; and our residence, as far as I can learn, is to be a half-furnished house in the midst of rice swamps, where our habitual company will be our slaves and our occasional visitors an alligator or two from the Altamaha.

[7] *Journal*, ed. Trewin, pp. 128–9.

CHAPTER 12

A Miserable Journey Southwards
1838

'It was no joke', said Fanny at the end of the thousand mile, nine day journey to the family plantations on Butler's and St. Simon's Islands off the coast of Georgia in December 1838. There were seven in the party: herself, Pierce Butler, his brother John, Sally, aged nearly four, the baby Fan, seven months old and still breast-fed, the children's nurse, Margery, and an elderly Butler aunt on her way to Charleston. They travelled by railroad, steam-boat and horse-drawn coach by night and day, stopping occasionally at dirty inns and eating often disgusting food. What follows are some high-lights – or more properly low-lights – from the 12,000 word-long account of the journey she wrote for Harriet.

Philadelphia to Baltimore

Persons obliged to travel during the intense cold of an American winter in the Northern states should clothe themselves accordingly and so do away with the present system of warming close and crowded [railroad] carriages with sheet-iron stoves heated with anthracite coal. No words can describe the foulness of the atmosphere, thus robbed of all vitality by the vicious properties of that dreadful combustible, and tainted beside with the poison from so many pairs of human lungs. Any attempt to open a window is met with a universal scowl and shudder; and indeed, it is but incurring the risk of one's death of cold instead of one's death of heat.

The carriage looks like a long greenhouse on wheels; the seats, each for two persons (a pretty tight fit too) are placed down the whole length of the vehicle, leaving a species of aisle in the middle for the uneasy to fidget up and down, for the tobacco-chewers to spit in and for a whole tribe of little itinerants to rush through, distributing their wares at every place where the train stops.

Attached to the Baltimore cars was a separate compartment for women, of comfortable dimensions and without a stove. Here I betook myself with my children, performing our journey with ease enough.

We crossed one or two inlets of the Chesapeake, of considerable width, upon bridges which consist merely of wooden piles driven into the river, across which the iron rails are laid, only just raising the train above the level of the water. To traverse with an immense train at full steam-speed one of the creeks is far from agreeable, let one be never so little nervous.

Aboard the steamboat at Baltimore, we obtained an unutterably hard beef-steak for our dinner, having had nothing on the road, and found ourselves but little fortified by the sight of what we really could not swallow. Between six and seven, however, occurred that most comprehensive repast, a steamboat tea. I had a most comical squabble with the stewardess, a dirty, funny, good-humoured negress who was driven almost wild by exorbitant demands for towels, of which she assured me that one was quite an ample allowance. I counted no less than seven handsome looking-glasses, while one towel was considered all that was requisite for each washing-room. This addition to ornament and neglect of comfort and convenience is a strong characteristic of Americans at present, luxuries often abounding where decencies cannot be procured.

Through North Carolina
After crossing the Roanoke we stopped at a small knot of houses, which, although christened Weldon and therefore pretending to be a place, was rather the place where a place was intended to be. Two or three rough pine station houses, a few miserable dwellings and one exceedingly dirty-looking old wooden house whither we directed our steps as to the inn.

The women were shown up a filthy flight of wooden stairs into a dilapidated room, the plastered walls of which were all smeared and discoloured, the windows begrimed and dark with dirt. Upon the three beds which nearly filled up this wretched apartment lay tattered articles of male and female apparel; and here we drew round the pine wood fire which blazed up the chimney, sending a ruddy glow of comfort even through this disgusting den. We were to wait here for the arrival of the cars from a branch railroad; in the meantime a so-called dinner was provided for us. Of the horrible dirt of everything at this meal, from the eatables themselves to the table-cloth and the clothes of the negroes who waited upon us, it would be impossible to give any idea.

Our male fellow travellers no sooner had despatched their dinner than they withdrew in a body to the other end of the apartment and, large rattling folding drawers being drawn across the room, the separation of men and women so rigidly observed by all travelling Americans took place. This is a most peculiar and amusing custom, though sometimes I have been not a little inclined to quarrel with it, inasmuch as it effectually deprives one of the assistance of the men under whose protection one is travelling, as well as all the advantages or pleasure of their society. Twice during this southward trip my companion has been most peremptorily ordered to withdraw from the apartment where he was conversing with me by coloured cabin girls, who told him that it was against the rules for any gentleman to come into the ladies' room.

The gentlemen are entrenched in a similar manner. If a woman has occasion to speak with the person with whom she is travelling, her entrance into the male den, if she has courage to venture there, is the signal for a universal stare and a whisper.

Our sole resource on the present occasion was to retire to the horrible hole above stairs where we had at first taken refuge, and here remained until the arrival of the train. My poor little children, overcome with sleep, were carried, and we walked, to the railroad, and by great good fortune obtained a compartment to ourselves.

It was now between eight and nine o'clock and perfectly dark. Between twelve and one the engine stopped and it was announced that we had travelled as far upon the railroad as was yet completed and that we must now transfer ourselves to stage-coaches; so in the dead middle of the night we crept out of the train and, taking our children in our arms, walked to an open space in the woods, where three four-horse coaches stood waiting for us.

The horrors of that night's journey I shall not easily forget. The road lay through swamps and was frequently under water. It was made of logs of wood (a corduroy road) and was so dreadfully rough and unequal that the drawing of a coach over it seemed perfectly miraculous. I expected at every moment to be overturned into the marsh.

We had especially requested that we might have a coach to ourselves. The outside seat of this was, however, appropriated

by someone, for our coachman who was travelling with us was
obliged to take a seat inside with us. Towards daylight the unfortunate individuals outside became so perished with cold that
they changed places, and thus the privacy of our carriage was
invaded, in spite of the promise to the contrary. As I am nursing
my baby and have been compelled to travel all day and all night,
of course this was a circumstance of no small annoyance. But as
subsequently I had to travel in a railroad carriage that held
upwards of twenty people, I had to resign myself to this among
other miseries of this most miserable journey.

As we alighted from our coach we encountered the comical
spectacle of two coachloads of gentlemen who had travelled the
same route as ourselves, with wrist bands and coat cuffs turned
back, performing their morning ablutions at a long wooden
dresser in the open air, though the morning was piercing cold.
The women were shown into one small room, the whole furniture of which consisted of a chair and wooden bench; upon the
latter stood one basin, one ewer and a relic of soap, apparently of
great antiquity. We were immediately summoned down to breakfast; but as we had travelled all night and all the previous day,
and were to travel all the ensuing day and night, I preferred
washing to eating and determined, if I could not do both, at least
to accomplish the first. There was neither towel, nor glass for
one's teeth, nor hostess or chambermaid to appeal to. As I leaned
over the banisters in a state of considerable despondency, I
espied a man who appeared to be the host and to him I ventured
to prefer my humble petition for a clean towel. He immediately
snatched from the dresser where the gentlemen had been washing a wet and dirty towel and offered it to me. Upon my suggestion that it was not *clean* he looked at me from head to foot in
ineffable amazement.

Of the breakfast in this place no words can give any idea. There
were plates full of unutterable-looking things which made one
feel as if one should never swallow food again. There were some
eggs, begrimed with smoke and covered with cinders; some
unbaked dough, cut into little lumps, by way of bread; and a hard
white substance calling itself butter, which had an infinitely
nearer resemblance to tallow. The mixture presented to us by
way of tea was absolutely undrinkable; and when I begged for a
glass of milk, they brought a tumbler covered with dust and dirt,
full of such sour stuff that I was obliged to put it aside. Thus
refreshed we set off again through the eternal pine lands.

A short distance beyond a small place called Waynesborough we were desired to alight and walk over a bridge which was in so rotten a condition as to render it very probable that it would give way under our weight. This bridge is built at considerable height over a broad and rapid stream called the Neuse, the colour of whose water we had an excellent opportunity of admiring through the numerous holes in the plankage, over which we walked as lightly and rapidly as we could, stopping afterwards to see our coach come at foot's pace after us.

It was near sunset when we reached the railroad. The train had not arrived, and we sat in the coaches, the day gradually drooping, the evening air becoming colder and the howling wilderness around us becoming more dismal every moment. In the meantime the coaches were surrounded by a troop of gazing boors who had come from far and wide to see the hot water coaches come up for only the third time into their savage solitude. A more forlorn, fierce, poor and wild-looking set of people, short of absolute savages, I never saw. The men were clothed in the coarsest manner, and the women also, with the grotesque addition of pink and blue silk bonnets, with artificial flowers and imitation-blonde veils.

It was now becoming dark and the male members of our caravan held council round a pine fire as to what had better be adopted for shelter during the night. After some debate it was recollected that Colonel ———, a man of some standing in the neighbourhood, had a farm about a mile distant and thither we repaired. An empty truck stood at hand upon the iron road, and to this the luggage and the women were transferred. A number of negroes were pressed into service and pushed it along; and the gentlemen, walking, brought up the rear.

I don't know that I ever in my life felt so completely desolate as during that half hour's slow progress. The last embers of daylight were dying out in dusky red streaks along the horizon and the dreary waste around us looked like the very shaggy edge of all creation. The men who pushed us along encouraged each other with wild shouts and yells. The road crossed one or two deep ravines and morasses at considerable height and, as it was not completed and nothing but the iron rails were laid across piles, it was a considerable risk to run along these narrow ledges urging our car along.

Presently we beheld a cluster of houses in the fields. To the principal one I made my way, followed by the rest of the women, and entering the house without ceremony, ushered them into a large species of wooden room, where blazed a huge pine fire. Sitting in the corner of the vast chimney was an old ruddy-faced man, with silver hair and a good-humoured countenance, who, welcoming us with ready hospitality, announced himself as Colonel —— and invited us to draw near the fire.

The worthy colonel seemed in no way dismayed at this sudden inbreak of distressed women, very soon followed by the gentlemen. He replied to their hesitating demands for something to eat by ordering to the right and left a tribe of staring negroes who bustled about preparing supper. His residence, considering his rank, was quite the most primitive imaginable – a rough brick and plank chamber of considerable dimensions, not even whitewashed. The windows would close neither at the top nor the bottom and were so broken as to admit delightful currents of air. In one corner stood a primitive looking bed, whilst in the opposite one an old case clock was ticking away its time and its master's with cheerful monotony. The walls were hung with a curious miscellany of physic phials, turkey-feather fans, bunches of dried herbs and the colonel's arsenal, in the shape of one or two old guns, etc.

My veneration waxed deep when the old man proclaimed himself one of the heroes of the revolution – a fellow fighter with Washington. I, who had been flippantly bandying jokes and had proceeded some way in a lively flirtation with this illustrious American, grew thrice respectful and hardly ventured to raise either my eyes or my voice as I enquired if he lived alone in this remote place. Yes, alone now; his wife had been dead nigh upon two years.

Suddenly we were broken in upon by the arrival of the train. It was past eight o'clock. If we delayed we should have to travel all night; but then, the Colonel pressed us to stay and sup. The gentlemen were famished and well inclined to stay; the ladies were famished too, for we had eaten nothing all day. The bustle of preparation began afresh; the negro girls shambled in and out more vigorously than ever, and finally we were called to eat – dirty water, I cannot call it tea, old cheese, bad butter and old dry biscuits. The hospitable colonel merely asked half a dollar apiece; paying which we departed with our enthusiasm a little damped for the warrior of the revolution. A tinge of rather deeper misgivings stole over our minds on learning that three of the sable damsels were the colonel's own progeny. I believe only three –

though the young negro girl whose loquacity made us aware of that fact added, with a burst of commendable pride and gratitude, 'Indeed, he is a father to us all!' Whether she spoke figuratively or literally we could not determine.

Charleston
This city is the oldest I have yet seen in America. Its appearance is highly picturesque, a word which can apply to none other of the American towns; and although the place is certainly pervaded with an air of decay, it is a genteel infirmity, as might be that of a distressed elderly gentlewoman. It has none of the smug mercantile primness of the northern cities, but a look of state, as of quondam wealth and importance, a little gone down in the world, yet still remembering its former dignity. Charleston has an air of eccentricity too, and peculiarity, which formerly were not deemed unbecoming the well-born and well-bred gentlewoman – none of the vulgar dread of vulgar opinion, forcing those who are possessed by it to conform to a general standard of manners. Every house seems to be built to the owner's particular taste; in one street you seem to be in an old English town and in another in some continental city of France or Italy.

There are several public buildings of considerable architectural pretension, all apparently of some antiquity except a handsome edifice not yet completed and intended for a guard house. Its extensive dimensions excited our surprise, but a man informed us that they not unfrequently had between fifty and sixty persons (coloured and white) brought in by patrol in one night. 'But', objected we, 'the coloured people are not allowed out without passes after nine o'clock.' 'Yes,' he replied, 'but they will do it nevertheless, and every night numbers are brought in who are endeavouring to evade the patrol.'

No doubt these precautions are but trifling drawbacks upon the manifold blessings of slavery; still I should prefer going to sleep without the apprehension of my servants cutting my throat in my bed even to having a guard provided to prevent them doing so.

Arrival
On Sunday morning the day broke most brilliantly over those Southern waters, and as the sun rose the atmosphere became clear and warm, as in the early northern summer. [The final stage

of the journey, from Charleston to Savannah and on to the little port of Darien on the delta of the Altamaha river, had been made in two days by small coastal craft.] As we grazed the wharf it seemed to me as if we had touched the outer bound of civilised creation. As soon as we showed ourselves on deck we were hailed by a shout from the men in two pretty boats, and the vociferations of 'Oh massa! How do you do, massa? Oh lilly missis! Me too glad to see you!' accompanied with certain inter-jectional shrieks, whoops, whistles and grunts that could only be written down in negro language, made me aware of our vicinity to our journey's end. The strangeness of the scene, the rapid retrospect which my mind hurried through of the past few years of my life, the singular contrasts they presented to my memory, the affectionate shouts of welcome of the poor people who seemed to hail us as descending divinities, affected me so much that I burst into tears and could hardly answer their demon-strations of delight.

We were presently transferred into the larger of the two boats and, the smaller one being freighted with our luggage, we pulled out from Darien. We crossed the river and entered a small arm of it which presently assumed the appearance of a canal – which indeed it is, having been dug by General Oglethorpe's men (tradition says in one night) and afforded him the only means of escape from the Spaniards and Indians who surrounded him on all sides and felt secure against all possibility of his eluding them. General Oglethorpe was the first British governor of Georgia; Wesley's friend and disciple.

After emerging from the cut we crossed another arm of the Altamaha and approached the reedy banks of Butler's Island, passing the rice-mill and the buildings surrounding it, all of which, it being Sunday, were closed.

As we neared the bank the steersman took up a huge conch and sounded out our approach. A pretty schooner, which carries the produce of the estate to Charleston and Savannah, lay alongside the wharf which began to be crowded with negroes, jumping, dancing, shouting, laughing and clapping their hands and using the most extravagant and ludicrous gestures to express their ecstasy at our arrival.

On our landing the crowd thronged about us like a swarm of bees; we were seized, pulled, pushed, carried, dragged and all but lifted in the air by the clamorous multitude. I was afraid my children would be smothered. Fortunately the overseer and the captain of the little schooner came to our assistance, and by their good offices the babies and nurse were protected through the crowd. They seized our clothes, kissed them – then our hands, and almost wrung them off. One tall, gaunt negress flew to us, parting the throng on either side, and embraced us in her arms.

I believe I was almost frightened, and it was not until we were safely housed and the door shut upon our riotous escort that we indulged in a fit of laughing, quite as full, on my part, of nervousness as of amusement.

CHAPTER 13

'The Grievous Sin against Humanity' 1838–1839

Butler's Island, Georgia, January 9th, 1839

Dearest Emily,[1] We all arrived here safely on Sunday last, and my thoughts are engrossed with the condition of the people from whose labour we draw our subsistence; of which, now I am here, I feel ashamed.

The place itself if one of the wildest corners of creation. It is a sort of hasty pudding of amphibious elements, composed of a huge rolling river, thick and turbid with mud, and stretches of mud banks scarcely reclaimed from the water. The river wants *straining*, and the land *draining* to make either of them properly wet or dry.

The island, which is only a portion of our Georgia estate, contains several thousand acres and is about eight miles round, and formed of nothing but the deposits of the Altamaha, whose brimming waters roll round it and every now and then threaten to submerge it. The whole island is a swamp, dyked and trenched and divided by ditches and a canal, by means of which the rice fields are periodically overflowed. A duck, an eel or a frog might find life here as in paradise.

January 8th, 1839

Dearest Harriet, . . . We live here in a very strange manner. The house we inhabit is inferior to the poorest farm house in any part of England. The little furniture is of the coarsest and roughest description, and the household services are performed by negroes who run in and out, generally bare-footed and always filthy. This unlimited supply of trained savages (for that is what they really are) is anything but a luxury for me. Their ignorance, dirt and stupidity seem to me as intolerable as the unjust laws which condemn them to be ignorant, filthy and stupid.

I had desired very earnestly to have the opportunity of judging this matter of slavery for myself; not, of course, that I ever

[1] Emily Fitzhugh, a girlhood friend.

135

doubted that to keep human beings as slaves was in itself wrong, but I supposed that I might discover at any rate circumstances of palliation in the condition of the negroes. Hitherto this has not been the case. The wrong strikes me more forcibly every hour I live here; and the evil effect of such a state of things upon the *whites*, who inflict the wrong, impresses me as I did not anticipate it would, with still more force.

The negroes here, who see me row and walk in the hot sun, lift heavy burthens and make various exertions which are supposed to be their peculiar *privilege*, frequently remonstrate with me, with the remark, 'What for you do work, missis? You hab niggers enough to wait upon you!' You may suppose how agreeable such remonstrances are to me.

After these two letters, Fanny seldom wrote to her English friends. Instead she spent her evenings keeping a detailed record of her experiences – hastily written jottings 'with constant additional notes inserted in a very irregular fashion'. Later, in Philadelphia, these were tidied and copied in the form of a series of 'letters' to her friend Elizabeth Sedgwick [sister-in-law of the novelist Catherine] in Massachusetts. Although the manuscript was widely read among New England abolitionists, it was not published until 1863.

This often highly emotional document ran to about 100,000 words, prefaced by a long analysis of Fanny's moral objections to slavery. 'Assuredly I am going prejudiced against slavery', she wrote in it, 'for I am an Englishwoman, in whom the absence of such a prejudice would be disgraceful. Nevertheless, I go prepared to find many mitigations in practice to the general injustice and cruelty of the system – much kindness on the part of the masters and much content on that of the slaves'.

She was to be disappointed. In her account of the fifteen-week stay on the plantations she could report but few examples of the masters' kindness and the slaves' contentment. Profoundly distressed by almost everything she saw, she certainly kept her promise to 'report every detail of the working of slavery that comes under my notice'.

Inevitably there was much repetition, since the pattern of the miseries and brutalities she witnessed with growing horror varied little from case to case or place to place, whether on the rice-growing plantaion on Butler's Island or on St. Simon's Island, where the staple crop was cotton.

The following chapter includes the more representative rather than the more sensational of Fanny's observations. It also reflects her growing disillusionment with her husband's role as slave-owner, as well as the rare moments on the islands which gave her real pleasure.

Butler's Island, December 30th, 1838–February 16th, 1839
I walked down the settlement towards the infirmary or hospital, calling in at one or two of the houses along the row. These cabins consist of one room, about twelve feet by fifteen, with a couple of closets smaller than the staterooms of a ship, divided off by rough wooden partitions, in which the inhabitants sleep. They have almost all a rude bedstead, with the grey moss of the forests for mattress, and filthy, pestilential-looking blankets for cover. Two families (sometimes eight or ten in number) reside in one of these huts, which are mere wooden frames pinned, as it were, to the earth by a brick chimney outside. A wide ditch runs immediately at the back, filled and emptied daily by the tide. Attached to each hovel is a small scrap of ground for a garden, which is however for the most part untended and uncultivated.

Such of these dwellings as I visited today were filthy and wretched in the extreme. On the floor, or squatting round the cold hearth, would be four or five little children from four to ten years old, the latter all with babies in their arms, the care of the infants being taken from the mothers (who are driven afield as soon as they recover from child labour) and devolved upon these poor little nurses, whose business it is to watch the infant and carry it to its mother whenever it may require nourishment. To these hardly human little beings I addressed my remonstrances about the filth, cold and unnecessary wretchedness of their rooms, bidding the older boys and girls kindle up the fire, sweep the floor and expel the poultry. For a long time my words seemed unintelligible to them, till, when I began to sweep, make up the fire, etc., they first fell to laughing and then to imitating me. The incrustations of dirt on their hands, feet and faces were my next object of attack, and the stupid Negro practice of keeping the babies with their feet bare and their heads, already well capped by nature with their woolly hair, wrapped in half a dozen hot coverings.

The infirmary is a large two-story building, built of white-washed wood, and contains four large-sized rooms. In the first, only half of the six casements were glazed and these were obscured with dirt almost as much as the others were darkened by the dingy shutters which the shivering inmates had fastened in order to protect themselves from the cold. In the enormous chimney glimmered the powerless embers of a few sticks of wood, round which as many of the sick women as could approach were cowering, some on wooden settles, most of them on the ground. Those who were too ill to rise lay prostrate on the floor, without bed, mattress or pillow, buried in tattered and filthy blankets.

Here, in their hour of suffering, lay those whose health and strength are spent in unrequited labour for us – those whose husbands, fathers, brothers and sons were even at that hour sweating over the earth, whose produce was to buy for us all the luxuries that health can revel in, all the comforts which can alleviate sickness. I stood in the midst of them, perfectly unable to speak, the tears pouring from my eyes. Here lay women expecting every hour the terrors and agonies of childbirth, others who were groaning over the anguish and bitter disappointment of miscarriages. Here lay some burning with fever, others chilled with cold and aching with rheumatism, upon the cold, hard ground.

Now pray take notice that this is the hospital of an estate where the owners are supposed to be humane, the overseer efficent and kind and the Negroes remarkably well cared for and comfortable.

As soon as I had recovered from my dismay, I bade old Rose, the midwife who has charge of this room, open the shutters to let in the light. I proceeded to make up the fire, but, upon my lifting a log, there was one universal outcry of horror, and old Rose, attempting to snatch it from me, exclaimed, 'Let alone, missis. What for you lift wood? You have nigger enough, missis, to do it.' I hereupon had to explain my view of the purposes for which hands and arms were appended to our bodies, and forthwith began making Rose tidy up the miserable apartment. It was all I could do, and I passed on to the other room on the ground floor and to the two above, one of which is for the men who are ill.

They were all in the same deplorable condition, the upper rooms being rather the more miserable as none of the windows were glazed at all, and they had therefore only the alternative of utter darkness or killing draughts from the unsheltered casements. In all, filth, disorder and misery abounded. The floor was the only bed and scanty begrimed rags the only covering. I left this refuge for Mr. Butler's sick dependents with my clothes covered with dust and full of vermin, and with a heavy heart enough.

I was glad to return to the house, where I gave vent to my

indignation to Mr. Butler and his overseer, Mr. O . . . who here is a member of the family. The latter told me that, from his first entering his employment within the last year, the hospital had appeared to him to require a reform and that he had proposed it to the former manager and to Mr. Butler's brother, who is part proprietor of the estate. But, receiving no encouragement, he had supposed it was a matter of indifference to the owners and had left it as he had found it.

With regard to the indifference of our former manager, Mr. King, he was an excellent overseer because the estate returned a full income under his management. Such men have nothing to do with sick slaves.

I am learning to row here, for, circumscribed as my walks necessarily are and impossible as it is to resort to my favourite exercise on horseback on the narrow dykes, I must do something to prevent my blood from stagnating.

I forgot to tell you that in the hospital were several sick babies whose mothers were permitted to suspend their field labour to nurse them. Upon my addressing some remonstrances to one of these, Harriet, who, besides having a sick child was ill herself, about the horribly dirty condition of her baby, she assured me that it was impossible for them to keep their children clean; that they went out to work at daybreak and did not get their tasks done till evening, and that then they were too worn out to do anything but throw themselves down and sleep. This I mentioned on my return from the hospital, and the overseer appeared extremely annoyed and assured me that it was not true.

*

This morning I paid my second visit to the infirmary and found that there had been some faint attempt at sweeping and cleaning. The poor woman Harriet, however, was crying bitterly. More by signs and dumb show than words, she and old Rose informed me that the overseer had flogged her that morning for having told me that the women had not time to keep their children clean.

Among the patients in the next ward there was a young girl whose hands and feet were literally rotting away piecemeal from a horrible disease which, when it attacks the joints of the toes and fingers. the pieces absolutely decay and come off, leaving the limb a maimed and horrible stump. Another disease of which they complained much was a species of lock-jaw, to which the babies frequently fall victim in the first or second week after birth.

Pleurisy, or a tendency to it, seems very common; also peripneumonia which is terribly prevalent and generally fatal. Rheumatism is almost universal and attacks indiscriminately young and old. A great number of the women are victims to falling of the womb and weakness in the spine; but these are necessary results of their laborious existence.

*

I have ingeniously contrived to introduce bribery, corruption and pauperism, all of a breath, upon this island which until my advent was as innocent of these pollutions, I suppose, as Prospero's island. Wishing to appeal to some perception perhaps a little less dim in their minds than the abstract loveliness of cleanliness, I have proclaimed to all the little baby nurses that I will give a cent to every little boy or girl whose baby's face shall be clean, and one to every individual with clean face and hands of their own. This morning I was surrounded by a swarm of children carrying their little charges on their backs and in their arms, the shining and in many cases wet faces and hands of the latter bearing ample testimony to the ablutions that had been inflicted upon them.

The black babies of a year or two old are very pretty; they have for the most part beautiful eyes and eyelashes, pearly, perfect teeth which they retain after their other juvenile graces have left them; their skins are all infinitely finer and softer than the skins of white people. I have seen many babies on this plantation who were quite as pretty as white children. This very day I kissed a little sleeping creature that lay on its mother's knee in the infirmary – as beautiful a specimen of a sleeping infant as any I ever saw. The caress excited the irrepressible delight of all the women present – poor creatures! – who seemed to forget that I was a woman and had children myself, and bore a woman's and a mother's heart to them and theirs.

*

Toward sunset I went to the river to take my rowing lesson. A darling little canoe, which carries two oars and a steersman and rejoices in the appropriate title of the *Dolphin*, is my especial vessel, and I contrived to row upward of half a mile with help and instruction from Jack, my particular slave who has been appointed to attend me in my roamings about the island. We coasted the reed-crowned edge to a large rice mill, the enormous wheel of which is turned by the tide. The steps of the landing were covered with young women and boys and girls drawing water. A very small cedar pail – a piggin – serves to scoop up the river water; and having filled a large bucket they transfer this to their heads, and thus laden march home with the purifying element – what to do with it I cannot imagine, for evidence of its ever having been introduced into their dwellings I saw none. They surrounded me with shrieks of joy, uttering exclamations of delight and amazement at my rowing. Considering that they dig, delve, carry burdens and perform many more athletic exercises than pulling a light oar, I was rather amused at this; but it was the singular fact of seeing a white woman stretch her sinews in any toilsome exercise which astonished them, accustomed as they are to see both men and women of the privileged skin eschew the slightest shadow of labour as a thing not only painful but degrading.

*

In the afternoon I and Jack rowed ourselves over to Darien. It is a Saturday, when the slaves are permitted to come over to the town to purchase such things as they may require and can afford, and to dispose of their poultry, moss and eggs. I met many of them paddling themselves singly in their slight canoes, scooped out of the trunk of a tree, and parties of three or four rowing-boats of their own building, laden with purchases, singing, laughing and apparently enjoying their holiday to the utmost. They hailed me with shouts of delight and many were the injunctions bawled after Jack to 'mind and take good care of missis!' We returned through the glory of a sunset all amber-coloured and rosy, and found that one of the slaves, a young lad for whom Mr. Butler has a particular regard, was dangerously ill. Dr. Holmes was sent for and there is every probability that he, Mr. Butler and Mr. O——— will be up all night with the poor fellow.

*

Today being Sunday, a large boat of Mr. Butler's people from St. Simon's Island came up, to go to church at Darien and pay their respects to their master and see their new missis. The same scene was acted over again that occurred on our arrival. A crowd clustered round the house door, to whom I and my babies were produced, and with every individual of whom we had to shake hands half a dozen times. They brought us presents of eggs (their only wealth) and one young lad had a beautiful pair of chickens which he offered most earnestly to Sally. We took one of them not to mortify him and, a green ribbon being tied round its leg, it became a sacred fowl, 'little missis's chicken'.

Dr. Holmes came again today to see the poor sick boy, who is bidding fair to recover. He entertained me with an account of the Darien society, its aristocracies and democracies, its little grandeurs and smaller pettinesses, its social jealousies and delicate divisions of genteel, genteeler, genteelest. 'For me', added the worthy doctor, 'I cannot well enter into the spirit of these nice distinctions; my house is perhaps the only one in Darien where you would find all these opposite and contending elements combined.'

After church the people came back from Darien. They are only allowed to go once a month. On the intermediate Sundays they assemble at the house of London, Mr. Butler's head cooper, an excellent and pious man who, heaven knows how, has obtained some little knowledge of reading, and who reads prayers and the Bible to his fellow slaves, and addresses them with extemporaneous exhortations.

I do not think that a residence on a slave plantation is likely to be advantageous to a child like my oldest. I was observing her today among her swarthy worshippers and saw with dismay the universal eagerness with which they sprang to obey her little gestures of command. She said something about a swing, and in less than five minutes headman Frank had it erected and a dozen young slaves were ready to swing little missis. Think of learning to rule despotically your fellow creatures before the first lesson of self-government has been well spelled over! It makes me tremble, but I shall find a remedy or remove myself and the child from this misery and ruin.

The Sunday trim of these poor people presents the most ludicrous combination of incongruities you can conceive – frills, flounces, ribbons; combs stuck in their woolly heads; filthy finery, every colour of the rainbow; head handkerchiefs that put one's very eyes out from a mile off; chintzes with sprawling patterns; beads, bugles, flaring sashes and little fanciful aprons which finish these incongruous toilets with a sort of airy grace.

*

I passed up the 'street' at between eleven o'clock and noon, when the people were taking their first meal in the day. By the bye,

Elizabeth, how do you think your farmers would relish labouring hard all day upon two meals of Indian corn or hominy? Such is the regulation on this plantation, and I beg you to bear in mind that the Negroes here are generally considered well off. They go to the fields at daybreak, carrying with them their allowance of food for the day, which, towards noon, and *not till then*, they eat, cooking it over a fire which they kindle as best they can where they are working. Their second meal is at night, having worked *at the very least* six hours without intermission since their noonday meal (properly called, for it is meal and nothing else). Those that I passed today were sitting on their doorsteps or on the ground eating. Chairs, tables, plates, knives, forks they had none; they ate out of their little cedar tubs or an iron pot, some with broken iron spoons, more with pieces of wood and all the children with their fingers.

I must not forget to tell you of a magnificent bald-headed eagle which Mr. Butler called me out early this morning to look at. I had never before seen alive one of these national types of yours, and stood entranced as the noble creature swept, like a black cloud, over the river, his bald white head bent forward and shining in the sun, and his fierce eyes and beak directed toward one of the beautiful wild ducks on the water.

*

I really never was so busy in all my life as I am here. I sit at the receipt of custom (involuntarily enough) from morning till night. No time, no place affords me a respite from my innumerable petitioners. Whether I be asleep or awake, reading, eating or walking – in the kitchen, my bedroom, the parlour – they flock in with urgent entreaties and pitiful stories, and my conscience forbids my ever postponing their business; for, with what shame and grief I say it, by their unpaid labour I live – their nakedness clothes me, and their heavy toil maintains me in luxurious idleness.

Mr. Butler has been most gratified today by the arrival of Mr. King who, with his father, was for nineteen years the sole manager of these estates, and discharged his task with great ability. How far he understood his duties to the slaves, or whether indeed an overseer can in the nature of things acknowledge any duty to them, is another matter. He is a remarkable man and much respected for his integrity. The mere fact of his having personally governed seven hundred people scattered over three tracts of land at considerable distance from one another certainly bespeaks efficiency and energy of a very uncommon order.

After dinner Mr. King gave me a lively description of the yeomanry of Georgia, more properly termed pinelanders. Have you visions of well-to-do farmers with comfortable homesteads, decent habits, industrious, intelligent, cheerful and thrifty? Such is not the yeomanry of Georgia. Labour here being the especial portion of slaves, no white man of any class puts hand to work of any kind soever. This is an exceedingly dignified way of proving their gentility for the lazy planters; but the effect on the poorer whites is terrible. Too poor to possess land or slaves and having no means of living in the towns, they squat either on other men's land or government districts – always here swamp or pine barren – till ejected by the rightful proprietors. These wretched creatures will not labour for their own subsistence. They are hardly protected from the weather by the rude shelters they frame for themselves in the midst of the dreary woods. Their food is chiefly supplied by shooting wildfowl and venison and stealing from the plantations nearest at hand. Their clothes hang about them in tatters, and the combined squalor and fierceness of their appearance is really frightful.

This population is the direct growth of slavery. The planters are loud in their execrations of these miserable vagabonds; yet they do not see that so long as labour is considered the disgraceful portion of slaves, these free men will hold it nobler to starve or steal than till the earth.

This led us to the subject of slavery; and you may be sure I listened with infinite interest to the opinions of a man of uncommon shrewdness and sagacity who was born in the very bosom of it and has passed his whole life among slaves. This was his verdict: 'I hate slavery with all my heart. I consider it an absolute curse wherever it exists. It will keep those states where it exists fifty years behind the others in improvement and prosperity'. Further on he made this remarkable observation: 'As for its being an irremediable evil – a thing not to be helped or got rid of – that's all nonsense, for as soon as people become convinced that it is in their interest to get rid of it, they will find the means to do so, depend upon it.'

Fanny's initial good opinion of Roswell King Junior was soon shaken by the sight of several children bearing a striking resemblance to him and by what she heard of his behaviour as overseer: that, for instance,

1(a) Charles Kemble (Fanny's father) as Romeo, Covent Garden 1814

1 (b) Mrs Charles Kemble, née Maria Theresa Decamp

1(c) Fanny's receipt for £910 salary for 182 performances at Covent Garden, October 1829 to May 1830

Theatre Royal, Covent-Garden, 29 May 1830.

Memorandum for £.910 : .. :— received by me from the Proprietors of the Theatre Royal, Covent-Garden—amount of my Salary from 5th October 1829 to 28 May 1830. 182 Nights at £ 5. per Night.

Frances Ann Kemble

John Hayter delt.
On Stone by

2 Fanny as Juliet, 1829

3 Fanny Kemble: from the painting by Alonzo Chaffee
based on the sketch by Sir Thomas Lawrence

4 The Trial Scene from *Henry VIII*, Covent Garden 1831,
with Fanny as Queen Katherine:
from the lithograph by Henry Andrews

5 Pierce Butler

6 Butler Place, Fanny's home near Philadelphia

7 Fanny Kemble in middle age

8 Fanny Kemble
reading Shakespeare,
St James's Theatre,
London, July 1850

he had taken as mistress the wife of headman Frank whom she much admired; that he would kick the older women, curse them, turn their clothes over their heads, flog them himself and abuse them shamefully, no matter what condition they were in. She could not, however, deny his efficiency as overseer.

Mr. Butler was called out this evening to listen to a complaint of overwork from a gang of pregnant women. I did not stay to listen to the details of their petition, for I am unable to command myself on such occasions. Mr. Butler seemed positively degraded in my eyes as he stood enforcing upon these women the necessity of fulfilling their appointed tasks. How honourable he would have appeared to me begrimed with the sweat and toil of the coarsest manual labour, to what he then seemed, setting forth to these wretched, ignorant women, as a duty, their unpaid, exacted labour! I hope this sojourn among Mr. Butler's slaves may not lessen my respect for him, but I fear it.

*

I have been engaged in receiving and returning visits, for even to this *ultima Thule* of all civilisation do these polite usages extend. I have been called upon by several families residing in and about Darien, and rowed over in due form to acknowledge the honour. The whole town lies in a bed of sand; at every step I took my feet were ankle deep in it and I had cause to rejoice that I was booted for the occasion. Our worthy doctor, whose lady I was going to visit, did nothing but regret that I had not allowed him to provide me with a carriage, though the distance is not a quarter of a mile. The magnitude of the exertion seemed to fill him with amazement, and he over and over again repeated how impossible it would be to prevail on any of the ladies here to take such a walk. Our doctor's wife is a New England woman; she gave me some violets and narcissus and expressed, like her husband, a thousand regrets at my having walked so far.

*

Everything today was in a high fever of preparation for the ball in honour of our arrival. It took place in one of the rooms of the infirmary whose few occupants had been removed and, without any very tender consideration for their not very remote though invisible sufferings, the dancing commenced. It is impossible to describe the things these people did with their bodies – the contortions, springs and flings and kicks and capers – and above all with their faces, the whites of their eyes and the whites of their teeth. The languishing elegance of some, the painstaking labori-ousness of others – and above all the feats of a certain enthusiastic banjo player, who seemed to thump his instrument with every part of his body at once, at last so utterly overcame any attempt at decorous gravity on my part that I was obliged to secede; and considering what the atmosphere was that we inhaled during the exhibition, it is only wonderful that we were not made ill by the double effort – not to laugh and, if possible, not to breathe.

*

Rowing yesterday evening through a beautiful sunset into a more beautiful moonrise, my two sable boatmen entertained me with alternate strophe and antistrophe of poetical description of my personal attractions, in which my 'wire waist' [her stays] recurred repeatedly. Occasionally I am celebrated in these rowing chants as 'Massa's darling' and Sally comes in for endless glorification on account of the brilliant beauty of her complexion. The other day, after the usual tribute to her roses and lilies, came the following rather significant couplet:
                    Little Missis Sally,
                    That's a ruling lady.
At which all the white teeth simultaneously lightened from the black visages, while the subject of this equivocal commendation sat with infantine solemnity surveying her dependents with imperturbable gravity.

    Yesterday I cut out a dress for one of the women. I have already spent considerable time in what the French call 'confectioning' baby bundles, i.e. the rough and simple tiny habiliments of coarse cotton and scarlet flannel which form a baby's layette here and of which I have run up some scores; but my present task was more difficult. Tall, straight, well-made, profoundly serious, she stood like a bronze statue, while I, mounted on a stool, pinned and measured, and cut and shaped, and had the satisfaction of seeing the fine proportions of my black goddess quite becomingly clothed in a tight-fitting body of the gayest chintz, which she really contrived to put together quite creditably.

*

We have had a death among the people since I last wrote. A very valuable slave called Shadrach was seized with pneumonia. The doctor came repeatedly from Darien and on the last night of the poor fellow's life Mr. Butler himself watched with him. His burial took place last evening. Just as the twilight was thickening into darkness I went with Mr. Butler to the cottage of the cooper London who was to perform the burial service. The coffin was laid on trestles in front of the cottage, and a large assemblage of people had gathered round. Many of the men carried pinewood torches, the fitful glare of which glanced over the strange assembly. Every pair of large white-rimmed eyes turned upon Mr. Butler and myself. Presently the whole congregation uplifted their voices in a hymn, the first high wailing notes of which sent a thrill through all my nerves. When the chant ceased cooper London began a prayer and all the people knelt down in the sand, as I did also. Mr. Butler alone remained standing in the presence of the dead man and the living God to whom his slaves were now appealing. It was a sort of conventional Methodist prayer, and probably quite as conventional as the rest was the closing invocation of God's blessing upon their master, their mistress and our own children; but this fairly overcame my composure and I began to cry bitterly.

The coffin was taken to the people's burial ground, where London read aloud portions of the funeral service from the Prayer Book. I knelt again while the words 'I am the resurrection and the life' sounded over the prostrate throng and mingled with the heavy flowing of the vast river sweeping through the darkness by which we were now encompassed beyond the immediate circle of our torch-bearers. There was something painful to me in Mr. Butler's standing while we all knelt on the earth; for, though in any church in Philadelphia he would have stood during the praying of any minister, here I wished he would have knelt, to have given his slaves some token of his belief that – in the sight of the Master to whom we were addressing our worship – all men are equal.

The service ended with a short address from London upon Lazarus and the confirmation which the story of his resurrection afforded our hopes. The words were simple and rustic, but there was nothing in the slightest degree incongruous or grotesque in the matter or manner, and the exhortations not to steal or lie, or neglect to work well for massa with which the glorious hope of immortality was blended in the poor slave preacher's address. When the coffin was lowered the grave was found to be partially filled with water. This seemed to shock and distress the people and for the first time during the whole ceremony there were sounds of crying and exclamations of grief. I could not speak to Mr. Butler, but continued to cry as we walked silently home; and, whatever his cogitations were, they did not take the usual form with him of wordy demonstration. And so we returned from one of the most striking religious ceremonies at which I ever assisted.

*

Having made a fresh purchase of fishing tackle, Jack and I betook ourselves to the river and succeeded in securing some immense catfish. The dexterity necessary for taking them off the hook so as to avoid the spikes on their backs and the spikes on their gills, the former having to be pressed down and the two others pressed up before you can get any purchase on the slimy beast – this makes the catching of catfish questionable sport. Then too, they hiss and spit and swear at one, and are altogether devilish in their aspect and demeanour. Nor are they good for food, except, as Jack said with much humility, 'Good for coloured folks, missis; me 'spect not good enough for white people'.

*

I was accosted by poor old Theresa who had complained to me of her back being broken by hard work and childbearing. She was in a dreadful state of excitement because she said Mr. O—— had ordered her to be flogged for complaining to me as she did. [Like Harriet, who had been flogged for the same reason some weeks earlier.] It seems to me that I have come down here to be tortured, for this punishing of these wretched creatures for crying out to me for help is really converting me into a source of increased misery to them. It is almost more than I can endure to hear such stories; and although I dare say Mr. Butler gives me little credit for prudence or self-command, I have some, and exercise it too, when I listen to such tales as these with my teeth set fast and my lips closed. Whatever I may do to the master, I hold my tongue to the slaves and I wonder how I do it.

A variety of improvements are about to be made to the infirmary. There is to be a third story for the least distressing cases, and the destitute apartments are to be furnished with bedsteads, mattresses, pillows and blankets. I feel a little comforted for the many heartaches my life here inflicts upon me.

I have had a long and painful conversation with Mr. Butler about the flogging inflicted on the wretched Theresa. He pronounced the whole transaction perfectly satisfactory and *en règle*. To this I retorted the manifest injustice of unpaid and enforced labour, the brutal inhumanity of allowing a man to strip and lash a woman, the mother of ten children, and to exact from her toil which was to maintain in luxury two idle young men, the owners of the plantation. I said I thought this must be abhorrent to any manly or humane man. Mr. Butler said he thought it was disagreeable, and left me to my reflections with that concession. These discussions are terrible: they throw me into perfect agonies of distress for the slaves; for myself whose intervention in their behalf sometimes seems to me worse than useless; for Mr. Butler whose share in this horrible system fills me by turns with indignation and pity. But after all, what can he do? How can he help it all? Born and bred in America, how should he care or wish to help it? Of course he does not, and I am in despair that he does not: *et voilà*, it is a happy and hopeful plight for us both.

*

Mr. Butler has for a little while been anxious that we should go down to St. Simon's Island, the cotton plantation, where we shall suffer less from the heat. It is fifteen miles down the river, a large island at the mouth of the Altamaha and he has gone to make arrangements for our departure thither.

The boat he went off in was large, broad and rather heavy; it serves as a sort of omnibus for the transfer of people, goods and necessaries from one island to the other. As it pushed off the men at the oars set up a chorus which they continued to chant in unison and in time with their stroke till the voices and oars were heard no more in the distance. The tune was a very distinct descendant of 'Coming through the Rye'. The words were astonishingly primitive, especially the first line which, when it burst from their eight throats in high unison sent me into fits of laughter.

> Jenny shake her toe at me,
>   Jenny gone away;
> Jenny shake her toe at me,
>   Jenny gone away.
> Hurrah! Miss Susy, oh!
>   Jenny gone away;
> Hurrah! Miss Susy, oh!
>   Jenny gone away.

What the obnoxious Jenny meant by shaking her toe I never could ascertain, but her going was an unmistakable subject of satisfaction, and the pause on the last 'Oh!' before the final announcement of her departure had really a good deal of dramatical and musical effect.

*

I was accosted by London with a request for a Prayer Book and Bible. I promised him his holy books and asked how he had learned to read, but found it impossible to get him to tell me. I wonder if he thought he should be putting his teacher, whoever he was, in danger of the penalty of the law against instructing slaves if he told me. Besides his other good qualities he appears to have that most unusual one of all in an uneducated person – discretion. He certainly is a most remarkable man.

You cannot imagine how great a triumph the virtue next to Godliness is making under my auspices and a judicious system of small bribery. I can hardly stir now without being assailed with cries of 'Missis, me mind child, me bery clean'. This virtue, if painful to the practicers, as no doubt it is, is expensive to me, and I shall have to try some moral influence equivalent in value to a cent current coin of the realm. What a poor chance the poor abstract idea runs!

*

There has been a terrible disturbance in consequence of the disappearance from undercook John's safe keeping of a ham Mr. Butler had committed to his charge. There is no doubt that he has made away with it: the very lies he told about it were curiously shallow, childlike and transparent. Mr. Butler was in a state of towering anger and, besides a flogging, sentenced the unhappy cook to degradation from his high and dignified position (and, alas! all its sweets of comparatively easy labour and good living from the remains of our table) to the hard toil and despised position of a common field hand.

In speaking of John's trespass to Mr. Butler this evening, I observed that the ignorance of these poor people ought to screen them from punishment. He replied that they knew well enough what was right and what was wrong. I asked how they could be expected to know it? He replied, by means of cooper London and the religious instruction he gave them. So, after all, the appeal is to be made to that moral and religious instruction which is withheld from them, and which, if they obtain it at all, is the result of their own unaided and unencouraged exertion. The more I see and hear and learn and ponder about slavery, the more impossible I find it to conceive how its practitioners and upholders are to justify their deeds before the tribunal of their own conscience or God's law. It is too dreadful to have those whom we love accomplices to his wickedness; it is too intolerable to find myself an involuntary accomplice to it.

*

St. Simon's Island,[2] *February 16th–April 19th, 1839*
We came down to St. Simon's Island yesterday afternoon, and I was thankful enough of the fifteen miles' row to rest in from the labour of leavetaking, which, combined with packing and preparing all our own personalities and those of the children, was no sinecure. At every moment one or other of the poor people rushed in to bid me good-bye. Many of their farewells were grotesque enough, some were pathetic, and all of them made me very sad. Poor people! how little I have done, how little I can do for them.

I have worked my fingers nearly off with making innumerable rolls of coarse little baby clothes for small new-born slaves, Margery diligently cutting and shaping and I as diligently stitching. We leave a good supply for the hospital.

The conch was sounded on our arrival, as at the rice island, and we made our descent on the famous long-staple cotton island of St. Simon's, where we presently took up our abode in what has all the appearance of an old, half-decayed, rattling farm house. This morning I peeped round its immediate neighbourhood and saw to my delight, within hail, some noble-looking evergreen oaks and close to the house itself a tiny would-be garden with one or two peach trees in full blossom, tufts of silver narcissus and jonquils, violets and an exquisite myrtle bush. After the rice island where the Altamaha kept looking over the dike at me as I

[2] The first English settlement at Frederica on St. Simon's Island was established as a military defence against the Spaniards in 1736 by General James Edward Oglethorpe, founder of the colony of Georgia. He had brought Charles and John Wesley to America, and the latter several times preached on the island. Aaron Burr spent a month at the Butler plantation at Hampton Point after the duel in which Hamilton was mortally wounded in 1804. Today St. Simon's is a fashionable holiday resort with an airport, luxury hotels, golf clubs and smart dress shops. President Jimmy Carter held pre-inauguration cabinet meetings there in December 1976.

sat in the house working or writing, it is pleasant to be on terra firma again and to know that the river is under my feet and not over my head.

The fame of my peculiar requisitions has preceded me here, for the babies presented to my admiring notice have all been without caps; also, however, without socks to their opposite little extremities, but that does not signify quite so much. The people too that I saw yesterday were remarkably clean and tidy; to be sure, it was Sunday. The whole day until quite late in the afternoon, the house was surrounded by a crowd of our poor dependents, until from sheer weariness I was obliged to shut the doors, an incessant stream poured in and out, whose various modes of salutation, greeting and welcome were more grotesque and pathetic at the same time than anything you can imagine.

I find here an immense proportion of old people. The work and climate of the rice plantation require the strongest of the able-bodied men and women of the estate. The cotton crop is no longer as paramount in value as it used to be and the climate, soil and labour of St. Simon's are better adapted to old, young and feeble cultivators.

When Major Butler, Mr. Butler's grandfather, first sent the produce of this plantation to England, it was of so fine a quality that it used to be quoted by itself on the Liverpool cotton market and was then worth half a guinea a pound; it is not now worth a shilling. Such a decrease, and the steady increase at the same time of the slave population (now numbering between seven and eight hundred bodies to clothe and house and feed) while the land is being exhausted by the wasteful nature of the agriculture itself – all this suggests a pretty serious prospect of declining prosperity. The rice plantations are a great thing to fall back on under these circumstances, and the rice crop is now quite as valuable, if not more so, as the cotton.

*

I write today in great depression and distress. I have had a most painful conversation with Mr. Butler, who has declined receiving any more of the people's petitions through me. The grief and indignation they cause me cannot always be done away with – though their expression may be silenced – by his angry exclamations of 'Why do you listen to such stuff? Why do you believe such trash? Don't you know the niggers are all d——d liars?' He desired me this morning to bring him no more complaints or requests of any sort, as the people had hitherto done very well without such an advocate, and as I was only kept in an incessant state of excitement with all the falsehoods they 'found they could make me believe'. How well they have done without my advocacy, the conditions I see with my own eyes demonstrate even more than their pitiful petitions. It is true that their sufferings, and still more the injustice done to the majority who cannot come to me for redress, have filled my heart with bitterness and indignation, until, I suppose, Mr. Butler is weary of hearing what he has never heard before: the voice of expostulation and importunate pleadings against wrongs that he will not even acknowledge, and for creatures whose common humanity with his own I half think he does not believe. I must return to the North. This is no place for me, since I was not born among slaves and cannot bear to live among them.

Perhaps after all what he says is true: when I am gone they will fall back into the desperate uncomplaining habit of suffering from which my coming among them, willing to hear and ready to help, has tempted them. He says that bringing their complaints to me, and the sight of my credulous commiseration, only tend to make them discontented and idle and bring renewed chastisement upon them, so that instead of really befriending them, I am only preparing more suffering when I leave and they can no more cry to me for help. And so I see nothing for it but to go and leave them to their fate. Perhaps too he is afraid of the mere contagion of freedom which breathes from the very existence of those who are free. My way of speaking to the people, of treating them, or living with them, the appeals I make to their sense of truth, of duty, of self-respect, the infinite compassion and the human consideration I feel for them – all these, as Mr. O—— once almost hinted, make my existence among slaves an element of danger to the 'institution'.

Yet I cannot give way to the bitter impatience I feel at my present position and come back to the North without leaving my babies; I must, for their sakes, remain where they are and learn this dreary lesson of suffering to the end.

Fanny had in fact actually tried to leave St. Simon's Island and had gone on hunger strike, refusing to eat food produced by slave labour, according to Pierce Butler's Statement *of his case for divorce published,in self-vindication he said, the year after it was over.*[3] *Her*

---

[3] Wright: *Fanny Kemble and the Lovely Land*, p. 83.

defence, Answer of Frances Anne Butler to the Libel of Pierce Butler praying for a Divorce *had had wide publicity in America and England.*

*

Often in the evening, when my bairns are asleep and I sit writing this daily history, the door of the great barnlike room is opened stealthily and men and women come trooping silently in, their naked feet falling all but inaudibly on the bare boards as they betake themselves to the hearth, where they squat on their hams in a circle, the bright blaze from the huge pine logs shining on their sooty limbs and faces and making them look like a ring of idols surrounding my domestic hearth. The candles on my table give only light enough for my own occupation, the firelight illuminates the rest of the apartment; and you cannot imagine anything stranger than the effect of all these glassy whites of eyes and grinning white teeth shining in the flickering light. I very often take no notice of them at all, and they seem quite absorbed in contemplating me. My evening dress probably excites their wonder and admiration no less than my rapid and continuous writing. Sometimes at the end of my day's journal I say, 'Well, what do you want?' when each black figure springs up as if moved by machinery and they all answer, 'Me come say ha'do, missis'; and then all troop out as noiselessly as they entered.

Some women visited me yesterday who were all in the family way and came to entreat me to use my influence with Mr. Butler to obtain for them a month's (instead of three week's) respite from labour in the field after child-bearing. A woman with a bright sweet face called Mary, and a very sweet voice, appealed to my own experience; and while she spoke of my babies and my carefully-tended, delicately nursed and tenderly watched confinement and convalescence, I held the table before me so hard in order not to cry that I think my fingers ought to have left a mark on it. All these women had large families, *all* of them had lost half their children and several had lost more.

Scarcely a day passed on which Fanny did not have a similar story to report. Indeed, on one evening she set down the case histories of no less than nine women who had asked for her help in a single day. Her deepest concern throughout her stay on the plantation was for the women, on whom, she soon came to believe, the principal hardships fell. The men, on the other hand, 'do not appear to me to be overworked. They lead a mere animal existence, in itself not particularly cruel or distressing', apart of course from the 'basic injustice' of slavery itself.

*

I am helped to bear all that is so very painful to me here by my constant enjoyment of the strange, wild scenery. I rode today across a salt marsh upon a raised causeway that was perfectly alive with land crabs, whose desperately active endeavours to avoid my horse's hoofs were so perfectly ludicrous that I literally laughed alound. The sides of this road were covered with a thick and close embroidery of vivid green and red: they made my horse's path look as if it were edged with an exquisite pattern of coral. It was like a thing in a fairy tale.

I suppose one secret of my being able to suffer as acutely as I do, without being made either ill or absolutely miserable, is the childish excitability of my temperament, and the sort of ecstasy which any beautiful thing gives me. No day, almost no hour, passes without some enjoyment of the sort this coral road gave me, and which returns again and again before my memory, delighting my fancy and stimulating my imagination. I sometimes despise myself for what seems an inconceivable rapidity of emotion, but I console myself by the reflection that it is a merciful system of compensation by which my whole nature, tortured as it was last night, can be absorbed this morning in a pleasurable contemplation of the capers of crabs and the colours of mosses as if nothing else existed in creation.

*

Only six weeks remained of the plantation visit after Pierce Butler's ultimatum. They were miserably unhappy. The petitioners still presented themselves in their dozens but Fanny was forbidden to intercede on their behalf; nor could she urge improvements to the St. Simon's hospital which she found in even worse case than that on Butler's Island. Instead she found her own ways of helping, not all of them to her husband's liking. On Sundays she held religious services, reading the scriptures to appreciative gatherings of tidy, decorous slaves. She ventured to pay wages to a gang of lads for cutting paths through the undergrowth. When a young house slave asked to be taught to read she had little hesitation in agreeing, though well aware that she would be breaking the law. 'I certainly intend to teach Aleck to read. I certainly won't tell Mr. Butler. I'll leave him to find out'.

Fanny's last 'letter' from the plantation ended, not with high-minded

reflections about slavery, but on a somewhat comical note. The day
before leaving she rode twenty-four miles on a visit to a neighbour and
came home hungry, to find 'not so much as a boiled potato to eat. I had
forgotten to order my dinner and my slaves, unauthorised, had not
ventured to prepare any'. But the postscript she added later was a sad
one.

*

I never returned to the plantation, nor ever again saw any of the
poor people among whom I lived during this winter but Jack,
once, under sad circumstances. The poor lad's health failed so
completely that his owners humanely brought him to the North,
to try what benefit he might derive from the change. This was
before the Fugitive Slave Bill, when, touching the soil of the
Northern states, a slave became free; and such was the apprehension felt lest Jack should be enlightened as to this fact by some
philanthropic abolitionist, that he was kept shut up in a high
upper room of a large empty house where even I was not allowed
to visit him. I heard at length of his being in Philadelphia; and
upon my distinct statement that I considered freeing their slaves
the business of Messrs. Butler themselves, and not mine, I was at
length permitted to see him. Poor fellow! coming to the North did
not prove to him the delight his eager desire had so often anticipated from it; nor, under such circumstances, is it perhaps
much to be wondered at that he benefited but little by the change
– he died not long after.

CHAPTER 14

Gathering Clouds
1839–1843

*During the six years after the return from Georgia in April 1839
Fanny had to face yet more abrupt changes of life style: 'days rolling on
in dreamy monotonous succession' followed by an outburst of hectic
gaiety in England and then again a long spell of solitude and misery.
In spite of everything she and Pierce were still in love, as both of them
later made very clear: otherwise the marriage could never have survived the strain of their frequent violent quarrels. The two had been
home for only four or five weeks when Pierce wrote urgently to
Elizabeth Sedgwick: 'I have done all that deep love for a wife, the
strongest affection for my children and an earnest desire to secure peace
and happiness for myself and them have dictated, but all has failed'.
Fanny had refused to sleep with him, he alleged, and had repeatedly
demanded to be allowed to return to England. She had said, 'You can
never repair the injury you have done in marrying me. I will not
remain here to be your housekeeper, your child's nurse or what you
make me that is still more degrading and revolting.' Pierce asked the
Sedgwicks to intervene. Elizabeth replied by urging Fanny to stay
with her husband and reproaching her with having allowed herself to
become irrational: she must fight against this and other morbid tendencies. Reminding her of her mother's mental instability, Elizabeth
concluded, 'My poor dear Fanny, my almost idolised friend, do let me
persuade you that your mind is diseased.'[1]*

*As always, only the barest hints of Fanny's emotional turmoil or of the
marital discord were allowed to emerge in her Records forty years later.
Hence the published letters to Harriet at this time are — for Fanny —
pedestrian and uninteresting. Except for the one all-absorbing topic
she had in any case little but trivialities to tell her friend.*

*In late summer a two months' stay at Lenox did much to soothe her
troubled spirits: 'I have good friends and my precious children, an
easy, cultivated, cheerful society, my capital horse, and in short most
good things I call mine — on this side of the water — with one heavy
exception. . . .', she wrote to Harriet.*

Fanny was entirely on her own at Butler Place during the early
[1] Wright, *op. cit.*, pp. 85, 86, 87.

157

months of 1840 when Pierce was away in Georgia. There he fell seriously ill. Fanny was remorseful, writing that she hoped he would be better when 'freed from the gloom and disquietude which my thrice unhappy temperament seems to throw over you . . . Oh my dearest, what can be done for you?'[2] For a time after his return relations were calmer. Meanwhile domestic problems loomed disproportionately large. The children's nurse Margery, who had helped her mistress through so many trials, reluctantly had to be dismissed for teaching little Sally Roman Catholicism: 'Though it would not mortally grieve me if hereafter my child were conscientiously to embrace Romanism, I have no desire that she should be educated in what I consider erroneous views on the most momentous of all subjects'. Fanny's household staff was reduced and, without a personal maid, she had to forego 'the usual decency' of changing for dinner, the housemaid being too clumsy to fasten the back of her dress on the new nurse's nights out. The Georgia journal was neatly transcribed: Fanny would have wished to enlarge and revise it during a second visit to the plantation but this was vetoed by her brother-in-law who considered her presence there to be 'a source of distress to myself, annoyance to others and a danger to the property'. Realising that her passionate anti-slavery arguments could only be counter-productive, she learnt to hold her tongue; and from family loyalty she refused pressing requests to publish the journal: 'I do not think I have a right to exhibit the interior management and economy of our property to the world at large as a sample of southern slavery'.

The monotonous days at Butler Place ended late in 1840 with the news that Charles Kemble was on his deathbed. The Butlers arrived in London just before Christmas to find him so ill that at first Fanny was not permitted to see him. Before long, however, the old man was back on his feet and able to join the Butlers in the house Pierce had rented in Clarges Street, off Piccadilly. Harriet St. Leger came for a long stay, and in April Adelaide Kemble, Fanny's sister, now a prima donna, arrived in London fresh from triumphs at the Fenice in Venice, the Scala in Milan and the San Carlo in Naples.

Clarges Street, [London] May 3rd, 1841
Dearest Harriet, Adelaide sits in the next room at her piano, singing and giving a taste of her quality to Charles Greville,[3] who

[2] *ibid.*, p. 89.
[3] Charles Greville (1784–1865). Clerk to the Council 1821–59. Intimate with statesmen of both Whig and Tory parties and author of the *Greville Memoirs*. He and his brother Henry were old friends of the Kembles. 'He was a sort of universal referee in the society to which he belonged,' observed Fanny, 'he knew the secrets of everybody, which everyone seemed willing that he should know'.

as you know is an important person in all sorts of matters. She is singing most beautifully, and the passionate words of love, longing, grief and joy light up her whole countenance with a perfect blaze of emotion. As for me, the tears stream over my face and I can hardly prevent myself from sobbing aloud. She has grown very large. She looks very well and handsome and has acquired something completely foreign in her tone and manner, and even accent. She complains of the darkness of our skies and the dullness of our mode of life here as intolerable and oppressive to the last degree.

May 21st

We are lifted off our feet by a perfect torrent of engagements, of visits, of going out and receiving; our house is full from morning till night of people coming to sing with or listen to my sister. Now let me tell you how I am surrounded at this minute while I write to you. At my very table sit Trelawny and Charles Young,[4] talking to me and to each other; further on, towards my father, Mr. Charles Greville and an Italian singer on one side of my sister; and on the other an Italian painter; then Mary Anne Thackeray. Furthermore the door has just closed upon an English youth who sings almost at well as an Italian, with whom my sister has been singing her heart out for the last two hours. Tomorrow evening we have a gathering here, I beg you to believe, nothing under the rank of a viscount. Friday, my sister sings at the Palace, and we are all enveloped in a golden cloud of fashionable hard work, which rather delights my father. As for me, I am bewildered by the whirl in which we live, which I find a rather trying contrast to my late solitary existence in America.

June 1841

A concert was given yesterday for the benefit of the Poles, the Duchess of Sutherland condescending to lend Stafford House provided the assemblage was quite select and limited to four hundred people. Rachel was to recite, Liszt to play, and my sister to sing. A large assembly of our finest (and bluntest) people was not a bad audience, in a worldly sense, for her *début*. She sang beautifully and was extremely admired and praised and petted. The whole scene was of the gayest and most splendid possible, the entertainment taking place in the great hall and staircase of

[4] Charles Young (1777–1856). Actor and an old friend. Fanny had been his leading lady at his farewell performance of Macbeth at Covent Garden in 1832.

Stafford House, with its scarlet floor-cloths and marble stairs and balustrades, pillars of scagliola and fretted roof of gold and white, and skylight surrounded and supported by gigantic gilt caryatids. The wide, noble flights of steps and long broad galleries, with the sunlight raining down on the panels and pillars of the magnificent hall, on the beautiful faces of the women, on the soft sheen and brilliant varied colouring of their clothes and on the perfect masses of flowers in every niche and corner – it was really one of the gayest and grandest shows you can imagine.

The first time Sally heard her aunt sing was one night after she was in bed – she sleeps in my room, where one does not lose a note of the music below. When I went up I found her wide awake and she started up in bed, exclaiming, 'Well, how many angels have you got down there, I should like to know?'

Adelaide has gone out with Mary Anne Thackeray to buy cheap gowns at a bankrupt's shop in Regent Street; the piano is silent and I can hear myself think.

June 23rd, 1841

Everybody here is raving about Rachel.[5] I have only seen her once on the stage, and heard her declaim at Stafford House at the concert for the Poles. Her appearance is very striking; she is of good height, too thin for beauty but not for dignity or grace; her want of chest and breadth indeed almost suggest a tendency to pulmonary disease, coupled with her pallor and her youth (she is only just twenty). Her voice is most remarkable; it wants brilliance, variety and tenderness, but it is like a fine, deep-toned bell, and expresses admirably the passions in the delineation of which she excels – scorn, hatred, revenge, vitriolic irony, concentrated rage, seething jealousy and a fierce love which seems in its excess allied to all the evil which sometimes springs from that bittersweet root. Pierce was so enchanted with her that he took me to call upon her, and I was very much pleased with the quiet grace and dignity, the excellent *bon ton* of her manners and deportment. She is completely the rage in London now; all the fine ladies and gentlemen crazy after her, the Queen throwing her roses on the stage out of her own bouquet, and viscountesses and marchionesses driving her about to show her all the lions of the town.

[5] Elisa Félix Rachel (1821–58), celebrated French actress.

July 28th, 1841

My sister has concluded an extremely advantageous engagement with Covent Garden, at a very handsome salary. This is in every way delightful to me. It keeps her in England; it places her where she will meet with respect and kindness, both from the public and from members of her own profession. Covent Garden is in some measure our vantage ground and I am glad that she should thence make her first appeal to an English audience.

For five or six weeks in the late summer of 1841 the Butlers were among a large party which accompanied Adelaide and the pianist Liszt on a concert tour of the Rhineland. Fanny was slightly disturbed at feeling less than her usual wild enthusiasm for scenic grandeurs and romantic ruins, being more concerned about where, how and on what her children were to dine.[6] About Liszt, however, she had no reservations.

(*Records*) The time we spent on the Rhine afforded me an opportunity of almost intimate acquaintance with the celebrated musician. Our expedition partook more of the character of a party of pleasure than a business speculation, though Liszt's and my sister's performances were professional exhibitions of the highest order. Nothing could exceed the charm of our delightful travelling through that lovely scenery and sojourning in those picturesque antique towns, where the fine concerts of our two artists enchanted us even more from personal sympathy than the most enthusiastic audiences who thronged to hear them. One day at Coblentz we were sitting in our drawing room together, the maestro as usual smoking his long pipe, when a sudden burst of music made us open the window and go out on the balcony, when Liszt was greeted by a magnificent chorus of nearly two hundred men's voices; they sang to perfection, each with his small sheet of music and sheltered light in his hand.

Of all the pianists I have ever heard, and I have heard all the most celebrated of my time, he was undoubtedly the first for fire, power and brilliancy of execution. It was difficult to believe that he had no more than the average number of fingers or that they

[6] Thackeray wrote to Edward Fitzgerald on 'October something 1841 . . . I saw Fanny Buttler [*sic*] and Adelaide K. at Frankfurt. A. looking very well: but Fanny I did not even know, she was changed so – as dirty as a housemaid and in a housemaid's costume. She won't forgive me for not knowing her and would hardly speak to me in consquints [*sic*]'. *Letters*, Vol. II, pp. 38–9. A surprising comment in view of Fanny's love of dress and her insistence during her travels on having soap and water to wash with.

were of average length – but that indeed they were not: he had stretched his hands like a pair of kid gloves and accomplished the most incredible distances while executing, in the interval between them, inconceivable musical feats with his three middle fingers.

Liszt became, at the very opening of his career, so immediately a miracle, and then an oracle in the artistic and great world of Paris, that he was allowed to impose his own terms upon its judgment; and suffering himself the worse consequences of success, he achieved too early a fame for his permanent reputation. A want of sobriety, a fantastical seeking after strange effect – in short the characteristics of artistic *charlatanerie* – mixed themselves up with all he did, and inevitably deteriorated the fine original gifts of his genius. The exaggeration and false taste which were covered by his marvellous facility and strength gradually became more and more predominant in his performances, and turned them almost into caricatures of the first wonderful specimens of ability which had amazed the musical world.

He could not go on being for ever more astonishing than before, and he paid the penalty of having made that his principal aim. In the summer of 1841, however, Liszt was but on the edge of this descent; his genius, his youth, his personal beauty and the vivid charm of his manner and conversation had made him the idol of society as well as the artistic world, and he was radiant with the fire of his great natural gifts and dazzling with the success that had crowned them. His conversation was sparkling and dazzling and full of startling paradoxes. He was a brilliant creature.

I never saw Liszt again until the summer of 1870. I had gone to the theatre in Munich with my daughter and her husband to hear the *Rheingold* and Sally exclaimed, 'There is Liszt'. The increased age, the clerical dress, had effected but little change in the striking general appearance which my daughter (who had never seen him since she was a child) recognised immediately. I went round to his box and the next day he called at our hotel and sat with us a long time. His conversation was curiously cautious and guarded, and every expression of opinion given with extreme reserve, instead of the uncompromising fearlessness of his earlier years. The abbé was indeed quite another from the Liszt of our summer on the Rhine.

Adelaide made her professional début in London on November 2nd, 1841, singing the title role in *Norma* in English at

Covent Garden. My sister's success was triumphant and the fortunes of the unfortunate theatre, which were again at the lowest ebb, revived under the influence of her popularity and the overflowing houses that night after night crowded to hear her. Her performances were among my most delightful pleasures during a season in which I enjoyed the companionship of my dear friend Harriet and a great deal of pleasant social intercourse with the most interesting and agreeable people of the great gay London world.

Bowood [Wiltshire], December 19th 1841

My dear Theodore,[7] . . . We are staying just now with Lord and Lady Lansdowne in this home of terrestrial delights. Inside the house all is tasteful and intellectual magnificence – such pictures, such statues! They are amiable, good, pleasant and in every way distinguished people, and I like them very much. He is one of our leading Whig statesmen, a munificent patron of the arts, at whose house eminences of all sorts are cordially received. Lady Lansdowne is a specimen Englishwoman of her class, refined, intelligent, well-bred and most charming.

Bowood, December 21st, 1841

Dearest Harriet, . . . This morning I took a brisk walk along the sunny terrace to a lawn that slopes gently to a sheet of water where swans and wild-fowl sail and sport about. The whole scene, tipped with sparkling frost and shining under a brilliant sky seemed very charming to me, and to Sally too, who exclaimed, 'Well, this is my idea of heaven! I do think this might be called Paradise, or that garden that Adam and Eve were put into'.

You ask if Lady Holland is at Bowood. No, she has returned home by land [at the beginning of railroad travelling, persons who still preferred posting on the high road were said to go by land], not choosing to risk her precious body on the railway[8] without Brunel's personal escort to keep it in order and prevent it from doing her any accident. He, having had the happiness of travelling down to Bowood with her, which she insisted upon,

[7] Theodore Sedgwick, brother-in-law of Elizabeth, who was looking after Fanny's small financial interests in the United States.

[8] The thirteen miles which took the Great Western Railway, built by Brunel, as far as Chippenham, the station for Bowood, had been open only seven months. The journey to London, some ninety miles, took three hours twenty-three minutes, and a first class ticket cost 24s. 6d.

naturally enough declined coming down again from London to see her safe home; so, not being able to accomplish his fetching her back to town, she contrived to extort from him a letter stating that, owing to the late heavy rains, her journey back to London would probably be both tedious and uncomfortable, and advising her by all means to go home 'by land', which, considering that the Great Western is his own road – his iron child, so to speak – is, I think a pretty good specimen of her omnipotence. I never knew such a terrified, terrible, foolish old woman in all my life.

There is here the goodliest company conceivable: Rogers, Moore, Macaulay, Charles Austen, Mr. Dundas, Charles Greville, dear old Miss Fox (Lord Holland's sister), whom I love, and Lady Harriet Baring, whom I do not love, which does not prevent her from being a very clever woman, etc. It is a brilliant party, but they are all so preternaturally witty and wise that, to tell you the truth, they occasionally give me the mind-ache.

(*Records*) I remember my amazement at finding Macaulay always in the same position on the hearth-rug, always talking, always answering everybody's questions about everything, always pouring forth eloquent knowledge. As one approached the room the loud, even, declamatory sound of his voice made itself heard like the uninterrupted flow of a fountain. He stood there from morning till evening, like a knight in the lists, challenging and accepting the challenge of all comers. As the volume of his voice was full and sonorous, he had immense advantages in sound as well as sense over his adversaries.[9]

Harley Street,[10] *London, December 26th, 1841*
Dear Harriet, . . . I have been nurse almost all day. Anne went to church and I walked with the children to the broad gravel walk in

[9] Greville's comment echoed Fanny's. 'Macaulay went the day before Christmas, and it was wonderful how quiet the house seemed after he was gone. Rogers was all alive again, Austen and Dundas talked much more than they would have done, and on the whole we were well without him . . . I never passed a week with so much good talk, almost all literary and miscellaneous, very little political, no scandal, no gossip.' (*Memoirs* (ed. Strachey), Vol. IV, p. 439.) Greville also noted that on December 21st 'Mrs Butler read the last three acts of *Much Ado about Nothing*, having read the first two the night before. Her reading is admirable, voice beautiful, equally happy in the humorous and the pathetick parts.' Later she started *The Hunchback* but when she was to have finished 'ran restive from the room, pretending that some of the party did not like it, and no persuasion could induce her to go on' (p. 437).

[10] The Butlers moved house several times during their two and a half years in London.

the Regent's Park; the day was bright and sunny above but exceedingly muddy and hateful underfoot. The servants having their Christmas dinner today, I offered to take entire charge of the children if Anne liked to join the party downstairs. They prolonged the social meal or their after-dinner converse for considerably more than two hours. Since that I have been reading to Sally and it is now time for me to dress for dinner. I shall go to bed early and very glad I shall be to shut up shop, for this has been a very heavy day. How well nurses ought to be paid!

January 31st 1842

My father, I am sorry to say, gets no rent from the theatre. The nights on which my sister does not sing the house is literally empty. Alas, it is the old story over again: that whole ruinous concern is propped only by her. That property is like some fate to which our whole family are subject, by which we are every one of us destined to be borne down by turn, after vainly dedicating ourselves to its rescue.

> *In the face of vehement family protests, Charles Kemble had once more undertaken the management of Covent Garden. The theatre closed the following November and he found himself accountable for a considerable sum of money in spite of having been assured that he would not be held financially responsible for any failure.*

February 4th, 1842

Like a fool, I have been to *see a sight* and feel so tired and have such a headache that it serves me right.

Our dear friend Harness[11] occupies a pleasant apartment in the Council Office Building, the windows of which look out on Whitehall. Here he begged me to bring the children, that we might see the Queen and the King of Prussia and all the great folks go to the opening of Parliament. But the carriage was ordered half an hour later than we ought to have started, and the coachman ordered to take us down Whitehall, though Harness had warned me that we could not come that way. We were of

[11] The Rev. William Harness (1790–1869), friend of Byron and Shakespearean scholar. Fanny says that he refused from conscientious motives to hold more than one living although offered several by influential friends. He had accepted from Lord Lansdowne his civil post at the Council Office, this not being against his moral scruples. 'His means were always small, his charities great and his genial hospitality unfailing. He was one of the most modest, unpretending, honourable human beings I have ever known.'

course turned back by the police and retraced our steps to the Carlton steps. Here, with the two children and Anne and the footman, I made my way through the crowd – but oh! what a crowd! When we got down into the park, the only clear space was the narrow line left open for the carriages and some were passing at a rapid trot. I assure you, Harriet, the children were not half a foot from one of those huge carriage horses, nor was there any means of retreat: the living mass behind us was as compact as bricks and mortar. At a favourable moment we rushed across the road into the protecting arms of some benevolent policeman, were seized and dragged and pushed and pulled and finally made our way through the crowd on the other side of the road, and then ran without stopping to our destination. On reaching it, I shook so that I could hardly stand and the imperturbable Anne actually burst into tears.

I was much surprised at the entire want of excitement and enthusiasm in the vast multitude who thronged and all but choked the Queen's way. All hats were lifted, but there was not a hatful of cheers, and the whole thing produced a disagreeable effect of coldness, indifference or constraint. Harness said that it was nineteenth century breeding which was too exquisite to allow even of the mob's shouting. He is a Tory. T—— M——, who is a Whig, thought the silence spoke of Paisley starvation and Windsor banquets.

Grimsthorpe [Lincolnshire] March 27th 1842
Belvoir [where the Butlers had been staying with the Duke of Rutland] is a beautiful place; the situation is noble and the views from the windows of the castle, and the terraces and gardens hanging on the steep hill crowned by it are charming. The interior is handsome and in good taste; and the whole mode of life stately and splendid, as well as extremely pleasant and comfortable. The Duke and his family are courteous hosts and the society free from stiffness or constraint. I enjoyed my visit very much.

Every morning the Duke's band marched round the castle, playing all sorts of sprightly music to summon us to breakfast, and we had the same agreeable warning that dinner was ready. As soon as the dessert was placed on the table singers came in and performed four very sweet pieces of music. This, with intervals for conversation, filled the time before the ladies left the table. In the evening we had music, of course, and one evening we adjourned to the ball room where we danced all night, the

Duke leading down a country dance, in which his housemaids and men-cooks were vigorously figuring at the same time. Whenever my sister sang, the servants all assembled on a large staircase and appeared among her most enthusiastic hearers.

(*Records*) My first introduction to 'afternoon tea' took place at Belvoir, when I received on several occasions private and rather mysterious invitations to the Duchess of Bedford's room and found her with a 'small and select' circle of female guests, busily employed brewing and drinking tea, with her grace's own private tea kettle. I do not believe that the now universally observed institution of 'five o'clock tea' dates further back in the annals of English civilisation than this very private and, I think, rather shamefaced practice of it.

Harley Street, March 31st, 1842
My dear Theodore, . . . My father is in wonderful health, looks and spirits, considering that this time last year he was very little better than dead. My sister is working very hard and successfully and proposing, after two more years of assiduous labour to retire on a moderate income [the figure Adelaide always mentioned was £300 a year] to Italy, where she would rather live than anywhere else. But oh dear me! how well I remember the day when that was my own vision of the future, and only see what a different thing it has turned out!

So much for private interests. As for public ones, alas! Sir Robert Peel is losing both his health and his temper, they say, and no wonder! His modification of the corn laws and new tariff are abominations to his own party, and his income tax an abomination to the nation at large.[12] I cannot conceive a more detestable position than his, except perhaps that of the country itself. Poverty and discontent in great masses of people; a pitiless opposition, snapping up and worrying to pieces every measure proposed by the Ministry; a determined, troublesome and increasing Radical party; a Minister [Peel], hated personally by his own party, with hardly an individual of his own political persuasion in either House who does not feel himself personally aggrieved by one or other of his measures of reform. Yet that Minister is the only man in England able to stand up at the head of public affairs, and the defeat of his measures would, I believe, produce instan-

---

[12] Peel had on March 11th 1842 reduced import duties on 769 articles and imposed an income tax of 7*d*. in the £ for three years.

taneously such disorder and dismay as England has not seen for many a year, not indeed since the last great Reform crisis. All this makes me pity everybody connected with the present Government and Sir Robert Peel more than anybody else.

April 17th, 1842

My dearest Harriet, . . . I was sitting doing worsted work in the parlour yesterday evening, when all my people were away. After they were gone, I was seized with a perfect nervous panic and could not bring myself to stir from the chair where they had left me. As to going up into the drawing-room, it was out of the question: I fancied every step of the stairs would have morsels of flesh lying on it, and the banisters would all be smeared with blood and hairs. In short, I had a fit of the horrors and sat the whole blessed evening in a perfect nightmare of horrible fancies. At one moment I had the greatest mind in the world to send for a cab and go to Covent Garden Theatre and sit in Adelaide's dressing room; but I was ashamed to give way to my nerves in that cowardly fashion and certainly passed a most miserable evening.

May 1st, 1842

You ask about my going to the Drawing Room. It happened thus: the Duke of Rutland dined at the Palace and, speaking of the party at Belvoir, mentioned me, when the Queen asked why I didn't have myself presented. He called next day at our house, but we did not see him and he left a message for me to the effect that her Majesty's interest about me (curiosity would have been the more exact word, I suspect) rendered it imperative that I should go to the Drawing Room. Wherefore, having no objection whatever to go to Court (except the expense of my dress, as I had already exceeded my year's allowance) I referred the matter to my supreme authority and it was settled that I was to go.

I suffered agonies of nervousness and, I rather think, did all sorts of awkward things; but so, I dare say, do other people in the same predicament. One thing I can tell you, if her Majesty has seen me, I have not seen her. I did not look at my sovereign lady. I kissed a soft white hand which I believe was hers; I saw a pair of very handsome legs in very fine silk stockings which I am convinced were not hers, but am inclined to attribute to Prince Albert; and this is all I perceived of the whole royal family of England, for I made a sweeping curtsey and came away with no impression but that of a crowded mass of full-dressed confusion, and neither know how I got in or out of it.

May 6th, 1842

The carriage is waiting to take Pierce to the Levée and I am waiting till it comes back to go upon my thousand and one daily errands. Mr. Everett,[13] our friend, presents Pierce, and I thought Anne would have fallen down in a fit when she heard that the ceremony consisted in going down on one knee and kissing the Queen's hand. She did not mind my doing it in the least in the world, but her indignation has been unbounded at the idea of a free-born American citizen submitting to such degradation.

You asked me how I managed about diamonds to go to Court in. I hired a set. They were only a necklace and earrings, which I wore as a bandescu, stitched on scarlet velvet and as drops in the middle of scarlet velvet bows in my hair, and my dress, being white satin and point lace, trimmed with white Roman pearls, it all looked nice enough. The value of the jewels was only £700, but I am sure they gave me £7000 of misery, and if her Majesty had but known the anguish I endured in showing my respect for her by false appearances, the very least she could have done would have been to have bought the jewels and given them to me.

May 14th, 1842

You ask whether it is a blessing or a curse not to provide one's own means of subsistence. I think it is a great blessing to be able and allowed to do so. Certainly my *pecuniary* position now would seem to most people very far preferable to my former one; but having *earned* money, and therefore most legitimately *owned* it, I never can conceive that I have any right to the money of another person. I cannot help regretting that I did not reserve out of my former earnings at least such a yearly sum as would have covered my personal expenses, [Fanny had made over to her father the £3000 she made out of the American tours in 1832–4] and having those notions, which impair the comfort of *being maintained*, I am sometimes sorry that I no longer possess my former convenient power of coining.

Being rather in want of money I am about to endeavour to make practicable for the English stage a French piece by Alexandre Dumas called *Mademoiselle de Belle Isle* which, except for one insuperably objectionable incident which I have done my best to

[13] Edward Everett, American Minister in London.

modify, is dramatically speaking one of the most cleverly constructed plays I have seen for a long while. [May 29th] If I could *earn* £200 now I should be glad. My bill at Mme. Dévy's [for her court dress] is £97 and I am determined *my brains* shall pay for it. Therefore also I have given my father a ballet on the subject of Pocohontas and have offered my review of Victor Hugo to John [her brother] for the British Quarterly Review of which he is the editor. He has promised me sixteen guineas for it if it suits him. I have drawn and sketched a play in five acts, a sequel to the story of Kotzebue's *Stranger* which I hope to make a good work of. Thus, you see, my brains are not altogether idle; and with all this I am rehearsing *The Hunchback* with amateurs for three and four hours at a time, attending to my own dresses and Adelaide's (who will attend to nothing), returning visits and going out to dinners and parties innumerable.

My dinner has intervened, my dear, and moreover a permission from my sister to inform you that *she is engaged to be married.*

Adelaide's fiancé was Edward Sartoris,[14] *an amiable but shadowy man of ample private means who was always very kind to Fanny. She was happy at her sister's obvious happiness but, in the light of her own experience, had grave doubts which a few months later found expression in a letter to her old friend Lady Dacre — 'Granny' as she often called her.*

My dearest Granny, I went in the evening to hear my sister sing Norma for the last time and cried most bitterly. I caught myself saying while the tears streamed down my face, 'If only she is happy, after all!' (but oh, that *if*!) It seemed amazing to abdicate a secure fortune and such a power – power to do anything so excellently (putting its recognition by the public entirely out of account) for that fearful risk. God help us all! I was surprised to

[14] One at least of the Kembles' friends heard the news of the engagement with utter amazement: '*That walking Pea Jacket*', Lady Monson called Edward Sartoris in a letter to Anna Jameson, '*not* handsome, *not* ugly, *not* fat, *not* thin, *not* pleasant, *not* unpleasant – in short the only quality about him not negative that he always had his hands in his P. Jacket. . . that *man* Sartoris (I hope he positively is that, by the way, but I never thought of him as any particular *sex* even) has always given me the idea of *not* being otherwise than a good *moral* sort of thing, may, I think, make Adelaide happy.' (Erskine: *Anna Jameson — Letters and Friendships*, p. 200.) Thackeray, however thought Sartoris 'everything that is good. There never was such a kind creature with such a scowling countenance. They give the pleasantest parties.' (*Letters and Private Papers*, Vol. III, p. 340.) This seems to have been the general opinion, both as regards the parties and Sartoris's good nature.

find how terrible it was to me to see my sister, that woman most dear to me, deliberately leave a path where the sure harvest of her labour is independent fortune for a life where, if she does not find happiness, what will atone to her for all that she will have left?

May 30th, 1842

Dearest Harriet, I received a very severe shock and one of rather paralysing effect upon my being reminded that whatever I write is not my legal property, but that of another. I cannot nevertheless persuade myself that that which I invent – *create*, in fact – can really belong to anyone but myself. Therefore if anything I wrote could earn me £97, I am afraid that I should consider that I and no one else had paid my bill.

In thinking over the position of women with regard to their right to their own earnings, I confess to something very like wrathful indignation; impotent wrath and vain indignation, to be sure – not less intense for that, however, for the injustice is undoubtedly great. It is true that, by our marriage bargain, men feed, clothe and house us and are answerable for our debts (not my milliner's bill though, if I can prevent it) and so, I suppose, have a right to pay themselves as best they can out of all we are or all we do. It is a pretty severe puzzle, and a deal of love must be thrown into one or other or both scales to make the balance hang tolerably even.

I went to the Duchess of Sutherland's fancy ball in my favourite costume, a Spanish dress which suited my finances as well as my fancy, my person and my purse; for I had to get but a short black satin skirt, having beautiful flounces of black lace, high comb, mantilla, and, in short, all things needful already in my own possession.

June 12th, 1842

You wanted to know how I felt acting the *Hunchback* again [in amateur theatricals got up by Lord and Lady Francis Egerton]. Why, so horribly nervous the first night that the chair shook under me while my hair was being dressed. After the performance my limbs ached as if I had been beaten with an iron bar. This, however, was only on the first night, and I suppose proceeded from the painful uncertainty I felt as to whether I had not utterly forgotten how to act. It is singular that no recollections or associations of past times were awakened by the performance. Beyond doing it as well as I could, I cared very little about it; it seemed a sort of routine business, just as it used to be, except for the inevitable unwholesome results of its being amusement instead of business; the late hours – three o'clock in the morning – and champagne and lobster salad suppers, instead of my former professional decent tea and to bed, after my work, before twelve o'clock.

Beneath the unremitting superficial glitter of her life at this time, Fanny was in fact in a constant 'horrible state of mental anguish', as can be seen from the nightmarish evening she had described to Harriet in April. Relations with Pierce were at rock bottom: twice, he alleged in his Statement, she had again made abortive attempts to run away. The couple's estrangement was common knowledge in London. Charles Greville, that inveterate gossip, gave an outsider's black and white assessment of the situation in his diary on December 8th, 1842: [Mrs. Butler] 'has discovered that she had married a weak, dawdling, ignorant, violent-tempered man who is utterly unsuited to her and she to him . . . With all her prodigious talents, her fine feeling, noble sentiments and lively imagination, she has no tact, no judgment, no discretion. She has acted like a fool and he is now become a brute. The consequence is that she is supremely and hopelessly wretched; she sees her husband brutal and unkind to her, ruining himself and the children by his lazy, stupid mismanagement of his affairs; and she lives in perpetual terror lest their alienation should at last mount to such a height that their living together may become impossible, and that she shall be separated from her children for whom alone she desires to exist. Among the most prominent causes of their disunion is her violent and undisguised detestation of slavery, while he is a great slave-holder.'[15]

There had indeed been more trouble about slavery — a complicated business starting with a request from an American abolitionist to publish part of her plantation diary in which at first Fanny seems to have behaved correctly but which Pierce and later she herself aggravated into a bitter quarrel. Her feelings for her husband were, however, by no means as cut and dried as Greville made out. True, their frequent rows 'so nearly deprived me of my senses as to be on the point of destroying myself', she asserted — yet having walked out on him for the second time and taken refuge with her sister, she wrote again and again beseeching a reconciliation: 'Oh! Pierce! — Pierce! I look at our children and tremble . . . For God's sake, and for your children's sake and for your own sake, Pierce! my husband, oh, still my most tenderly beloved! Let us still be wise before it is too late.'[6]

[15] *Op. cit.,* Vol. V, pp. 60–3.   [16] *Mrs. Butler's Answer,* p. 34.

Unmoved, Pierce stood firmly on his rights as a man and a husband.
'On my soul and conscience I have done everything in my power to make
you happy . . . I have not succeeded . . . The fault has been entirely
your own . . . If you will govern your irritable temper, and if you can
consent to submit your will to mine, we may be reconciled and happy. I
firmly believe that husband and wife cannot live together upon any
other terms.' [17] *Fanny, promising 'compliance and obedience in all things*
where my conscience does not forbid them' and assuring him that she
would 'endeavour' to control her temper, proposed that she should
return to his abode, to live there in a separate establishment; or alter-
natively that he should give her an allowance to enable her to lodge with
her father without imposing upon his limited means. She added a further
appeal: 'Having never loved any human being as I have loved you,
you can never be to me like any other human being, it is utterly
impossible that I should ever regard you with indifference, my
whole existence having once had you for its sole object; and all its
thoughts, hopes, affections having, in their full harvest, been
yours . . . I cannot behold you without emotion; my heart still answers
to your voice, my blood in my veins to your footsteps.' [18] *There being*
no reply, Fanny presented herself on Pierce's doorstep at midnight
and was taken in. Thereafter, to outward appearances at least, the
couple were reunited, giving two extravagant farewell parties before
they left for home in the early summer of 1843.

April 15th, 1843
My dearest Hal [Harriet], In the evening our first grand party of
the season came off. Nearly two hundred people came and
seemed, upon the whole, tolerably well amused. Adelaide and
Miss Masson and I sang, and Benedict played, and it all went off
very well. There were six policemen at the door and Irish Jack
O'Lanterns without count; the refreshment table was exceedingly elegantly set out by Gunter – at a price we do not yet know.

April 27th, 1843
Anyone would suppose I was in great spirits, for I fly about,
singing at the top of my voice, and only stop every now and then
to pump up a sigh as big as the house and clear my eyes of the
tears that are blinding me. Occasionally, too, a feeling of my last
moments here and my leave taking of my father and sister shoots
suddenly through my mind and turns me dead sick; but all is well
with me, on the whole, nevertheless. Our second party took

[17] Wright, *op. cit.*, p. 100.   [18] *Answer*, p. 36.

place yesterday evening and we had all our grandee friends and fine-folk acquaintances.

April [misdated May] 30th, 1843

You ask how our second party went off. Why, very well. It was much fuller than the other, and in the hopes of inducing people to 'spread themselves', we had the refreshments put into my drawing-room; but they still persisted in sticking all in the room with the piano, which rather annoyed me, because I hate the proximity of 'important human beings'. Our company stayed very late, till near two o'clock; and upon a remark being made about the much smaller consumption of refreshments than at our first party, our butler very oracularly responded, 'Quite a different class of people, Sir'; which mode of accounting for the more delicate appetites of our more aristocratic guests, made with an ineffable air of cousinship to them all, sent me into fits of laughter.

On Friday we dined with my sister who had a large party in the evening; and as the hour for breaking up arrived and I saw those pleasant, kindly acquaintances pass one after another through the door, I felt as if I was watching the vanishing of some pleasant vision. The nearest and dearest of these phantasmagoria are yet around me but in three days the last will have disappeared from my eyes, for who can tell how long? if not for ever!

CHAPTER 15

Collapse of a Marriage
1843–1845

Philadelphia, May 23rd, 1843

My dearest Hal, You will want to know of our sea-faring. Mine was truly miserable as it always is. [This in spite of the fact that the Butlers were crossing the Atlantic for the first time by steamship, with the voyage lasting only half as long as previous trips under sail.] I contrived to crawl out of my bunk two days before we reached Halifax. I was sitting disconsolate, with my head in my hands, in a small cabin on deck to which I had been carried up from below, when Mr. Cunard, the originator of the Atlantic Steam Mail packet, came in and with many words of kindness carried me up to his house in Halifax, whence I returned to the ship for two days more misery with a bunch of exquisite flowers. The children bore the voyage as well as could be expected; sick one half-hour and stuffing the next; little Fan *pervading* the ship from stem to stern, like Ariel, and generally presiding at the officers' mess in undismayed she-loneliness.

While in Boston I made a pilgrimage to dear Dall's grave: a bitter and sad few minutes I spent, lying upon that ground beneath which she lay and from which her example seemed to me to rise in all the brightness of its perfect lovingness and self-denial. The oftener I think of her, the more admirable her life appears to me. From her grave her lovely virtues seemed to call to me to get up and be of good cheer, and strive to forget myself, even as perfectly as she had done . . . How bitter and dark a thing life is to some of God's poor creatures.

Bitter and dark Fanny's life was indeed to become. By now the marriage was incontestably breaking up, with overt animosity replacing the love the couple still felt for each other even during the worst of their quarrels in London. The next two and a half years are a long and complicated story of relentless in-fighting on both sides. As a result of Pierce Butler's extravagances in England, Butler Place had to be let and the family lived in boarding houses, an existence Fanny hated and

175

which she endured only for the sake of her children. Sarah and Fan, now aged twelve and ten, became the sole reason for her remaining in Philadelphia; she was determined not to desert them. Pierce was equally determined that she should have as little contact with them as possible. Even when they lived under the same roof she was scarcely allowed to see them. There were humiliating scenes: on one occasion, for instance, when she met them in the street with their governess they passed her without a word: 'I heard her say, "Go on"; and though my younger child called out, "There is my mother", the governess re-iterated her command. I ran after them and overtook them; and, upon asking my elder child how she could bring herself to insult and wound me in so cruel a manner, she replied that she had acted in obedience to the governess, whose orders her father had told her she was to obey.'[1] The occasional holidays Fanny was allowed to spend in her children's company and annual breaks with the Sedgwicks at Lenox were her only pleasures during these increasingly miserable years.

Yellow Springs, Pennsylvania, July 6th, 1843
Dearest Harriet, I am sitting on the piazza (so-called) of one of a group of tumbledown lodging houses and hotels which, embosomed in a beautiful valley in Pennsylvania, and having in the midst of them an exquisite spring of mineral water, rejoices in the title of 'Yellow Springs'. Before me stretches about a quarter of an acre of uneven ground, enclosed in a dilapidated whitewashed wooden paling and clothed, except for several mangy bare patches, with rank, weedy grass, untended shrubs and neglected trees. Behind me is a whitewashed room about fifteen feet by twelve, containing a rickety horse-hair sofa, all worn and torn into prickly ridges, six rheumatic wooden chairs, a lame table covered with a plaid shawl of my own. In this room Miss Hall and Sally are busily engaged in lessons.

Some years ago this place was a fashionable resort for the Philadelphians, but other watering places have carried off its fashion, and it has been almost deserted for some time past; and except invalids unable to go far from the city and people who wish to get fresh air for their children without being at a distance from their business, very few visitors come here.[2]

[1] *Answer*, p. 10.

[2] One of the few was a Mrs. Charles Ingersoll who later told Fenimore Cooper: 'It seems Mrs. Butler is a good fisherman, and she made a great deal of *cancan* by wearing pantaloons, with boots and straps, a man's hat, with blouse overall. She rode miles on horseback alone, in petticoats, and fished in pantaloons, which Charles said was unreasonable, if not in bad taste. Still, Mrs. Charles says she is charming.' *Correspondence of James Fenimore Cooper*, Vol. I, p. 515.

This morning the children took me up a hill at the back of the house, from which there is a charming prospect of a rich rolling country in fine cultivation. After our walk I went with them to the cold bath, a beautiful deep spring of water, as clear as crystal and almost as cold as ice, surrounded by whitewashed walls which screen it only from earthly observers. Into the lucid, liquid gem I gave my chickens and myself three breathless dips – it is too cold to do more.

Philadelphia, August 15th, 1843

My dear Theodore, Yesterday, at three o'clock, I was told that we must all return to town by five, which accordingly was accomplished, not without strenuous exertion and considerable inconvenience. I do not know in the least whether we are to remain here now, or go elsewhere, or what is to become of us. It has been an annoyance to me to leave the Yellow Springs, independently of the hurried and disagreeable mode of our doing so. I like the country and have been almost happy once or twice while riding over the hills and through the valleys.

August 22nd, 1843

Dearest Harriet, . . . Your question about society here puzzles me a good deal, from the difficulty of making you understand the absolute absence of anything to which you would give that name. During a certain part of the year certain wealthy individuals give a certain number of entertainments, evening parties, balls, etc, but it does not strike me that social intercourse is easy at all here. I have hitherto always lived in the country, and have supposed that the mere civil formality at which my intercourse with most Philadelphians stopped short would lead to more intimate intercourse if ever I lived in the city. I now perceive, however, that their communion with each other is limited to an exchange of morning visits, of course almost exclusively among the women, and that society, such as you and I understand it, does not exist here. Yet of course there must be the materials for it – clever and pleasant men and women. I had sometimes thought that in the city I should find some compensation in the society which I hoped I might be able to gather around me, but I am quite deprived of any such recourse by my present situation in a boarding-house. Here I inhabit my bedroom, contriving, for sightliness' sake, to sleep on a wretched sofa bed, that my room by day may look as decent as possible, but where the presence of washhand-stand and toilette apparatus necessarily enforces the absence of visitors except in public rooms. I have received a great many morning visits and one or two invitations to evening parties, but I do not like to accept civilities which I have no means of reciprocating, and so I have as little to expect in the way of social recreation as I think anybody living in a large town can have.

Of the discomfort and disorder of our mode of life I cannot easily give you a notion, for you know nothing of the sort, and, until now, neither did I. The absence of decent regularity in our habits and the slovenliness of our whole existence is particularly trying to me, who have a morbid love of order and regularity, and a positive delight in the decencies and elegancies of civilised life.

September 1st, 1843
My dear Theodore, . . . Rooms have been hired for us three miles beyond West Chester, which is seven miles from the nearest railroad station on the Columbia railroad, altogether about forty miles from town, and for want of regular traffic and proper means of conveyance, an exceedingly tedious and unpleasant drive thence to the farm. Here there is indeed pure air for the children and blessed relief from the confinement of the city, but so uncivilised a life that it keeps me in a constant state of amazement.

We eat at the hours and at the table of these worthy people, and I am a little starved as I find it difficult to get up a dinner appetite before one o'clock, and after that nothing is known in the shape of food but tea at six o'clock. We eat with *two-pronged forks* – i.e. we who are 'sophisticate' do. The more sensible Arcadians, of course, eat exclusively with their knives. The farming men and boys come in to the table from their work, without their coats and with their shirt-sleeves rolled up above the elbows; and my own nursemaid and the servant of all work of the house, and any visitors who may look in upon our hostess all sit down with us to feed; which, I confess, makes me a little melancholy. It is nonsense talking about positive equality; these people are sorry associates for me, and so, I am sure, am I for them.

Today, I came to town to endeavour to procure some of the common necessaries that we require: table implements that we can eat with, and lights by which we may be able to pursue our occupations after dark.

Philadelphia, October 10th, 1843

My dearest Hal, How much I thank you for your generosity to me! for the watch you are sending me, which I have not yet received. I shall feel most anxious till it arrives, and then I think I shall sleep with it round my neck, so great will be my horror of having it stolen from me in this wretched and disorderly boarding house, where I am in perpetual misery lest I should have left any closet or drawer in my bedroom unfastened, and where we are obliged to lock our sitting room if we leave it for a quarter of an hour, lest our property should be stolen out of it – a state of anxious and suspicious caution which is as odious as it is troublesome.

When I arrived in New York last Sunday morning on my return from Berkshire and was preparing to start for Philadelphia next day, I found I was to stay in New York to meet and greet Mr. Macready, who is just landed in America and to whom we are to give an entertainment at the Astor House as we have no house in Philadelphia to which we can invite him.

I forget whether I told you that I had taken Margery[3] up to Lenox with me, in the hope that the change of air and scene might be of benefit to her, but ever since her return she has been ill in bed, poor thing! and though the only servant girl she had has left her and she is in the most forlorn and wretched condition possible, neither her mother nor her sisters have been near to help or comfort her – such is the Roman Catholic horror of a divorced woman, for she has at length obtained her divorce from her worthless husband. And so, I suppose, they will let her die, such being, it seems, their notion of what is right.

Fanny must have dated this letter incorrectly. According to Macready, the dinner took place on September 30th,[4] Mr. and Mrs. Longfellow being among the other guests: 'Mrs. Butler spoke admirably well, but quite like a man', noted Macready, 'She is a woman of extraordinary mind; what she said on most subjects was true — the stern truth, but what in the spirit of charity should not have been said in the presence of one who was obliged to listen to it. Alas!'

Wednesday, May 15th, 1844

Dear Mrs. Jameson, My last letter to you was pretty nearly filled with dismal private affairs, and now, Heaven knows, all resi-

---

[3] Margery O'Brien, the children's nurse, who had made a disastrous marriage after being dismissed by Fanny early in 1840.
[4] *Journal* (ed. Trewin), p. 204.

dents in Philadelphia have a gloomy story to tell of public ones. We have had fearful riots here between the low American population and the imported population from Ireland, who have also taken the opportunity of the present anarchy to indulge in violent exhibitions of their own special home-brewed feud of Protestant against Catholic. A few nights ago there was a general mob-crusade against the Catholic churches, several of which, as well as various private dwellings, were burnt to the ground. The city was lighted from river to river with the glare of these conflagrations – this city of 'brotherly love'; whole streets looking like pandemonium avenues of brass and copper in the lurid reflected light. Your people [Mrs. Jameson was Irish] have lost little of their agreeable combined facetiousness and ferocity: while a large Catholic church was burning the Orange party caused a band of music to play 'Boyne Water', and when a cross fell from the porch above the building, these same Christian folk gave three cheers.

My own affairs are far from flourishing, and I am heartily glad to have anything else to speak of, little cheerful as that anything else may be.

July 14th, 1844

My dearest Hal, About a month ago the town was lighted from one end to the other with the burning of Catholic churches; and now, within the last week, the outrages have recommenced with more fury than ever, because, for a wonder, the militia did actually fire upon the mob.

It is absurd, and yet sad enough, that not six months ago, 'Repeal Unions' – Irish Repeal Unions – were being formed all over this country in favour of and in sympathy with the poor, oppressed Roman Catholics in Ireland; 'professional' politicians made their cause, and England's oppression of them, regular popularity capital; writing and speechifying in the most violent manner, and with the most crass ignorance upon the subject of their wrongs and the tyranny they endured from our government; and now Philadelphia *flares* from river to river with the burning of Catholic churches, and the Catholics are shot down in the streets and their houses pillaged in broad daylight.

You ask me if I apportion my time among my various occupations with the same systematic regularity as formerly. I endeavour to do so, but find it almost impossible. I read but little. My leisure is principally given to my German, in which I am making some little progress. I walk with the children before breakfast – i.e. from seven till eight. Three times a week I take them to the market to buy fruit and flowers, an errand that I like as well as they do. The three other mornings we walk in the square opposite this house. After breakfast they now pass the mornings with their governess or nurse. For the past two months I have ridden every day, but have unhappily disabled my horse, poor fellow, by galloping him during a sudden heavy rain shower over a slippery road, in which process he injured one of his hip joints, not incurably, I trust, but so as to deprive me of him for at least six months.

(*Records*) My dear and noble horse never recovered from his injury, but was obliged to be shot. He had been sold [by Pierce] and I had ransomed him back by the publication of a small volume of poems which gave me the price demanded for him by the livery stable owner who had bought him. He was beautiful and powerful, almost a perfect creature and I loved him very much. [Fanny had owned Forrester for eight years. She had written earlier, 'he grins with delight like a dog when I talk to him and pat him. He is a bright bay, with black legs and mane, tall and large and built like a hunter. I do not like to think what would become of me if anything were to happen to him.']

I shall walk now after breakfast, as, my rides being suppressed, my walks with the chicks are not exercise enough for me. I take the children out again at half-past six, and at half-past seven come in to my dinner; after dinner I go to my piano and go to bed early – *et voilà*!

Almost all the people I know are out of town now, and I do not see a human creature. The heat is intense and the air foul and stifling, and we are gasping for breath and withering away in this city atmosphere.

So, miserably, ends Fanny's last letter — or at any rate her last published letter — from Philadelphia for many years to come. When she wrote it she was still living apart from her children and husband, who had recently taken a house in the city. Negotiations went on for months about her joining them there, but Pierce laid down conditions she hesitated to accept, chief of which were that she was to conform absolutely to all his domestic arrangements, including the upbringing of the children, and that she was to have nothing more to do with her old and trusted friends the Sedgwicks — 'those low-bred, vulgar meddlers', he called them. At last, desperate to be with the girls again, she brought herself to accept his terms; but there were endless procrastinations and when at last she moved in, Pierce made life so impossible that in six months she was out again. She was, she later asserted, constantly humiliated in front of the children; she was allowed no authority over them — less than none, in fact, since her instructions and wishes were often countermanded. Except at meals, all communication between husband and wife was in writing, and the atmosphere may be judged by the opening of one of his letters to her: 'It is impossible to make any impression on one whose mental and moral obliquity blinds her to all the vices of her nature, whose reason is sophistry, and whose religion is cant, and whose unbounded self-esteem renders her happy and satisfied in all her wrong doings; therefore I have no hope that you will ever comprehend, much less fulfill, your duties as a mother.'[5]

With scarcely an opportunity of fulfilling any duties as a mother, Fanny soon realised that 'my remaining here being not only useless henceforward, and undoubtedly prejudicial to the children, I shall comply with my father's desire and the advice of my friends and family and return to England.'[6]

Having borrowed the money for her passage, she sailed for home in October, 1845, facing a glum future. A prompt and pressing invitation from Adelaide and her brother-in-law who had settled in Rome came as the perfect answer to her problems. Thither, in December, she accordingly set out, accompanied only by her maid.

[5] *Answer*, p. 23.   [6] *Op. cit.*, p. 52.

Part Three

CHAPTER 16

Interlude in Italy
1845–1846

For no other reason than to earn herself badly needed money Fanny kept a journal of her eleven-month stay in Italy. 'I have a great contempt for this process', she informed Harriet, 'and a greater contempt for the barren balderdash I write, but exchange is no robbery and if a bookseller will buy my trash I will sell it to him.'

Balderdash is too strong a word, but A Year of Consolation *is admittedly uninspired; the many discursive accounts of sight-seeing and excursions often seem no more than perfunctory — the inevitable ingredients of every mid-Victorian travel book. Yet Fanny had too lively a mind and too acute an eye not to have been stimulated by many of her new and strange experiences, and when her imagination was really caught she could usually rise to the occasion.*

The journey was in itself a formidable undertaking for two unaccompanied women in midwinter in the year 1845. Their way took them by diligence as far as Lyons, down the Saône and Rhône to Marseilles and thence by sea to Civita Vecchia, the port for Rome. Characteristically Fanny chose to make a detour in central France through country highly recommended for its beauty by friends who had passed that way in summer, only to find herself benighted in a squalid inn whose ruffianly host charged extortionately for transporting the travellers onwards in a broken-down cart. Bitterly cold, mistress and maid feared instant assassination; the scenery however — or what could be glimpsed of it under the snow — almost came up to expectations.

Otherwise the long journey was uncomfortable rather than alarming. Once they did not see a bed for four nights running and often they travelled round the clock. The food was mostly execrable and the prices exorbitant. Fellow travellers were impertinent and inconsiderate, and Fanny noted with disgust that the French were as prone as the Americans to the constant hawking and spitting she had so loudly deplored in the United States. On the other hand she frequently found herself reflecting that in that vast country a woman might travel anywhere alone 'with as much safety as though she were the sister or daughter of every man she meets.'

On the evening of January 16th, 1846, three weeks after setting out
from England, Fanny and her maid arrived, weary but safe and sound,
within the gates of Rome — a moment Fanny had longed for all her life.

St. Peter's stood over against us, towering into a violet-coloured sky – and it was real – and I really saw it. I was in Rome, and it was the very Rome of my imagination. The dark, stinking streets through which we now rattled, however, were new experiences. My sister's servant met me at the Custom House, and at length, in an open carriage, we rolled up steep and slippery pavements to the Pincio where, at a lighted window, I saw a woman's figure. I scrambled up three flights of stone stairs and so into my sister's arms, worn out and ready to die with the fatigue of coming and the emotion of being come.

*

I had seen my sister's children asleep in their cribs last night; their cooing and chirping woke me in the morning. While I was still in my dressing-gown Edward called me out to see the view. We are on the very top of the Pincio. Rome lay like a map at our feet, bathed far and near with glorious sunlight. Our apartment reminds me of all the houses I ever was in in the southern states of America – large, lofty rooms with not a window or door that can shut; coarse, common carpets over a layer of straw – in short, the whole untidy discomfort which characterises the dwellings of all southern people, as far as my observation goes.

Now for the compensations: my bed-room door and window open upon a terraced garden at least forty feet above the street, full of orange and lemon trees, magnolias, myrtles, oleanders and camellias, roses and violets in bloom. A fountain trickles under the superintendence of a statue into a marble shell. The coloured tiles of all our ante-rooms delight me, so do the gay painted ceilings. The little room where I bathe is a perfect delight, with its walls covered with fresco cupids and dolphins and baskets with flowers strung together by waving patterns of wreaths and garlands.

This afternoon we drove out through the streets of Rome.

Driving or walking endless miles about Rome, sightseeing, visiting,
going on expeditions near and far — such was the pattern of Fanny's
stay with Adelaide and Edward Sartoris in the eternal city. So peaceful
did her life become that at times she felt she almost understood the
'delight of listless apathy'. But 'up and be doing' had always been her

*motto, and soon she was off to visit another museum, look at another
picture or gallop yet again over the Campagna.*

*

The great, wide, beautiful stairs leading up from the Piazza di
Spagna to the door of our lodging are the favourite haunt of all
the painters' models – old men with grizzled beards and hair, and
lads with blue-black locks falling round the most wonderful eyes
ever beheld; girls in the picturesque costume of the lower orders
here, with splendid heads and shoulders and scarlet jackets and
daggers thrust through their hair; here they sit and stand and
lounge and loll in the sun; screaming, shouting, laughing or
dozing like cats with half-closed eyes on the worn stone steps; or
with true brotherly humanity exploring the animated nature of
each other's elf locks – beautiful, beastly creatures.

With these specimens of all that is finest in form and colour lie a
rabble of hideous deformities whose sole occupation it is to extort
money: women with huge goitres, men with withered arms,
idiots lolling out their tongues and goggling their eyes; the blind,
the maimed, babies in arms and old creatures on crutches – all
swarm round the wretched wayfarer and with vociferous out-
cries persecute him for alms. Words only fit for dogs do not repel
them, nor the threatening arm and lifted hand. They have lost all
sense of shame; they are triple-cased in the impervious cal-
lousness of the lowest degradation.

*

On St. Valentine's day, the first day of the Carnival – at about
two o'clock, with our carriage duly lined with white calico and my
green velvet bonnet covered with the same, we set forth to
observe the solemnities. On the seat opposite was a large tray
heaped with small bunches of fresh flowers; under the seat were
two baskets filled with sugar plums, some of them the size of very
large bullets – formidable missiles, as we found when we
received a volley of them. At our feet was a large basket filled with
confetti – a species of small shot made of dried peas and covered
with flour, in throwing handfuls of which consists the chief
warfare of the Corso. A couple of wire masks, rounded to fit the
face, coloured pink to become it and furnished with a handle,
completed our equipment. Thus we descended to the field of
battle, our dresses being as nearly white as possible, and my
sister having a large white burnous and I a large white shawl on. '

We had the privilege of occupying a balcony at a house in the Corso. We had no sooner taken our stations there when from a neighbouring balcony a shower of sweetmeats and flowers assailed us and we found ourselves the mark of a little man who, with a delighted countenance, kept exercising his skill on us and enjoying apparently equally our awkwardness in missing him. While busily engaged with him, sundry treacherous shots reached us from another direction and we found that we were commanded by a balcony opposite and higher than ours from which sundry demure gentlefolk were pelting us. Every window was filled with spectators, every balcony adorned with hangings of crimson and gold or rose and white, and tapestry and curtains were put in requisition to render commodious and gay every point where a station could be obtained.

We soon left our balcony, got into our carriage and joined the stream of absurdity in the street below. It is well to see the *coup d'oeil* from the shelter of a balcony, but it is infinitely more amusing to be among the people themselves, whose great good humour, fantastic and grotesque gaiety, droll fancies and withal decent deportment no foreigner can form the least idea of without having seen it; whereas in England drunkenness, riot and violence would have been the inevitable result of this universal licence.

As daylight thickened we regained our balcony to see the race of the Barberi. A cannon gave the signal for clearing the Corso and at length the shout of a thousand voices announced the start, and presently down the crowded, gaping street rushed eleven or twelve horses, covered with ribbons, artificial flowers, streaks of bright red paint and other decorations. To these were added appendages of a less harmless character: crackers and squibs igniting and going off as they ran; and onions, stuck full of pins and needles hanging on their manes or flanks, performed the part of spurs whose impulse became more sharp and constant in proportion as the terrified creatures increased their speed. This part of the ceremonies may be an improvement upon the former custom of making the unfortunate Jews race through the Corso for the edification of their Christian fellow creatures; but it is still, in its present less offensive form, the least agreeable part of the Carnival to me.

Our return home was anything but as triumphant as our going forth. Hoarse with laughing; our arms aching with hurling things; our shawls awry; our bonnets battered and dented into cocked hats; our very stays filled with confetti which had fallen into our bosoms and down our backs. A more complete sample of 'After the Battle' I never saw. To be sure, we brought home sundry most elegant little boxes and baskets full of bonbons which we piled like a trophy before Edward, who, having done his Carnival thoroughly some years ago, looks with eyes of superior wisdom upon our folly in doing ours now.

After this fashion passed all the days of this strange Saturnalia. In the evening we went three times to the masked ball at the theatre. We took a box each time and, provided with black dominoes, hoods and masks, entertained ourselves with mystifying some of our friends and being mystified by them. Our box was filled with a perpetual stream of men and women, but I must say their conversations were not up to the pitch of brilliant wit and fanciful humour which the licence of the occasion and our old playwrights had led me to anticipate. The Italians who visited us were quite as dull as the British.

*

A Year of Consolation is a strangely impersonal document. Fanny tells little or nothing about herself or Adelaide, even less about her affectionate and generous brother-in-law Edward to whom the book is dedicated, and virtually nothing about their many friends and acquaintances. Yet, surprisingly, she did not hesitate to include, among the many poems scattered throughout the book, several which plainly revealed her constant misery at her separation from her daughters.

UPON A BRANCH OF FLOWERING ACACIA

The blossoms hang again upon the tree,
As when with their sweet breath they greeted me
Against my casement, on that sunny morn,
When thou, first blossom of my spring, wast born.
As I lay, panting from the fierce strife
With death and agony that won thy life,
Their snowy clusters hung on their brown bough
E'en as upon my breast, my May-bud, thou.
They seem to me thy sisters, Oh, my child!
And now the air, full of their fragrance mild,
Recalls that hour, a tenfold agony
Pulls at my heart-strings, as I think of thee.
Was it in vain! Oh, was it all in vain!

That night of hope and terror and of pain. . . .
Alone, heart-broken, on a distant shore
Thy childless mother sits lamenting o'er
Flowers, which the spring calls from this foreign earth,
Thy twins, that crowned the morning of thy birth.
How is it with thee? – lost – lost – precious one!
In thy fresh springtime growing up alone?
What warmth enfolds thee? – what sweet dews are shed,
Like love and patience over thy young head?
What holy springs feed thy deep inner life?
What shelters thee from passion's deadly strife?
What guards thy growth, straight, strong, full and free,
Lovely and glorious, oh, my fair young tree?

*

On Good Friday Fanny was enthralled and at the same time dismayed by a spectacle the like of which she had never before seen — the ancient ceremony of the washing of the feet, performed by Roman ladies belonging to a charitable sisterhood.

The ladies were attired either in coloured cotton gowns or black silk, with red aprons. We descended a narrow stairs into a low whitewashed room with a stone floor, around which ran a wooden bench upon which, with their shoes and stockings off, sat a number of the poor women for whose supposed benefit the ceremony was about to take place. I say supposed, for nobody, looking at the scene with the eye of common sense, would have seen anything but awkwardness, embarrassment and a sort of terrified surprise, fatigue and shy dismay in these poor creatures, as they sat with their bare feet under the gaze of the chattering, giggling women who filled the room. Each of these pilgrims must have walked an hundred miles to entitle them to the hospitality of this institution which, besides the problematical comfort of this public feet-washing, provided them with the less doubtful accommodation of food and lodging for three days. Most of them were in the meanest and coarsest peasant's apparel; many of them looked ill and faint; all of them weary and stupefied by the strangeness of the scene. Before each knelt the lady who was to wash her feet, with hands crossed upon her breast in the attitude of prayer. In the midst of the room swarmed and flitted, like a parcel of flies, the foreign gazers; and to and fro through the idle crowd, like so many bees, buzzed and hummed the red-apron'd ladies hospitallers. Presently one of the gentlemen in a geranium-red blouse (I presume of course a priest) pronounced a short prayer and the word of command 'Lavate' was given, when the process of cleansing began, during which the same minister read aloud by the light of a candle a sort of church service.

In the great room where the pilgrims were to have supper the tables were set by ladies of various rank and nobility, and great trays full of dishes of food were brought in in endless succession. The poor creatures who had gone through their washing were all penned together like so many cattle; and so weary were they with their long foot-travel and these prolonged ceremonies that many of them fell together in deep sleep and could hardly be awakened when called to take their places at the tables. Even then, with the savoury and smoking plates of soup under their noses, there occurred a most tantalising delay occasioned by the non-arrival of the Cardinal whose special office it was to pronounce a benediction on the food placed before them. This dignitary having finally arrived and the blessing duly uttered, we departed, leaving the hungry to the enjoyment of their meal and the charitable to the consciousness of their virtue.

*

In May the Sartoris household moved to Frascati to spend the summer of 1846 in an apartment in a dilapidated but beautiful palace which had been a favourite residence of Pauline Borghese, Napoleon's favourite sister. With them were 'a happy company of friends from whose national and individual dissimilarities no element of discord arose, but only variety of harmony during an uninterrupted season of delightful intercourse.'

How charming the life was, with its monotony and variety, like that of beautiful nature itself. The early morning walk, through dewy vineyards, where I forestalled my breakfast, picking from the purple and amber bunches the finest grapes all bathed in bloom and freshness, or breaking from the branches over my head the heavy-hanging luscious figs, while my eyes slowly wandered from the Sabine hills to the Alban mountain and from the shining glorious campagna to the glittering Mediterranean. Then the noon-day plunge into the cool fountain with the beautiful children, their rosy limbs shining through the clear water. Then the readings and the music – that exquisite voice enchanting the hours with the songs of every land; the infinite anecdote, the varied learning. . . . How many, many elements of pleasure and happiness were there! It was a perfect life, and to have led it for several months is a miracle.

*

Our quiet *villegiatura* is becoming much excited and disturbed by the news of all that is going on in Rome. The circumstances gradually beginning to transpire of the Pope's death [Pope Gregory XVI] are really most curious. It is now pretty openly stated that he literally died for want of assistance and, partly if not absolutely, for want of food. His favourite attendant, a man whom he had raised from the condition of servant to that of confidential advisor, having amassed a fortune by every species of iniquity, began, it is conjectured, to be weary of his service. During the last two days of the Pope's illness he declared that his Holiness had strictly enjoined him to allow ingress to no one. Thus deterred, the cardinals, his friends and counsellors turned from the forbidden door. The condition of the poor old Pope's body when it was embalmed proved that he must have been without nourishment for a considerable time and that there is every probability that he died of exhaustion and inanition.

The office of the Guardia Nobile during these dreadfully hot days has been something intolerable: their constant guard, relieving each other only every four hours, round the bier upon which the Pope's body lies in the Sistine Chapel, where the incessant thronging of the curious and the pious, combined with the distressing and nauseous effluvium from the corpse itself and the heat of the weather, have really made their duty most onerous.

We have just had a visit from Monsignor——who belonged to the household of the late Gregory XVI and always appeared to be in a state of perfect loyalty to him. Now, however, he confesses that the torment of living in a state of perpetual fear and falsehood to which he was condemned was not to be described, and that a man could not speak to his most intimate acquaintance on any matter touching the government, for that ruin might have been the consequence of an unguarded word to persons whom one would have supposed the least likely to betray one.

The matter now, it seems, is quite otherwise. Immediately after the amnesty [one of the first acts of the newly elected Pius IX had been to declare an amnesty for political prisoners], the men who had recovered their liberty flocked to the churches and received the sacrament with extreme devotion. Monsignor said that Heaven had certainly appointed this man to the exigency of the times, for that the whole Papal government was tottering to its foundations. If anything can save it, I suppose this may. Monsignor told us several anecdotes of the Pope's benevolence and activity. On fixed days of the week he receives all persons who wish to see him, hears their grievances and, warning them that any attempt to impose upon him or alter the truth will be detected and punished, takes their names and has their business inquired into and put to rights.

We have also seen —— who is open-mouthed in his enthusiasm for the Pope. He said that people were coming daily from Bologna and Ancona and various of the hitherto most disaffected districts of the Papal territory with enthusiastic demonstrations of loyalty and devotion. Instead of the spirit of distrust and jealousy which existed between the people of Rome and those of the provinces, a kindly feeling of free brotherhood now seems to animate them all towards each other.

*

The summer in Frascati ended, Fanny spent her remaining weeks in Rome revisiting galleries and museums and discovering new ones. Not everything she saw pleased her, for 'all representations of Christ are intolerable to me, all representations of his agony absolutely intolerable' and it is scarcely possible to avoid these in Rome; but otherwise she was in ecstasies. As the end of her stay drew near she contrived to spend two hours each morning in the Vatican before the doors opened to the public: 'For a whole month these galleries, these halls, these vast marble staircases and all the glorious company of divine creations within them have been mine. I have lived as it were, in Olympus. I do not know how I shall ever live among mere mortals again'.

At Adelaide's hospitable home, however, there was but one subject of conversation — the new Pope, his liberality and the much needed reforms he had already begun to introduce in Rome and the Papal States. Coming down from the heights, Fanny gathered 'all the information and every anecdote I have been able to obtain relating to him' from the mere mortals she met there. Though much of what she heard was no more than gossip, she was still able to make a very fair assessment of Pius IX's short and long-term prospects.

The measures of public improvement most urgently needed both for the city and for the country have obtained ready sanction. Gas in the streets of Rome and railroads in the Roman states will soon bear witness to a more enlightened spirit; and while the one will tend to increase the order, comfort and security of the city, the other will awaken the dormant energies of the inhabitants, quickening all the commercial energies of the various cities, hitherto deplorably stagnant, by opening lines of rapid communication from Civita Vecchia to Ancona. A rumour has been current for some time that the Pope intends to organise a representative government by permitting the various states and towns in his dominion to send deputies to Rome to represent the grievances and wants of the people. This would indeed be an amazing step forward. It is moreover added that, being warned that this would probably induce the people to demand a constitution, he replied with much tranquillity that he did not know that it might not be a very good thing for them to have one.

There is something in the unbounded expectations of Pius IX's own subjects – mixing up, as they undoubtedly do, the idea of his religious sovereignty with that of his political power and capacity – extremely touching to one who perceives the enormous disparity between the two. The anomaly as well as the difficulty of his position strikes me forcibly. I have seen the Roman Catholic religion in the United States, the faith of implicit obedience and absolute subserviency encountering the political spirit of unbridled democracy – perhaps the most remarkable of all the social phenonema that country presents. The Roman Catholic religion can subsist and greatly prosper, even in republican America, but it is because it is there a religion and not a government: as religion it is the most pliant, insinuating, pervading and powerful that has yet existed; as government it is rigid, despotic and incapable of either receiving or accepting the impulse towards universal freedom which the world in these latter times seems to obey. The Bishop of Rome may yet be the powerful head of the most powerful sect of Christendom; I doubt whether he can ever be the enlightened sovereign of a people with free institutions. Therefore it is that the acclamations which precede and follow the present Pope's footsteps seem sad to me, for they seem to demand impossibilities and to foretell disappointments.[1]

[1] Fanny's intuition was borne out by events within two years. In 1848, the year of revolutions, Pius IX's chief minister, Rossi, was assassinated and the Pope forced to flee to the Kingdom of Naples. His once liberal outlook became increasingly reactionary; and his notorious *Syllabus of Errors* denouncing liberal trends in 1864 paved the way towards the proclamation of the dogma of Papal Infallibility at the first Vatican Council of 1870. His loss of temporal power in the city of Rome and the Papal States shortly thereafter was a blow from which he never recovered.

7th December, 1846. I went to the fountain of Trevi – for those who drink of its sweet waters return, it is said, to Rome. It was a dark and gloomy day and raining fast; but I knelt nevertheless upon the edge of the beautiful fountain to drink to my return.

On the 8th of December I left Rome.

It had indeed been a year of consolation. Italy had brought refreshment and a measure of peace to Fanny's battered spirit. 'In spite of abiding sorrow', she had written to Harriet from Frascati in the summer, 'I have often hours of vivid enjoyment; momentary flashes, bright gleams of exquisite pleasure; and whatever bitterness lies at my heart's core, it still leaves above it a surface of sensibility which reflects a sort of ecstasy at every ray of light and every form of beauty'. She had written in the same vein during the miserable months on the Georgian plantation eight years earlier.

CHAPTER 17

Back to the Stage
1847–1848

Fanny had had frequent experience of moving almost overnight from one world to another, and now she faced perhaps the biggest change of all — from lady of leisure in Italy to professional actress in the English provinces, a career she in any case did not relish. Not that she seems to have been downhearted, or if she was she managed not to show it: when Henry Greville called on her soon after her return her conversation was as amusing as ever — 'she is so eloquent, so droll, so sad, so gay, so unlike the rest of the world'.[1] A pleasant surprise was the almost immediate sale of the Italian journal to the Dover Street publisher and bookseller, Edward Moxon, who offered far more than she had expected for the manuscript, sight unseen. Her most pressing need, however, was to find an opening in the theatre and here the omens were not propitious.

(*Records*) A stout, middle-aged [Fanny was just thirty-eight], not particularly good-looking woman such as I then was is not a very attractive representative of Juliet or Julia; nor had I, in the retirement of private life, improved by study or experience my talent for acting, such as it was. I had hardly entered the theatre, and my thoughts had as seldom reverted to anything connected with my former occupation. While losing, therefore, the few personal qualifications (of which the principal one was youth) I ever possessed for the younger heroines of the drama, I had gained but age as a representative of its weightier female personages – Lady Macbeth, Queen Katherine, etc.

I had the additional disadvantage of being an extremely incompetent woman of business; and having now to make my own bargains in the market of public exhibition, I did so with total want of knowledge and experience to guide me in my dealings with the persons from whom I now had to seek employment.

[1] *Diary*, p. 182.

Such bargaining was distasteful to Fanny, especially when she had to haggle with such 'persons' as Alfred Bunn, the vulgar and quarrelsome theatrical manager whom Macready was not alone in considering a blackguard. On January 14th, little more than a fortnight after Fanny's return, the latter wrote in his journal: 'Saw correspondence between Fanny Butler *and Mr. Bunn, she asking £100 a night, he declining in a letter written, of course, in* bad English *and offering £50!'*[2]

Yet, in spite of such set-backs and the impossibility of finding work in London, it was not long before Mr. Knowles of the Manchester theatre offered £40 a night 'with which very liberal remuneration I was more than satisfied'.

10 Park Place, February 1st, 1847

I feel almost certain, my dear Hal, that it will be better for me to be alone when I come out in Manchester than to have you with me. My strength is much impaired, my nerves are terribly shattered, and to see reflected in eyes that I love that pity for me which I shall feel only too keenly for myself might completely break down my courage. I am glad for this reason that I am to come out in Manchester and not in London where, although I might not distinguish them, I should know that not a few who cared for me were among my spectators.

My work, however, has a more encouraging aspect. It is an immense thing to be still able to work at all and keep myself from helpless dependence on anyone. The occupation will, I am persuaded, be good rather than bad for me; for though one may be strong against sorrow, sorrow and inactivity combined are too much for any strength.

Albion Hotel, Manchester, 15th February, 1847

My kind friend Henry Greville and that very charming young Alfred Potocki, brother of the Austrian Ambassadress and a great friend of Henry's, came down with me half way yesterday. They come tomorrow to see the play, so that I shall have the comfort of people that I like, and not the trial of people that I love, near me on that occasion. I am not very nervous about my *plunge*; the only thing I dread is the noise (noise of any sort being what my nerves can no longer endure at all) which I am afraid may greet me. Any loud sound shakes me from head to foot. I have gained some self-possession and strength in these past years, and I hope my

[2] *Journal* (ed. Trewin), p. 240.

acting itself, as well as my comfort in acting, may benefit by my
increased self-command.[3]

Albion Hotel, Manchester, February 17th
My dear Lady Dacre,[4] I acted *The Hunchback* last night (for the first
time for thirteen years); got up this morning with a dreadful
cough and sore throat; rehearsed Lady Macbeth and Juliana in
The Honeymoon (a *dancing* part!); have written to three managers
from whom I have received 'proposals', have despatched accounts
of myself to my father and sundry of my friends; have corrected
forty pages of proof of my Italian journal, have received sundry
visits (amongst others, that of a doctor) and have wished that I
had not so much to do.

The theatre here is beautiful; the company very fair; the plays
are well and carefully got up. The audience were most exceedingly kind and I think I have every reason to be thankful and more
than satisfied. The Manager wants to renew my engagement
which is a sign, I suppose, that he is satisfied.

Thursday, 18th
My dear Hal, . . . The proprietor and manager of the theatre is an
enterprising, intelligent man who knows the value of liberality
and that generosity is sometimes the most remunerative as well
as the most popular line of action. He is a shrewd man of business, a little rough, but kindly withal. Everybody in the theatre is
civil and good to me and I am heartily grateful to them all. The
company is a very fair one indeed and might be an excellent one if
they were not all too great geniuses either to learn or rehearse
their parts. The French do not put the flimsiest vaudeville on the
stage without rehearsing it for three weeks; and I am going to act
this evening in the *Honeymoon* with a gentleman who has not
thought fit to attend at rehearsal, so that, though I was there, I
may say in fact that I have had no rehearsal of it.

Oh my dear Hal, I strive to judge of my position as reasonably
as I can! I do hope that, in spite of the loss of youth, of person and
feeling, I may be able to fill some parts better than I did formerly. I
have no longer any nervousness to contend with – only the sense

[3] 'She of course had an immense reception, which overcame her so much that
she acted the first scenes of the play with less effect than usual, but, recovering
herself by degrees, she came out with all her former spirit and energy in the last
two acts.' Henry Greville, *op. cit.*, p. 191.
[4] Barbarina Brand, Lady Dacre (1768–1854), poet and dramatist and the very old
friend whom Fanny often addressed as 'Granny'.

of duty I owe to my employers and spectators, to take the utmost pains to do my work as well as I possibly can for them.

My physical power of delivery is not diminished, which is good for tragedy; my self-possession is increased, which ought to be good for comedy, and I do trust I may succeed at least sufficiently to be able, by going from one place to another and returning to America when I have worn out my public favour here – say in two years – to make what will enable me to live independently, though probably upon very small means.

Birmingham, Sunday 28th

My dear Lady Dacre, I played last night for the last time in Manchester. The house was immensely full, and when I went on the stage after the piece, so loud and cordial were they that, what with the exhaustion of a whole day's packing (which I have to do for myself, my maid being utterly incompetent), and getting through my part, the whole thing was too much for me, and I turned quite faint and all but fell down on the stage. But I am not a fainting woman and so only went into violent hysterics as soon as I was carried into my dressing room.

I came to this place today and feel indescribably cheerless and lonely in my strange inn. I only act here one night, and then go to Liverpool where the master of the Adelphi Hotel is a person to whom I have been known for many years, in whose house I have been with my children, and where I shall feel less friendlessly forlorn than I do here.

Adelphi Hotel, Liverpool, Sunday 7th [March]

Dearest Harriet, The manager of the Princes Theatre, where I am engaged to act in London, will not allow me to act for the proposed charity at the St. James Theatre [to raise money for Irish Famine Relief]. I offered to give up the engagement with him, rather than break my promise to the amateurs; but he will not permit me to appear anywhere else before that takes place. I think he is injuring himself by baulking a pet plan of amusement in which all manner of fine folks, and the Queen herself, had been induced to interest themselves; and I think his preventing me acting for this charity will injure him much more than my appearance before coming out at his theatre could have done. But of course he must be judge of his own interest; and having entered into an engagement with him, I cannot render myself liable to squabbles, and perhaps a lawsuit with him, about it. All these petty worries and annoyances torment and confuse me a good deal. I have a very poor brain for business, and there is something in the ignoble vulgarity and coarseness of manner that I occasionally encounter that increases my inaptitude by the sort of dismay and disgust with which it fills me.

(*Records*) The amateur performance given at the St. James' Theatre [Fanny's arguments having prevailed] was Lord Ellesmere's translation of Victor Hugo's *Hernani* which had been acted sixteen years before under such different circumstances, as far as I was concerned, at Bridgewater House. It was upon this performance that Mr. Macready made such annihilating condemnation, not even excepting his friend and admirer, John Forster, whose mode of delivering the part of Don Ruez bore ludicrous witness to Macready's own influence and example, if not direct teaching. Macready does not even mention poor Forster. The entry in his diary runs thus: 'Went to the amateur play at the St. James' Theatre. The play . . . was in truth an *amateur* performance. Greville and Craven were very good amateurs, but tragedy by amateurs!'[5]

> *During the 'wandering, homeless year' that followed Fanny's comeback on the English stage, she dated her letters from nearly forty different towns, as far apart as Plymouth and Dundee, Dublin and Yarmouth. In some places she acted for as long as a fortnight; others were no more than one or two night stands. It was a hard life, 'rehearsing every morning, and sitting in a dull, dirty hired room, and acting that everlasting* Hunchback *in awful barns of theatres'. Though rail travel was quicker and easier than the stage coaches Fanny and her father had used on their provincial tours in 1830 and 1831, it was often cold and uncomfortable: she sometimes had to stretch out on the carriage floor on overnight journeys. But she started her perambulations at the right time of year and some of them were enjoyable.*

[5] Macready did in fact mention Forster – 'by far the best' – and continued with some unkind remarks about Fanny herself, tactfully omitted from the first edition of his letters and diaries in 1875: 'In Mrs Butler I saw *proof* that I had been *most honest* and *most discriminating* in my original judgment. *She is ignorant of of the very first rudiments of her art.* She is affected, monotonous, without one real impulse – never in the feeling of her character, never true in look, attitude or tone. She can never be an actress, and this I never ventured to think before.' (*Op. cit.*, pp. 241–2.) Fanny was, however, aware of part at least of Macready's criticism of her acting, and mentions several times that he had said she did not know the 'elements' of her profession.

Great Western Hotel, Bristol, May 30th

Dearest Harriet, The road from Birmingham here is quite pretty; the crops look extremely well and the little cottage gardens, which delight my heart with their cheerful tidiness, are so many nosegays of laburnum, honeysuckle and lilac.

The stokers on all the engines I saw this morning had adorned their huge iron dragons with great bunches of hawthorn and laburnum which hung their poor blossoms close to the hissing hot breath of the boilers and looked wretched enough. But this dressing up the engines, as formerly the stage coach horses used to be decked to their ears on May Day, was touching. I suppose the railroad men get fond of their particular engine, though they can't pat it and stroke it, as sailors do their ship.

May 31st

I have just come back from rehearsal, where I found a letter from Henry Greville, full of strictures on my carriage and deportment and earnestly entreating me to suffer his *coiffeur* ('a clean, tidy foreigner') to whitewash me after the approved French method, i.e. to anoint my skin with cold cream and then cover it with pearl powder; not only my face, but my arms, neck and shoulders. Don't you see me undergoing such a process?

(*Records*) Among the various changes [in the theatre] I had to encounter, one that might appear trivial occasioned me no little annoyance. The inevitable rouge, rendered indispensible by the gas-light illumination of the stage, has always been one of its disagreeables to me; but now I found that my fair theatrical contemporaries literally whitewashed their necks, shoulders, arms and hands – a practice which I found it impossible to adopt, and continued to confront my public in my own skin, looking, when in proximity with any feminine coadjutor, like a bronze fighter arm-in-arm with a plaster of paris cast.

Bath, June 2nd

Yesterday evening the weather was so beautifully bright that I could not bear to shut the shutters of my dressing room and light the gas, so I was sitting working, rouged and arrayed for my part when a small mob of poor little ragged urchins collected round the window and, clambering on each other's shoulders, clustered and hung like a swarm of begrimed bees at the window, to enjoy the sight of me and my finery. Bridget [her maid], who is fond of

children, turned the dresses that were hanging up right side out
and their comments were exceedingly funny and touching – how
they wondered if I put them beautiful dresses on one by one, or
over each other. The rose in my hair and the roses in my shoes
made them scream with delight. Poor little creatures! My heart
ached with compassion for them while they hung and clung in
ecstatic amazement at my frippery.

The house at Bristol the first night was wretched, my share of it
only £14. Here last night it was much better, but I do not yet know
the proceeds.

Royal Hotel, Plymouth, June 16th

The weather is cold and odiously tempestuous; in spite of which I
went into the sea yesterday and shall do so every day while I am
here; the freshness of the salt water is delicious.

. . . Both the Grevilles are friends of ours. Henry has a great
many good qualities, and though essentially a society man, has a
good deal of principle; he is not very clever, but bright and very
amiable. His brother Charles has better brains and is altogether a
cleverer person. He is a man of the world, and more selfishly
worldly, I think, than Henry, whose standard of right is considerably higher; indeed, Charles Greville's *right* always seems to
me a mere synonym for *expedient*, and when I tell him so he
invariably says 'they are the same thing', which I do not believe.
He is unfortunately deaf, but excellent company in spite of that.

Exeter, June 23rd

This is my holiday, and I have been spending it between two
famous nursery gardens and the Cathedral. These great gardeners showed me their choicest and rarest plants: such exquisite
and wonderful creatures, lovely to the eye and delicious to the
smell – Patagonians, Javanese, from Peru, from Chile, from Bor-
neo – the flower tribes of the whole earth. Then again, they
showed me little pots of fine sand, covered with bell-glasses,
where the eye could hardly detect a point of sickly green upon the
surface – the promise of some *unique* foreign flower sent from its
savage home in the forests of another hemisphere, to blossom at
the Chiswick horticultural exhibition and win medals for the
careful cultivators. One of these gentlemen showed me two
perishing-looking dried up *twigs* and said, 'those are the only
specimens of their kind in the kingdom. They come from Chile
and when healthy bear a splendid blossom as large as a tulip.

They are just between life and death. I fear we may kill them with kindness, we are so anxious about them'.

Orchard Street, [6] *[London], August 24th*
My father talks of giving up his readings, and I have therefore spoken to Mitchell, of the St. James's Theatre, about giving some myself. I find him very willing to undertake the whole 'speculation', not only in London but all over the provinces. Mr. Mitchell is a Liberal, and an honest man too, and I shall be quite safe in his hands.

It was with a new friend, also called Mitchell, that Fanny spent a short holiday in the Scottish border country in September, 1847. Mrs. Mitchell was her notion 'of what Mary Stuart must have looked like, but a marvellously wise and discreet body, mentally and morally, I should think, very unlike the bonnie Queen of Scots.' Fanny loved the countryside too, for its associations with Burns and Scott and its memories of the Scottish ballads and Thomas the Rhymer.

Carolside, September 5th
You ask me what I am doing, dear Hal. I am driving fifteen miles a day in an open britzska [a Polish type light, open carriage] on a bitter, blowing day, to return morning calls of neighbours, whose laudable desire is to 'keep the county lively'. I have taken several charming rides: the country is beautiful. I have caught a tolerably good cold – I mean, good of its kind – by wading knee deep in the [river] Leader and then standing on cold rocks fishing by the hour; in which process I did catch – cold, but nothing else; for, though the water is drowning deep in some beautiful brown pools, it is for the most part so shallow and everywhere so clear with the long drought that the spotted trout and silver eels see me quite as well as I see them and avoid me more successfully, but quite as zealously, as I seek them.

The only music I have is my own *forbye*, and a comic song or two, gasped and death-rattled out by poor old Sir Adam Fergusson, whom I met seventeen years ago at Sir Walter Scott's house, and who is still tottering on with inexhaustible spirits, but a body that seems quite threadbare, tattered and ready to fall to pieces with long and hard use.

[6] Fanny rented 18 Orchard Street from Lady Fitzhugh, her friend Emily's mother, and during 1847 it served as her base in London. She liked it particularly because one wall of the drawing room was covered with a painting of the city and bay of Naples – 'a pleasant object of contemplation on winter days'.

Howick Grange, November 14th

I arrived here about three hours ago and received a most painful blow in a letter from Henry Greville containing the news of Mendelssohn's death. When I think of that bright genius (he was the *only* man of genius I have known who seemed to me to fulfil the rightful moral conditions and obligations of one), by whose loss the whole civilised world is put in mourning; of his poor wife, so ardently attached to him; of his children; of my own dear sister and poor Edward, so deeply attached to him – I feel half stupid with pain.

Leeds, November 19th

I do not know what is to be done with Covent Garden. I suppose it will remain an opera house, for to fit it for that it has been made well-night unavailable for any other purpose, as I think we shall find on 7th December when a representation of 'Scenes' from Shakespeare's plays is to take place there, to raise funds for the purchase of the house Shakespeare was born in.

You know what my love and veneration for Shakespeare are, but I do not entirely sympathise with all that is being said and done about the four walls between which the king of poets came into his world. The thing is more distasteful to me because originally got up by an American charlatan of the first water, with a view to thrusting himself into notoriety by shrieking stupendous commonplaces about the house where Shakespeare was born. It has been taken up by a number of people who, with the exception of Macready, have the same petty personal objects in view. They have written to me to act the dying scene of Queen Katherine, to which I have agreed, not choosing to decline any part assigned to me in this 'Celebration', little as I sympathise with it.

18 Orchard Street, November 18th

I am not exempt from a feeling about 'illustrious localities' but the world seems to me so absolutely Shakespeare's domain and dwelling-place that I do not vividly associate him with those four walls between which he first saw the light of an English day. If the house he dwelt in in the maturity of his age and to which he retired to spend the evening of his life still existed, I should feel considerable emotion in being where his hours and days were spent when his mind had reached its zenith. A baby is the least intelligent form of a rational human being, and I do not care to contemplate him in that condition, in which I cannot recognise him – that is, with an undeveloped and dormant intelligence. Shakespeare's mere birthplace is not much to me, though I agree that it should be respectfully preserved and allowed to be visited by all who find satisfaction in such a pilgrimage.

He could not have been different from other babies, you know; nor indeed need be, for a *baby* – *any* baby – is a more wonderful thing even than Shakespeare.

Sunday 4th

In answer to your question of what 'coarsenesses' L—— finds in *A Year of Consolation*, I will give you an extract from her letter. 'There are a few expressions I should like to have stricken out, *par exemple* I hate the word *stink*, though I confess there is no other to answer its full import; and there are one or two passages, the careless manner of writing which astonishes me in you.' Now, Hal, I can only tell you that more than once I thought myself actually to blame for not giving with more detail the disgusting elements which in Rome mingle everywhere with what is sublime and exquisite; for it appeared to me that to describe one half of the truth only was to be an unfaithful painter. The place and the people can only be perfectly described through the whole, you know.

Hull, December 3rd, 1847

I have been spending the afternoon crying over the tender mercies of English Christians to their pauper population till my eyes smart and itch and I shall have neither sight nor voice to read *Coriolanus* this evening.[7] To this Hull Railway Hotel is attached a magnificent railway station (or rather vice versa) shaped like a horse-shoe with a spacious pavement roofed with a sky-light all round, of which I avail myself every day for my walking exercise.

Today I was accompanied by old Mr. Frost – a most charming, accomplished old gentleman and my Hull employer, President of the Literary and Scientific Institution before which I am giving my readings.

As we paced up and down, I remarked lying in a corner what I at first took to be a bundle of rags. On looking again, however, I perceived that there was a live creature in the rags – a boy whose attitude of suffering and weariness was the most wretched thing

[7] This is the first time that Fanny mentions actually giving a 'reading' as distinct from acting in a play. She says later that she gave her first reading at Highgate on 25th March, 1848, by which she probably meant her first on her father's territory in London.

you can imagine. I knelt down by him and asked what ailed him: he hardly lifted his face from his hands, and said, 'Headache', and then, coughing horribly, buried his miserable face again. Mr. Frost began to ask him questions, and then followed one of those piteous stories which makes one smart all over: parental desertion, mother marrying a second time, cruelty from the stepfather, beating, starving and abandonment. They had gone away to avoid paying the rent and left this boy to shift for himself. 'How long ago?' asked Mr. Frost. 'Before snow,' said the boy – the snow has been gone a fortnight and more, and for all that time the child had lived by begging and slept in barns and stables and passages. The interrogatory was a prolonged one: Mr. Frost is slow by age and cautious by profession, and a man by nature and so not irresistibly prompted to seize up such an unfortunate at once in his arms and adopt it for his own. Among other things the boy said, 'I wouldn't mind only for the little brother'. 'How old is he?' 'Going on two years.' 'Where is he?' 'Mother got him.' 'Oh well then, she'll take care of him.' 'No, she won't, he won't be having nothing to eat, I know he won't.' And the boy covered his face again in a sullen despair that was pitiful to see. He had been in the workhouse for two years, with his mother before she married this second husband, and on his saying that he had been sent to school and kindly treated and well-fed there, I asked if he would go back thither, and he said yes. So, rather to Mr. Frost's amazement, I think, I got a cab and put the child in, and we carried the small forsaken soul to the workhouse where we got him, with much difficulty, *temporarily* received. Would you believe it, Hal? – the wife of the master told us that this poor little creature had come to their gate the night before begging admittance; but that because he had not a *certain written order* from a certain officer, the rules prevented their receiving him, and he had been turned away *of course*.

After I returned, blubbering and blaspheming, to my inn, Mr. Frost went off in search of some further information about the child, which he presently brought back to me. 'Oh yes, the magistrate knew the child; he had *sent him to prison* already several times for being found lying at night on the wharves and about the streets'. So this poor little wretch was *sent to prison* because he literally had not where to lay his head. I wouldn't be a man for anything! They are so cruel, without even knowing that they are so: the habit of seeing sin and suffering is such a *heart-hardener*.

Well, the boy is safe in the workhouse now and is, according to his own wish, to be sent to sea, or put out apprentice to some trade. I have pledged one of my readings for purpose of outfit or entrance fee, and Mr. Frost has promised me not to lose sight of the child.

Do you remember what difficulty I had in rescuing that poor little wretch out of the streets of Glasgow? But then she had a *mother* who drove her into them day after day, to sing her starvation in the miserable mud and rain – luckily this poor Hull boy's mother had not this *interest* in him.

I went last night, it being my holiday, to hear Mr. Warren, the author of *Ten Thousand a Year*[8] and the Recorder of Hull, address the Mechanics' Institute on the duties, privileges, difficulties, dignity and consolations of labour. I sat on the platform, opposite that large concourse of working men and women – labourers well acquainted by daily experience with the subject of the eloquent speaker's discourses – and was deeply touched by the silent attention and intelligent interest with which, for two hours, they listened to his admirable address.

Norwich, January 20th, 1848

I left London for this place on Monday morning and, having a sulky and deliberate cab-driver, arrived at the station just five minutes after the train had departed. This kept me waiting from 11.30 till 3.30, during which time Hayes went out privately, and coming back with a paper of biscuits, pointed out a raspberry tart at the bottom and said, 'here is a little tart I have got on purpose for you.' Was not that courtly and kind of her?

Begun at Norwich, finished at Yarmouth, Friday 21st

I do but poorly at Norwich, my dearest Hal, in body and estate, having a wretched influenza, through which I am obliged to stand bare-necked and bare-armed and almost bare-footed on the stage (for the thin silk stockings and satin shoes are a poor protection), to houses as thin as my stockings; so that the money return for all this fatigue, discomfort and expense is but inconsiderable.

Yarmouth, 22nd

My very dear and most sententious friend, I never *do* run the time of my departure for railroad trains 'to the chances of free streets

---

[8] *Ten Thousand a Year* was a three-volume novel published in 1839, and not, as might be supposed from the context, a treatise on economics.

and fast-driving cab-men'; I always allow amply for all accidents as I have a greater horror of being hurried and jostled even than of being too late. But my driver was, I think, inexperienced as well as sulky. He was very young, and my recollection of the route, which I had traversed before, seemed to indicate that he did not take the most direct way.

I am often very cold and comfortless in these horrible theatres and shall be glad to get back to London. As soon as I am there I will take measures about my readings, which I think I had better begin in earnest with.

29 King Street,[9] *Saturday 12th February, 1848*

Did I tell you what a nice long visit I had from Thackeray the other day? Oh, have you read that *Vanity Fair* of his? It is wonderful! He was a schoolfellow of my brother John's, you know, and is a very old friend of mine, but I had not seen him for some time.

(*Records*) I wish to record a slight anecdote of my friend William Thackeray which illustrates his great kindness and amiability, his *sweetness* of temper and disposition. I met him a few days before he began his course of lectures on the English essayists and he asked me to come and hear him. He told me he was so nervous about it that he was afraid he should break down. I had an engagement which prevented me, but I promised to go and see him before he began, to cheer him.

He was to lecture at Willis Rooms, where I read, and I found him standing like a forlorn, disconsolate giant in the middle of the lecture room. 'Oh, Lord,' he exclaimed as he shook hands, 'I'm sick at my stomach with fright.' I spoke some words of encouragement and was going away, but he held my hand like a scared child, crying, 'Oh, don't leave me!' 'But,' said I, 'Thackeray, you mustn't stand here. Your audience are beginning to come in,' and I drew him into the retiring room. Here he began pacing up and down, literally wringing his hands in nervous distress. 'Oh,' he said, 'if only I could get at that confounded thing (his lecture) to have a last look at it.' 'Where is it?' 'On the reading desk.' I darted into the lecture room, hoping to snatch the manuscript without attracting the attention of the audience, with which the room was already nearly full. I had been used to deliver my reading seated at a very low table, but Thackeray gave his lectures standing and

[9] Where Fanny had taken lodgings after the expiry of the lease of the Orchard Street house.

had a reading desk adapted to his very tall stature, so that when I came to get his manuscript it was almost above my head. I made a half-jump and a clutch at it, when every leaf came fluttering separately down about me. I think I must have gone nearly on all fours in my agony to gather them up, and, retreating with them, held them out in dismay to poor Thackeray, crying 'Look what a dreadful thing I've done!' 'My dear soul,' said he, 'you couldn't have done better for me. I have just a quarter of an hour to wait here and it will take me about that to page this again. It's the best thing in the world that could have happened to me.' So I left him to give the first of that brilliant course of literary historical essays with which he enchanted and instructed countless audiences in England and America.

The last time I saw Thackeray he talked back to our early times and my coming out at Covent Garden, and how 'we all of us (said he, and what a noble company of young brains and hearts they were!) were in love with you, and had your portrait by Lawrence in our rooms' – which made me laugh and cry, and abuse him for tantalizing me with the ghost of a declaration at that late hour of both our days.

On February 21st, 1848 Fanny opened in a Shakespearean season with Macready at the Princess's Theatre. The two were far from compatible.

Friday 18th, 1848

Dearest Harriet, I have been this morning to a rehearsal of *Macbeth* at which Macready did not attend; so that in point of fact, as far as I was concerned, it was *nil*. I have another rehearsal tomorrow at which it is to be hoped he will attend, as otherwise my being there is quite a work of supererogation.

29 King Street, February 19th

I had a three hour rehearsal this morning, and Macready was there. He is less unfair in his mode of acting than I had been led to expect. He is not courteous or pleasant, or even well-bred; remains seated while one is standing talking to him; and a discussion having arisen as to the situation of a table which he wished on the stage and I wished removed, he exhibited considerable irritability and ill humour.

He is unnecessarily violent in acting, and I congratulated myself that as Lady Macbeth I could not possibly suffer from this; but was astonished and dismayed when, at the exclamation 'Bring forth men-children only', he seized me ferociously by the

wrist and compelled me to make a demi-volte or pirouette such as
I think that lady did surely never perform before.

Macready's entry in his Journal for the same day read: 'Rehearsed
Macbeth, Mrs. Butler as the Lady Macbeth. I have never seen anyone
so bad, so unnatural, so affected, so conceited. She alters the stage
arrangements without any ceremony, and in fact proceeds not only en
grande artiste, but en grande reine. She is disagreeable, but her
pride will have a yet deeper fall, I feel confident.'[10]

I don't know anything about the income tax. I am getting
frightfully behind the times, having read no *Times* for a long time.
It is deplorable to hear the despondency of all the public and
political men that I see.

I dined on Saturday at Lady Grey's, with the whole Grey
family.[11] All of them spoke of Cobden and Bright[12] as of another
Danton and Mirabeau, likened their Corn-Law League and peace
protests to the first measures of the first leaders of the French
Revolution, and predicted with woeful head-shaking a similar
end to their proceedings. I do not know whether this is an
injustice to the individuals in question, but it seems to me an
injustice to the whole people of England collectively and to their
own class, the aristocracy of England, which has invariably furnished liberal and devoted leaders to every step of popular progress. Such misgivings seem to me, too, quite unjust to the powerful, enlightened and wealthy class, which forms the sound
body of our sound-hearted nation: and equally unjust to those
below it in whom, in spite of much vice and more ignorance, of
poverty and degradation, the elements of evil do not exist in the
degree and with the virulence that spawned that hideous mob of
murderers who became at last the only government of revolutionary France. The antecedal causes have not existed here for such
revolts, and it is an insult to the whole English people to
prophesy thus of it.

What a fine thing faith in God is, even when one's own individual interests must perish, even though the temporary interests of one's country may appear threatened with adversity!
What an *uncommonly* fine thing it is under such circumstances to

[10] *Op. cit.*, p. 248.
[11] Widow of the second Earl Grey, Whig Prime Minister responsible for the
passing of the Reform Bill in 1832.
[12] Richard Cobden (1804–65) and John Bright (1811–89), leading members of the
Anti-Corn Law League and the leading representatives of the emergence of the
manufacturing classes in English politics after the Reform Act.

do right and to be able to do right and to be able to believe in right doing! As I listened to the persons by whom I was surrounded and considered their position and circumstances – their forks and spoons, their very good dinner and all their etceteras of luxury and enjoyment – I thought that, having all they have, if they had faith in God and in their fellow creatures besides, they would have the portion of those who have none of the good things of this world – they would have too much.

I did not impart these sentiments to my fellow guests at Lady Grey's, but kept them in my bosom and went to the opera.

Wednesday 23rd, 1848

Macready is not pleasant to act with, as he keeps no specific time for his exits and entrances, comes on while one is in the middle of a soliloquy and goes off while one is in the middle of a speech to him. He growls and prowls, and roams and foams about the stage, like a tiger in his cage, so that I never know what side of me he means to be; and keeps up a perpetual snarling and grumbling like the aforesaid tiger, so that I never feel sure that he *has done* and it is my turn to speak. I do not think fifty pounds a night would hire me to play another engagement with him; but fifty pounds a night is a consideration, four times a week, and I have never forgotten the French proverb: 'Il ne faut pas dire, fontaine, jamais de ton eau je ne boirai.'

I do not know how Desdemona might have affected me under other circumstances but my only feeling about acting it with Mr. Macready is dread of his personal violence. I quail at the idea of his laying hold of me in those terrible passionate scenes; for in *Macbeth* he pinched me black and blue and almost tore the point lace from my head.

Macready: 'February 24th. Mrs. Butler's rehearsal of Desdemona struck me as a very correct and forcible conception of that beautiful character, and if she would give herself up to the study of execution, she might yet become a very fine actress. Her intention, which is admirable, is seen in her acting the part; but her affected voice, her leaning her head, her walk, etc., so many affectations prevent her from being Desdemona'.[13]

King Street, Friday February 28th

I got through Desdemona very well, as far as my personal safety was concerned: for though I fell on the stage in real hysterics at

[13] *Op. cit.*, p. 248.

the end of one of those horrible scenes with Othello, Macready was more considerate than I had expected and did not really smother me in bed. I played the part fairly well and wish you had seen it. I really believe Macready cannot help being as odious as he is on the stage. He nearly made me faint last night in *Macbeth*, with crushing my broken finger, and by way of apology merely coolly observed that he could not answer for himself in such a scene and that I ought to wear a splint. If I act much more with him, I think I shall require several splints for several broken limbs. I do not mind his tiresome particularity on the stage, for, though it all goes to making himself the only object of everything and everybody, he works very hard and is zealous and conscientious. But I do think it rather *mean* of him to refuse to act in such plays as *King John* and *Much Ado about Nothing* to oblige me, while I have studied expressly for him Desdemona, Ophelia and Cordelia, parts quite out of my line, merely that his plays may be strengthened by my name.

(*Records*) I have always had a cordial esteem and respect for Mr. Macready's character, which has been increased by reading the record he has himself left of his life.[14] Of his merits as an actor I had not a very high opinion, though in one or two parts he was excellent. He was disqualified for sentimental tragedy by his appearance, and he was without comic power of any kind. His want of musical ear made his delivery of Shakespeare's blank verse defective, and painful to people better endowed in that respect. It may have been his consciousness of his imperfect declamation of blank verse that induced him to adopt what his admirers called the natural style of speaking it, which was simply chopping it up into prose. Mr. Macready's eye was as sensitive and cultivated as his ear was the reverse. He had a painter's feeling for colour and grouping and scenic effect; he was always picturesque in his appearance, dress, attitudes and movements; and all the pieces that were put upon the stage under his supervision were admirable for the appropriate harmony of the scenery, decorations, dresses and whole effect: they were carefully accurate and extremely beautiful.

February 28th
You can imagine the state of perturbation and excitement London

[14] This was the 1875 expurgated version of Macready's memoirs.

is in with these Parisian events.[15] The universal cry is, 'What is the news?' People run from house to house to gather the latest intelligence. The streets are filled with bawling news-vendors, amid whose indistinct vociferations the attractively appealing words, 'Revolution! Republic! Massacre! Bloodshed!' are alone distinguishable.

March 7th, 1848

The retreat of the great political powers of darkness before the advance of freedom in Italy seems to me like a personal happiness to myself. I rejoice unspeakably in it. In Italy the people are rising against foreign tyranny, to get rid of foreign dominion. In France the revolution against power is passed, but that against property is yet to come. As for us, our revolt against iniquitous power ended with the final expulsion of the Stuarts; but we have sundry details of that wholesale business yet to finish and there will be some sort of *property* revolution, in some mode or other.

The crying sin of modern Christian civilisation, the monstrous inequalities in the means of existence, will yet be dealt with by us English, among whom it is more flagrant than anywhere else on earth. It is the one revolution of which our social system seems to me to stand in need, the last that can be directly affected, if not effected, by legislative action upon the tenure of the land, the whole system of proprietorship of the soil, the spread of education, and the extension of the franchise: and as we are the richest and the poorest people in the world, the force must be great – I pray God that it may be gradual – that draws the opposite ends of the social scale into more humane nearness.

I cannot believe that any violent convulsions will attend inevitable necessary change here; for, in spite of the selfish passions of both rich and poor, our people do fear God more, I think, than any other European nation, and recognise a law of duty; and there is good sense and good principle enough in all classes, I believe, to meet even radical change with firmness and temperance.

Portsmouth, Wednesday

Dear Theodore, What a marvellous era in the world's history is this that we are living in! Kings, princes, potentates flying dismayed to the right and left, and nation after nation rising up,

[15] The French monarchy had fallen on February 24th, 1848 – the first revolution in that Year of Revolutions, which shook Europe from one end to the other.

demanding a freedom which God knows how few of them are capable of using.

The last month in Europe has been like the breathless reading of an exciting novel, and every day and hour almost teems with events that surpass in suddenness and importance all that has gone before.

Our country is wonderful: I mean, my blessed England receiving into her bosom the exiled minister and the dethroned King of France, and the detested Crown Prince of Prussia, with the dispassionate hospitality of a general house of refuge for ruined royalties.

The spirit and temper of this English people is noble in its steadfastness. Alone of all the thrones in Europe, that of our excellent Queen and her admirable consort stands unshaken; alone of all the political constitutions, that of the country they govern is threatened with no fatal convulsion; in the midst of the failing credit and disturbed financial interests of the Continent, our funds have been advancing in value, and our public credit rises as the aspect of affairs becomes more and more involved and threatening abroad.

Ireland is our weak point and, as we have to *atone* there for cruelty and injustice and neglect too long persisted in, that will be the quarter from which we shall receive our share of the national judgments which are being executed all over the world.

In England we shall have an extended right of suffrage, a smaller army, a cheaper government, reduced taxation and some modification of the land tenure, but no revolution and no fits, I think. Considerable changes we shall have, but the wisdom and wealth of our middle classes is a feature in our social existence without European parallel; it is the salvation of our country.

King Street, Saturday and Sunday, March 11th and 12th, 1848
Dearest Harriet, My father tells me he has definitely renounced all idea of reading again, so I took heart of grace to ask him to lend me the plays he read from, to mark mine by. My father's marks are most elaborate, but the plays are cruelly sacrificed to the exigencies of the performance – as much maimed, I think, as they are for stage representation. My father has executed this inevitably mangling process with extreme good judgment and taste, but it gives me the heart-ache, for all that. But he was *timed*, and that impatiently, by audiences who would barely sit two hours in

their places and required that the plays should be compressed into the measure of their *short* suffering capacity.

(*Records*) My first intention in undertaking my readings from Shakespeare was to make, as far as possible, of each play a thorough study in its entireness; such as a stage representation cannot, for obvious reasons, be. The dramatic effect, which of course suffers in the mere delivery from a reading-desk, would I hoped be in some measure compensated for by the possibility of retaining the whole beauty of the plays as poetical compositions. I very soon, however, found my project in making my readings 'studies of Shakespeare' for the public quite illusory.

To do so would have required that I should take two, and sometimes three, evenings for the delivery of one play; a circumstance which would have rendered it necessary for the same audience to attend two or three consecutive readings; and in many other respects I found the plan quite incompatible with the demand of the public, which was for a dramatic entertainment and not for a course of literary instruction. I was grievously disappointed, but could not help myself.

I was determined not to limit my repertory to the few most theatrically popular of Shakespeare's dramas, but to include in my course all his plays that it was possible to read with any hope of attracting or interesting an audience. My father had limited his range to a few of the most frequently acted plays: I delivered twenty-four. I invariably read them through in rotation, without repeating any of them: partly to make such of them as are seldom or never acted familiar to the public, and partly to avoid becoming mechanical or hackneyed myself in their delivery by perpetual repetition of the same pieces. I persisted in this system to the very considerable detriment of my gains.

The public *always* came in goodly numbers to hear *Macbeth*, *Hamlet*, *Romeo and Juliet* and *The Merchant of Venice*; and Mendelssohn's exquisite music, made an accompaniment to the *Midsummer Night's Dream*, rendered that a particularly popular performance. But to all the other plays the audiences were considerably less numerous – I often had but few listeners. Mr. Mitchell who for a considerable time *farmed* my readings, protested bitterly against this system, which involved of course less profits than he might have made by my repeating only the most popular plays. (Mr. Mitchell, court bookseller, Queen's publisher, box-letter to the nobility, general undertaker of pleasures and amusements for the fashionable world of London, was my manager and paymaster throughout all my public reading career in London.) But man does not live by bread alone, and for more than twenty years that I followed the trade of a wandering rhapsodist, I never consciously sacrificed my sense of what was due to my work for the sake of what I could make by it. My great reward has been passing a large portion of my life in familiar intercourse with that greatest and best English mind and heart, and living almost daily in that world above the world into which he lifted me.

Fanny gave her first London reading on March 25th, 1848. Mitchell had arranged an extensive programme of engagements for her, and she was looking forward eagerly to the long delayed arrival from Italy of Adelaide and her family, with whom she hoped to make her home. Then, in April, at the very moment when for the first time Fanny's course ahead seemed set fair, came the news from America that Pierce Butler was suing for divorce on the grounds of his wife's 'wilful and malicious' desertion.

CHAPTER 18

'Great Good Fortune'
1848–1874

Adelphi Hotel, May 10th, 1848

My dear Arthur,[1] I sail for America tomorrow. My sister will reach England exactly two days after I have left it, and only for the next six weeks I have engagements to read that would have paid me upwards of six hundred pounds, which I must now forgo and accept instead grief, vexation and loss. All is intolerable uncertainty before me; but you know I have good courage, faith and hope, the foundations of which cannot be shaken by human hands, so that nothing can go desperately wrong with me.

Nothing, in the long run, was to go desperately wrong with Fanny – on the contrary indeed, though she first had to live through nearly eighteen months of distress and anxiety. A divorce is always a painful experience, and Fanny's was more painful than most, conducted as it was with much washing of dirty linen and in the full glare of publicity. Yet the terse paragraph with which she concluded her Records of a Later Life *characteristically made no mention of the reason for her abrupt and unpremeditated departure for the United States:*

In the summer of 1848 I returned to America, where my great good fortune in the success of my public readings soon enabled me to realise my long-cherished hope of purchasing a small cottage and a few acres of land in the beautiful and beloved neighbourhood of Lenox.

Thus Fanny summarily dismissed what were in the long run to become the most rewarding years of her long and varied life. True, there was later to be a further instalment of the Records, *but surprisingly it includes not a single letter to Harriet before 1874, a gap perfunctorily filled by some thirty relatively uninformative letters to Arthur Malkin.*

[1] Arthur Malkin, an old family friend, and son of the Headmaster of Bury St. Edmund's Grammar School where her elder and for a time her younger brother had been educated.

217

It is inconceivable that Fanny should not have continued writing to Harriet with her usual regularity throughout this long period, so why did she include none of these letters in the last volume of her records? Most likely they were simply lost or forgotten when her correspondence was returned after Harriet's death, since she prints some hundreds written during her last years in America. She was rising eighty when she came to edit the final memoirs and seemingly too tired or bored to bother much about them. They are in fact thrown together with little regard for date or sequence, and afterwards she regretted having published them. They were, she thought, often too intimate and she had changed her mind about some of her earlier opinions.

It is ironical that, while the rest of Fanny's life (apart from her marital troubles) is so copiously documented from her own writings, she should have left virtually no personal account of these twenty-five years of success and contentment. Yet the Malkin letters and some of her haphazard recollections, set down then or at other times, provide a skeleton on which to hang her story; and enough of her friends have left their impressions of her to clothe that skeleton with some flesh.

For the first months after her return, while she was preparing her defence in the divorce case, Fanny stayed with the Sedgwicks at Lenox, but by early 1849, with money running short, she ventured on the first of her Shakespearian readings in America. It cannot have been easy, with her private life so much a matter for gossip; in Boston, for instance, where she first appeared in January, the magazine Littell's Living Age *published a long article about her case which, though sympathetic to her, revealed intimate details about the breakdown of her marriage. Still, she had loyal friends to support her.*

(*Records*) On one of my visits to Boston I was honoured with an invitation to read to the gentlemen of Harvard College. Longfellow was then Professor of Poetry there and led me to my reading desk, and from it, when the performance was over, to his own house, to an exquisitely prepared supper table where, seated between him and his wife, I received from her a lovely nosegay and from him the manuscript copy of the beautiful sonnet with which he has immortalised my Shakespeare readings.[2]

[2] Fanny Longfellow wrote to a friend on March 2nd, 1849: 'I sat directly under her and thought her face was never so beautiful as in Portia's speeches. . . . She came home with us afterwards and we had a very nice little supper. . . . She was in great spirits, as she always is after reading and seemed to enjoy it much. At the close I presented her with a bouquet and Henry with a sonnet which he read. She was much overcome and could hardly recover herself. Her affectionate nature is

After reading the sonnet on my readings, I told Longfellow that next time I was in Boston it should be something of his, a promise which I fulfilled by reading his exquisite poem of the 'Building of the Ship'. Among the audience of more than two thousand Longfellow and his wife sat just in front of me, his sweet and bright countenance beaming, I hoped with pleasure, and her fine eyes raised towards me, while tears fell from them like glistening dew in bright moonlight.[3]

The delightful evening [at Harvard] also saved me from great pain. Dr. Webster, the Professor of Chemistry, offered to lead me to my desk, which proposal I declined having previously accepted Longfellow's offer – but for which I should have put my hand in that of a murderer, and remembered my reading at Cambridge with horror for ever afterwards.

The murder of Dr. Parkman by Dr. Webster, who had borrowed money from him and so endeavoured to cancel the debt, created the most terrible sensation in a society of which all the members were related, connected or acquainted with each other. The unfortunate man was sentenced to death but escaped the disgrace of public execution by taking strychnine which was said to have been conveyed to him in prison.

At this time [February 1850] I gave a reading of *Macbeth* at which all the gentlemen engaged on each side of this dreadful suit were present, and was more impressed, as many of my audience told me they had been, by the awful tenour of the play than I ever was before or since – a deep groan from one of my listeners, a most distinguished and venerable member of the Boston bar, having been the only sound that broke the breathless silence of my audience in the terrible murder scene.

Not long after this the sky was darkened over my friend

easily touched by kindness and the tears flow at once.' *Op. cit.*, p. 149. Longfellow's sonnet ends:

O happy Poet! by no critic vext!
How must thy listening spirit now rejoice
To be interpreted by such a voice!

[3] Longfellow described Fanny 'standing out on the platform, book in hand, trembling, palpitating and weeping, and giving every word its true weight and *emphasis*.' (*Life*, p. 161.) Her declamatory style did not however please everyone. Henry Irving never forgot seeing her in London as a youth and much later mimicked her for Ellen Terry's amusement: 'After a portentous wait on swept a lady with an extraordinarily flashing eye, a masculine and muscular outside. Pounding her book with terrific energy, as if she wished to knock the stuffing out of it, she announced in thrilling tones "HAM-A-LETTE by WILL-Y-AM SHAK-ES-PEARE".' (Terry, *Memoirs*, p. 136.)

Longfellow's head by the tragical death of his beloved wife. Robert Mackintosh, who married Mrs. Longfellow's sister, stayed with me in Lenox on his way to join them in Cambridge. During this visit he spoke at length of the unusually fortunate and happy life of Longfellow, the blessed home, the devoted wife, the dear and lovely children, the affectionate esteem in which he was regarded, the favour with which his writings were received in Europe as well as in America, his distinguished social position and ample fortune – an existence which, with his own most amiable character, certainly combined all the elements of happiness possible in this world. A week later I got a letter from Mackintosh recalling this conversation and telling me that Fanny Longfellow was dead, burnt alive while playing with her children in the next room to the one where her husband was sleeping.[4]

After her promising start in Boston, Fanny ventured to face audiences in New York, where she had no close friends like the Longfellows to sustain her. An old acquaintance, however, was present at one of her first readings there – Philip Hone, whose dinner party she had so flippantly dismissed seventeen years earlier. He, unlike the rest of the 'fashionable world', was somewhat cynical about her instant success. 'Mrs. Butler, the veritable Fanny Kemble, has taken the city by storm', he wrote on March 13th, 1849. 'She reads Shakespeare's plays three evenings in the week and at noon on Mondays at the Stuyvesant Institution in Broadway. . . . Delicate women, grave gentlemen, belles, beaux and critics flock to the doors of entrance and rush into such places as they can find two or three hours before the lady's appearance. They are compensated for this tedious sitting on hard seats, squeezed by the crowd, by an hour's reading – very fine, certainly, for Fanny Kemble knows how to do it – of her favourite plays by the immortal bard. She makes two or three thousand dollars a week, and never was money so easily earned. . . . Shakespeare was never paid for writing his plays as Mrs. Butler is for reading them.'[5]

Meanwhile, the divorce hearing, already postponed, had been put off yet again; and it was not until the following September that Pierce

---

[4] Mrs. Longfellow did not in fact die until eleven years after Fanny's reading of 'The Building of the Ship', and the details of the death are also slightly wrong. Mrs. Longfellow's sleeve caught fire as she was sealing a packet containing a lock of one of her children's hair. She rushed to the library where her husband was sitting, but his efforts to extinguish the flames could not prevent her from being dreadfully burned. She died the following morning and was buried on July 13th, 1861, the eighteenth anniversary of her marriage. *Op. cit.*, p. 242.

[5] *Diary*, Vol. II, p. 357.

Butler was granted an uncontested divorce. [Under Pennsylvanian law two years 'wilful' desertion provided sufficient grounds for divorce.] The terms were, at first sight, reasonably favourable for Fanny. In return for not contesting the case she was to receive $1500 a year, to be able to see and write to her children, and they to her, at all times, and to have them with her every summer for two months. The reality turned out so differently, with Pierce Butler not at all keeping his side of the bargain, that Fanny reluctantly made up her mind to wait in the wings until the girls came of age – Sally was then fifteen and Fan two years younger. Accordingly she came back to England and, as Mrs. Kemble, once more set off on her 'laborious money-making', reading Shakespeare in theatres and halls all over the country.

Other matters besides Shakespeare and money-making were on her mind at this time. Once again she became, emotionally if not publicly, involved in the controversy over slavery. Harriet Beecher Stowe's novel, Uncle Tom's Cabin, *caused as much of a sensation in England as it had in America after its publication in 1852; and when in London* The Times *impugned its veracity, Fanny instantly fired off a broadside in its defence.*

Sir, As it is not to be supposed that you consciously afford the support of your great influence to misstatements, I request your attention to some remarks I wish to make on an article on a book called 'Uncle Tom's Cabin as It Is' in your paper of the 11th. In treating Mrs. Harriet Beecher Stowe's work as an exaggerated picture of the evils of slavery, I beg to assure you that you do her serious injustice: of the merits of her book as a work of art I have no desire to speak; but of its truth and moderation as a representation of the slave system in the United States I can testify with the experience of an eye-witness, having been a resident of the Southern states and had opportunities of observation such as no one who has not lived on a slave estate can have.

So began Fanny's 7,500 word letter to The Times. *It was never posted.[6] Having discovered the identity of the author of the offending articles, she decided that it was not worth while 'to send my letter for insertion, because, as that is the tone deliberately taken on the subject by that paper, my counterstatement would not, I imagine, be admitted into its columns. . . . The most charitable conjecture I can form is that . . . the statement put forward by* The Times *contradicting Mrs.*

[6] The letter was published as an appendix to the *Journal of a Residence on a Georgian Plantation* when this appeared in 1863.

Stowe's picture may be intended to soothe [American] irritation at the philanthropic zeal of our lady abolitionists.'

These 'lady abolitionists', headed by the Duchess of Sutherland, had drafted an anti-slavery petition under the title of An Affectionate and Christian Address of Many Thousands of Women in Great Britain and Ireland to Their Sisters, the Women of the United States of America. *'We appeal to you', it ran, 'as sisters, as wives and as mothers, to raise your voices to your fellow citizens and your prayers to God, for the removal of this affliction and disgrace from the Christian world'. Although the petition obtained 500,000 signatures, Fanny did not feel free to add hers. Her children were still in the charge of her slave-owning former husband and she dared not further imperil her already tenuous relationship with them.*

(*Records*) When the address, drawn up at Stafford House under the impulse of Mrs. Beecher Stowe's powerful novel, and under the auspices of Lord Shaftesbury and the Duchess of Sutherland (by Thackeray denominated the 'Womanifesto against Slavery') was brought to me for my signature, I was obliged to decline putting my name to it, though I felt very sure no other signer of that document knew more of the facts of American slavery, or abhorred it more, than I did; and also that no other of its signers knew, as I did, the indignant sense of offence which it would be sure to excite in those to whom it was addressed, nor its absolute futility as to the accomplishment of any good purpose and the bitter feeling it could not fail to arouse, even in the women of the Northern states, by the assumed moral superiority which it could be thought to imply.

Canterbury, September 26th, 1852
My dear Arthur, . . . How exceedingly little you know of the gastronomic resources of that most capital hotel, the Royal, at Lowestoft! Except the Bedford at Brighton, it is the most luxurious establishment in her Majesty's dominions and assuredly in the work I mean to publish by-and-by upon the hotels and inns of England, of which my peregrinations have afforded me a vast experience, I shall certainly award it a distinguished and honourable position.

If I had shown you my 'George', the jewel which I have lost, you would not have forgotten it. It was the exact counterpart of the ornament worn by our Knights of the Garter, but instead of being made with brilliants it was of solid gold. It would have covered the palm of your hand, and was so heavy that I could never wear it suspended round my neck, but was obliged to support it on my breast with a large pin or brooch. It was very precious to me. It is gone and a great vexation to me it is.

There is some talk of my going to Woodbridge, which I only rejoice at for the chance it will give me of seeing Edward Fitzgerald once more.

(*Records*) Mr. Edward Fitzgerald was an eccentric gentleman and man of genius.

A poet, a painter, a musician, an admirable scholar and writer, if he had not shunned notoriety as sedulously as most people seek it, he would have achieved a foremost place among the eminent men of his day. He led a curious life of almost entire estrangement from society, preferring the companionship of the rough sailors and fishermen of the Suffolk coast to that of lettered folk. He lived with them in the most friendly intimacy, helping them on their sea ventures, and cruising about with one, an especially fine sample of his sort, in a small fishing smack which Edward Fitzgerald's bounty had set afloat.[7]

His parents and mine were intimate friends and he, during the whole of his life, my brother's and mine. For many years before his death he made his home at Woodbridge, and when I read there his friendly devotion was the occasion of some embarrassment, for when I came on the platform and curtsied to my audience, Mr. Fitzgerald got up and bowed to me, his example being immediately followed by the whole room. I was not a little surprised, amused and confused by this courtesy on the part of my hearers who, I suppose, supposed that I was accustomed to be received standing by my listeners.

99 Eaton Place, Belgrave Square, Sunday October 17th, 1852
My dear Arthur, Let me first tell you that my Order of Knighthood is happily recovered and I shall again be the only woman besides our gracious lady the Queen who will wear St. George and the Dragon on her breast. It was discovered in a very old and curious carved oak wardrobe, which had sundry cracks and

[7] This paragraph was omitted from Fanny's *Records* at Fitzgerald's urgent request. 'He made me feel painfully', she recalled, 'that I had been guilty of the impertinence of praising'. (*Letters to Fanny Kemble*, footnote, pp. 94–5.) The two carried on a voluminous correspondence during the last twelve years of his life, and his delightfully idiosyncratic letters to her were published two years after his death in 1883. Unfortunately none of hers to him have survived.

crevices into one of which my knightly insignia slipped, and was found last week only by the merest chance by a housemaid.

(*Records*) I gave several readings in New York for the benefit of the St. George's Society, a benevolent institution founded and maintained by Englishmen for the assistance of their fellow countrymen in America, whose circumstances rendered them proper objects of charity or help.

The readings were very profitable to the charity, and some of the members called on me and told me that in recognition of the service which, they were good enough to say, I had rendered them they had intended to make me an honorary member, but had found it impossible to do so, the terms of their charter referring to male individuals only. They therefore gave me a gold badge similar to the silver one all of them wore. Afterwards I wore the noble ornament whenever I read one of Shakespeare's historical plays. My friend Henry Greville told me that once on going out from my reading he heard a gentleman maintain it was a foreign order given me by some royal or princely personage abroad. 'I tell you it isn't', was the testy reply, 'she was never *ordered* by anybody, at home or abroad,' 'which made me think', said my friend, 'that the gentleman knew you.'

Once again Fanny was almost completely out of touch with her daughters, hearing of them only through friends like Thackeray who made a point of visiting the Butlers while lecturing in America early in 1853. 'I went to see Pierce Butler, not of my own wish, but in order to try and see his girls and report on them. But one is at school and the other, though I asked particularly about her, said I remembered her as a child and so forth, I could not see. She passes for being very clever, is like her mother and her father is said to be very fond of her. . . . He wouldn't bring Sally down though, for all my asking, and I was obliged to go away. I purposely called on him on my last day in Philadelphia (he came to me on my first), because I knew he would be offering hospitality which would rather have choked me, you know.'[8] Early that same year Fanny went for a second long sojourn in Italy with Adelaide and Edward Sartoris.

Villa Correali, Sorrento, June 5th, 1853
My dear Arthur, . . . I found Adelaide and Edward and her children quite well and thriving. They have taken a house in Rome for next winter and, unless some most unforeseen cir-

[8] *Op. cit.*, p. 257.

cumstance prevents it, I shall spend my next winter there too.

The place where we now are is enchantingly beautiful. We have terraces that dominate over earth, sea and sky and are surrounded by loveliness and grandeur. The drawback – there is no beach and the cliffs being very high and all crowned with the gardens or orchards of private dwelling houses, one is debarred from that familiar intercourse with the sea which its proximity makes one particularly eager for. We shall, it is true, be able to bathe by passing through the orange orchard of an adjoining villa; but though we may get into the sea, we can hardly get by it; and our conversation with the nymph of these bright waters must be rather distant, or a plunge into her arms. One would desire a medium.

> *Villa Correali, Sorrento, August 8th, 1853*

You are quite right. Italy is to be eschewed in summer. Sorrento disagrees with me extremely; the volcanic atmosphere of the whole region is utterly repugnant to my constitution.

I have had a letter from Lady Ellesmere, with a long account of my girls whom she saw in Philadelphia; and I think, judging by that, Sally must be the prettiest and pleasantest thing she has seen on the other side of the Atlantic.

> *33 Via delle Mercedi, Rome, December 22nd, 1853*

We have not a very agreeable society here this winter, at least I think not, but then I am hard to please, and perhaps other people might think otherwise. Thackeray is here, and the Brownings, so it is not their fault if we are not both witty and poetical.

This somewhat jaundiced letter and young Anne Thackeray's recollections suggest that Fanny may have been more subdued than usual that winter, in spite of singing at the top of her voice on drives through the streets of Rome, to the girl's intense embarrassment. Years later Anne Ritchie, as she became, remembered her 'sitting dressed in a black dress, silently working all through the evening by her sister's fireside, and gravely stitching on and on, while all the brilliant company came and went, and the music came and went. In those days Mrs. Kemble had certain dresses she wore in rotation. If the black gown chanced to fall on a gala day she wore it, if the pale silk gown fell on a working day she wore it. . . . Another vivid impression I have is of an evening visit Mrs. Kemble paid Mrs. Browning in the quiet little room in the Bocca di Leoni, only lit by a couple of tapers and by the faint glow of the fire. I looked from one to the other: Mrs. Browning welcoming her guest, dim in her dusky gown unrelieved; Mrs. Kemble, upright and magnificent, robed on this occasion like some Roman empress, in stately crimson edged with gold.'[9]

Elizabeth Barrett Browning too seems to have received something of the impression of an empress: 'Fanny is looking magnificent, with her black hair and radiant smile. A very noble creature indeed. Somewhat unelastic, unpliant to the eye, attached to the old modes of thought and convention, but noble in quality and defects. I like her much. She thinks me credulous and full of dreams but does not despise me for that reason, which is good and tolerant of her, and pleasant too, for I should not be quite easy under her contempt. The Sartoris house has the best company in Rome, and exquisite music of course.'[10] The eccentric young American sculptress, Harriet Hosmer, was also a frequent guest at Adelaide's twice weekly parties: 'Mrs. Sartoris sings and Mrs. Kemble sometimes reads, and all in all, it is the perfection of everything that is most charming.'[11]

Back in England in the early summer of 1854, Fanny began to establish the pattern that her life was to follow for the next twenty years: profitable reading tours on both sides of the Atlantic, with summers in Lenox when in America and holidays in Switzerland, Italy and Scotland when based in London.

Meanwhile, however, there were family sorrows and joys. Her father, Charles Kemble, died at the age of 79 in November 1854; her brother Henry, for whom she had as a young woman so triumphantly bought a commission in the army, survived him by three years, having spent his last days in a mental home, and leaving two illegitimate children. Adelaide took care of the girl, while Fanny paid for the boy's education.[12]

When, in 1856, Sarah Butler came of age, mother and daughter were at last reunited for a long, happy summer at Lenox, after which Fanny set out on a tour of distant and hitherto unvisited parts of the United States.

---

[9] *Chapters from Some Memoirs*, pp. 198–9.
[10] *Letters of Elizabeth Barrett Browning*: ed. Kenyon, p. 150.
[11] *Letters and Memoirs*: ed. Carr, p. 32.
[12] Harry Kemble was the last of the family to become an actor. He was 'short, stout and an excellent comedian', but Fanny did not think much of her nephew's talents. 'She would say "My dear Harry, you are not a great actor", to which he always replied, "That is not the first time you have told me so." (Leigh, *Other Days*, p. 219.) Nevertheless she was very fond of him: 'he is peculiarly amiable in his manner, and gentle and courteous and kind to me. His temper appears perfectly even and sweet, and the reasonableness and sound common sense of all his views, though not perhaps an attractive quality in so young a man, is a very unusual and valuable one'.

Boston, Monday April 6th, 1857

My dear Arthur, . . . I have been to the great West this winter, to St. Louis, beyond the Mississippi, across the prairies and to the further shore of Lake Michigan, and very thankful indeed I am to be once more back in New England.

The hurry of life in the Western part of this country, the rapidity, energy and enterprise with which civilisation is there being carried forward baffles all description. Cities of magnificent streets and houses, with wharves and quays and warehouses and shops full of Paris luxuries, and railroads to and from them in every direction, and land worth its weight in gold by the foot, and populations of fifty and hundreds of thousands where, within the memory of man, no trace of civilisation existed, but the forest grew and the savage wandered.

I was at a place called Milwaukee, on Lake Michigan, a flourishing town where they invited me to read Shakespeare to them, which I mention as an indication of advanced civilisation; and one of the residents, a man not fifty years old, told me that he remembered the spot on which stood my hotel as a tangled wilderness through which ran an Indian trail. Does not all that sound wonderful?

P.S. I have been working hard all winter and half believe I shall die a rich woman.

New York, Sunday November 29th, 1857

The best part of my year is over, the summer with Sally, who returns to Philadelphia for the winter months on 1st December; after that I shall resume my readings and work hard, probably the whole time, till the summer months come round again, bringing for me the one blossom of my year.

I find living in America very irksome and I am often sadder that I ought to be, when I think that my home for the rest of my life must certainly be here even if I should revisit my own country, of which at present I see not the remotest chance.

It is not likely, my dear Arthur, let me live as I will, that I shall ever be a rich woman if I am to live in America. For instance, I have just arrived in New York where I shall probably spend the greater part of the winter at a hotel. I have a very lofty, airy, cheerful drawing room with three large looking-glasses set in superb frames, green and gold satin curtains and furniture, and carpet and rug of all the splendidest colours in the rainbow. The bedroom is a small closet without curtains to the window or bed, no fireplace and a washing-stand which is a fixture in a corner-cupboard. There is not even room nor any substitute for a towel horse. Does not this juxtaposition of such a drawing room and such a bedroom speak volumes for the love of finery and ignorance of all decent comfort, which alike are semi-barbarous? For this accommodation and a bedroom for Marie, I am expected to pay sixteen guineas a week, so that, you see, let me work as I will it is not possible for me to save much. I cannot help thinking sometimes of the amount of comfort, enjoyment and pleasure of all sorts I could command almost anywhere in Europe for the expense that here cannot procure me what we call the decencies of life, simply because they are not to be procured; and then I think my children are *dear* to me in the most literal sense of the word.

Syracuse, Sunday, April 18th, 1858

I am giving readings here just now, and was besought by a friend of mine, an excellent clergyman of this place, to bestow an hour's reading this morning on a convention of all the school-masters and school-mistresses of the county.

I found an assembly of nearly two hundred young men and women – intelligent, conceited, clever, eager-looking beings, with sallow cheeks, large heads, narrow chests and shoulders. There is something at once touching and ludicrous in the extreme in the desire exhibited at all times by the people of this country for the fine blossoms and jewels of civilisation and education and their neglect and ignorance of the roots and foundation of education and civilisation. My reading was in this wise:

'I will give you Hamlet's soliloquy and speech to the players.' Having finished them, 'the air of this room is pestiferous. You have no ventilation, and two rusty sheet-iron stoves all but red hot.'

'I will now read you the lament of her brothers over the supposed dead body of Imogen.' Having finished it, 'you have now thrown open windows at the top and bottom on opposite sides of the hall, producing violent draughts of cold air. Such of you as are exposed to them will get colds or rheumatism.'

'I will now read you Mercutio's speech about dreams.' Having finished it, 'there is a strong escape of gas in this room; the screws in the gas burners are none of them turned square; you are inhaling poison and I am being choked.'

'I will now read you Othello's defence before the Senate of Venice.'

This being ended, I shut my book and asked what use it was for them to listen to or learn poetical declamation while they were sitting there violating every principle of health and neglecting the most necessary of all elementary knowledge, that which concerns the well-being of themselves and their pupils. So much for my first and last public lecture on education. I felt so angry with them for what they *wanted to know* and for what they *did not know*!

After her younger daughter Fan came of age in 1859, Fanny took her to England and Europe for a year. They returned to America to find the elder married to Owen Wister, a Philadelphia doctor, and the whole of the country in turmoil.

Lenox, May 8th, 1860

The United States schism, my dear Arthur, has become a wide, yawning cleft. The whole spirit of the people is gone. It seems to me that slavery has made the Southerners insane egotists, and that the pursuit of gain has made the Northerners incapable egotists. Manliness, patriotism, honour, loyalty, appear to have been stifled out of these people by material success and their utter abdication to mere material prosperity. A grievous civil war, shattering their financial and commercial idols, and compelling them to find the connection between public safety and private virtue, may be the salvation of the country; a blessed, bitter blast of adversity, checking the insolent forwardness of their national spring, may yet preserve them from that which really seemed impending over the land: unripe rottenness, decay without duration or exertion to excuse and account for it, the most amazing and deplorable unworthiness of the most glorious advantages that have ever yet belonged to any nation of the world.

A short while ago I was in New York and Philadelphia giving away swords and pistols to young volunteers, soldiers, whom I remember boys in rounded jackets. Up here among the hills, the great hubbub that fills the land in its more populous regions comes but faintly. The tap of a drum along the village street at evening, calling the men to drill when they have done work, is our faint echo of the great national stir, and the vivid stars and stripes flying from the scattered farmhouses on the hillsides and valleys, the only visible sign of the strife that is preparing – indeed, that is already begun.

August 2nd, 1860

Oh, how I do wish I were going over the Col de Liseran with you, but I am not! I am going to the flattest region (figuratively as well

as literally) in the whole universe – the immediate neighbourhood of Philadelphia, to see my child Sally and her child, who is a
month old and towards whom I feel grandmotherly yearnings.[13]

November 24th, 1860

I trust that you will be starting for the Alps in August, 1862, which
I hope and mean to do then, if it should please God to spare my
life and health; for, though I am old and fat and rheumatic, and
shall then be older, fatter and rheumaticker, I will nevertheless go
over certain of those Swiss passes, if not on my own legs, why
then on mules' legs; and if not on mules' legs, why then on man's
legs in a *chaise-à-porteurs*, with sixteen men to carry me as I had
going up Vesuvius (in the night, to be sure); eight carried torches
(which were light), and eight carried me (which *were* heavy). Oh,
my dear Arthur, your letter positively makes me sick – sick to be
again on those mountains and in those valleys![14]

Our Prince of Wales, who has kept the whole land alive with
interest and excitement, must have reached home ere this. I
missed seeing him, which I was very sorry for; but Fan danced
with him at the New York Ball and I console myself with that
honour and glory, of which however she seems less sensible than
I am, for when I asked if she had laid up in lavender the satin
shoes in which she danced with such a partner, she shrugged her
shoulders and laughed, though she said he was a 'nice little
fellow, and danced very well'. Think, my dear Arthur, of the
shock to my rather superstitious respectful loyalty at hearing my
future sovereign, the future sovereign of England, Scotland,
Ireland, Wales and India, clapped on the shoulder by this mon-
key of a democratic damsel of mine.

*The American Civil War, already foreseen by Fanny, started in earnest
in April 1861 with the bombardment and surrender of Fort Sumter.*

September 15th, 1861

Our daily talk is of fights and flights, weapons and wounds. The
stars and stripes flaunt their gay colours from every farm roof

[13] According to Sidney Fisher, *Philadelphia Perspective*, p. 356, Sarah had been
'fractious and odd' before the birth. No preparations had been made and no baby
clothes provided. Though christened Owen, the boy was usually called Dan. He
became a writer, best known for his novel *The Virginian*.
[14] Arthur Malkin and his wife had been enthusiastic mountaineers for twenty
years; he was an early member of the Alpine Club. Fanny later joined them several
times in Switzerland, but it is unlikely that she ever climbed with them, as distinct
from scrambling up steep rocky paths.

among these peaceful hills and give a sort of gala effect to the quiet
New England villages embowered in maple and elm trees. It
would be pretty and pleasing but for the grievous suggestions
they awake of bitter civil war, of the cruel interruption of an
unparalleled national prosperity, of impending danger and
insecurity, of heavy immediate taxation, of probable loss of property and all the evils, public and personal, which spring from the
general disorganisation of the government and disrupture of the
national ties.

Of the ultimate success of the North I have not a shadow of
doubt. I hope to God that neither England nor any other power
will meddle in the matter – but above all not England. Thus, after
some good and bad fighting and an unlimited amount of brag and
bluster on both sides, the South – in spite of much better preparation, better soldiers, better officers and, above all, a much
more unanimous and *venomous* spirit of hostility – will be obliged
to knock under to the infinitely greater resources and less violent
but more enduring determination of the North. With the clearing
away of this storm, slavery will be swept from the acknowledged
institutions of America.

How nearly I am affected by all these disturbances you can
imagine when I tell you that Mr. Butler is a state prisoner, that he
was arrested a month ago on a charge of high treason, and that
my children left me last week to visit him in a fortress at the
entrance of the Bay of New York, to which they obtained access
only by special order from the President, and where they were
only permitted to see him in the presence of one of the officers of
the fort. The charge against him is that he acted as an agent for the
Southerners in a visit he paid to Georgia this spring, having
received large sums of money for the purchase and transmission
of arms. Knowing Mr. Butler's Southern sympathies, I think the
charge very likely to be true; whether it can be proved or not is
quite another question, and I think it probable that if it is not
proved, he will still be detained till the conclusion of the war as he
is not likely to accept any oath of allegiance to this government,
being a determined democrat and inimical, both on public and on
private grounds, to Mr. Lincoln and his ministers.

*Pierce Butler was not in fact incarcerated for the duration but released
after a month on pledging himself to do no act hostile to the federal
government. 'It is true that no overt acts of treason were committed by
Butler', wrote Sidney Fisher in his diary, 'nor was he committed for*

punishment or for trial, but as a precaution and because his general conversation was seditious and tended to strengthen the rebellion, and he is morally as much a traitor as any man in the Confederate army. His arrest had a very good effect here and his release will have a bad effect. It will be ascribed to the influence of his position and to his rich friends.'[15]

Pierce's personal affairs had not prospered since the divorce. In 1853 he had, according to Thackeray, lived in an elegant house and been 'very busy making money.' Three years later he had gambled it all away. The Butler estate was put in the hands of trustees and Pierce made a small allowance, but even so nearly half the Butler slaves had to be sold in 1859. To do him justice, Pierce objected strongly to the sale; and as the 439 men, women and children left the plantation where they had been born he handed each of them a dollar in silver quarters.

In the spring of 1862 Fanny crossed the Atlantic yet again in the company of her younger daughter. She remained in England until after the end of the war, but her thoughts were never far from the struggle in America. Profoundly distressed by the pro-Southern opinions she heard on all sides and by the apparent intention of the British government to recognise the Confederacy, she lobbied friends and politicians, sending Lord Clarendon, a member of the Cabinet, 'a fair and accurate account of the whole origin of the quarrel and the present state of the struggle,'[16] writing a long defence of emancipation for Charles Greville, and eventually deciding that the time had come to make her own experience of slavery known to a wider public.

(Records) The people among whom I then lived were, like most well-educated members of the upper classes of English society, Southern sympathisers. The ignorant and mischievous nonsense I was continually compelled to hear on the subject of slavery determined me to publish my own observation of it – not that I had any fallacious expectation of making converts, but that I felt constrained to bear my testimony to the miserable nature and results of the system, of which so many of my countrymen and women were becoming the sentimental apologists.[17]

[15] *Op. cit.*, p. 405.
[16] John Murray Forbes: *Letters and Recollections*, p. 26.
[17] How much, if any, influence Fanny's *Journal of a Residence on a Georgian Plantation* had in England or America is debatable, although it was widely read in both countries. John A. Scott, editor of the 1960 American edition of the *Journal* assesses it thus: 'Southerners have written, and some still believe, that Fanny Kemble single-handed prevented England's recognition of the Confederacy and hence turned the balance of advantage against the South. . . . On the other hand

I believe I was suspected of being *employed* to 'advocate' the Northern cause (an honour of which I was as little worthy as their cause was in need of such an advocate); my friend Lady Grey told me she had repeatedly heard it asserted that my journal was not a genuine record of my own experiences and observation, but 'cooked up' to serve the purpose of special party pleading. This, as she said, she was able to contradict upon her own authority, having heard me read the manuscript many years before.

The republication of this book in America had not been contemplated by me; my purpose and my desire being to make the facts it contains known in England. In the United States, by the year 1862, abundant miserable testimony of the same nature needed no confirmation of mine. My friend Mr. John Forbes of Boston, however, requested me to let him have it published in America, and I very gladly consented to do so.

Fanny's younger daughter spent a great part of the remaining war years with her in England and on the continent. Since Fan was now of age this must have been by her own choice; yet the relationship cannot have been easy and it says much for both of them that such long proximity remained possible at such a time, with Fanny everywhere parading her Northern sympathies and Fan, whether or not she paraded her equally strong loyalties, always staunchly supporting the Southern troops. 'I have had rather a difficult task,' Fanny wrote after the war had ended [June 1865], 'in sympathising with my daughter's grief at the overthrow of the Confederacy, while rejoicing with every thought and feeling of my own in the victory of the North. Surely there never was a more signal overthrow of the Devil and all his works in the world's history since it began, nor one for which good men and angels are bound to praise and bless God.'[18]

Less than a year after the Southern surrender the spirited and determined young Fan was on her way southwards with her father,

it has been argued that both in England and America the contemporary importance of the *Journal* was small, its sales minor and its influence negligible. . . . By May 1863, when Fanny's English edition appeared, the danger of English recognition of the Confederacy was past. The news of Gettysburg and Vicksburg, arriving in July, administered the *coup-de-grâce* to whatever hope remained. Fanny's *Journal* simply came on the scene too late to affect the outcome at all. But what is of more significance, the emancipation proclamation of January 1st, 1863, had let loose a flood of pro-Union sentiment in England. Now that the moral issue had been clearly raised, the English working class, with its deep-rooted antislavery traditions, rallied round the North and the spring of 1863 witnessed an avalanche of mass meetings supporting the proclamation.' (pp. li–lii.)

[18] Letter to Harriet Hosmer. *Op. cit.*, p. 212.

hoping to bring the ruined and deserted plantations once more into working order. These had been evacuated, but by the spring of 1866 most of the former slaves had returned, including many of those who, seven years earlier, had been sold to pay Pierce Butler's debts – which, Fan observed, 'speaks louder than words as to their feelings for their old master and former treatment. . . . The negroes seemed perfectly happy at getting back to the old place and having us there.'[19] *She stayed a year, making a pleasant home for her father out of their dilapidated house and, in spite of wretched servants and constant shortage of provisions, she was very happy.*

> Cold Spring, New York State, June 12th, 1867

My dear Arthur, . . . Fan has been back with us at the North for nearly a month now, and is busy preparing the old farmhouse, where she and her sister were born, for her summer residence. The place is lamentably run down and out of repair but she is fixing it, as folks here say, and means to inhabit it until Christmas, when she contemplates returning to the South. This pendulum sort of life seems not without attractions for the damsel, who finds in it variety and excitement, the indulgence of her unfortunate propensity for what she calls independence, and the exercise of a good many of her better qualities and faculties.

Pierce had remained on Butler's Island by himself when Fan went north. She had left only a few weeks before he fell seriously ill with 'country fever' from which he did not recover.[20] *Undeterred, Fan persisted in taking his place on the plantation the following winter, much heartened at first by the negroes' evident grief at the loss of their former master – 'their love for and belief in my father was beyond expression and made me love them more than I can say'. That love was to be sorely tried: the post-war honeymoon was ending, and Fan had to face problems that might well have daunted even the toughest of men.*

> New York, April 29th, probably 1868 [misdated 1865]

You cannot be sorrier than I was that Fan judged it expedient to go down to the plantation and spend the winter there. Her sister

[19] Leigh: *Ten Years on a Georgian Plantation Since the War*, p. 21.
[20] 'He was a man of strongly marked character', wrote Pierce Butler's close acquaintance Sidney Fisher on hearing of his death, 'with some good qualities and many faults. He led a very unsatisfactory life and threw away great advantages. He was handsome, clever, most gentlemanlike in his manners, but uneducated, obstinate, prejudiced and passionate. His daughters are in great grief.' *Op. cit.*, p. 531.

and all her friends advised and entreated her not to do so, but she thought it best and has been labouring hard to induce the former slaves to work steadily on the plantation. The consequence is that, having newly signed the contract to work there for this year, when her personal influence is withdrawn, as it must be when she comes north next week, they may altogether disregard the contract they made with her and leave the crop to take care of itself. She has simply deferred the settlement of the question – namely whether these poor people can be made to understand that freedom means leave to labour or leave to starve. She being down there has not helped to make them realise their new position as labourers but has simply tended to prolong the dependent feeling of the old relation without the possibility of bringing back the former relations between the negroes and their employers. Of course an estate cannot be made to depend on a woman's coaxing or scolding the cultivators, and hitherto Fan's mission at the South has been simply one of successful coaxing and scolding. Personal influence is one thing and the laws of labour another, and these are what the poor negroes have yet to learn.

Fan's labour force, however, had needed more than mere coaxing and scolding during her first winter by herself on the plantation. There had been ugly moments when she came to share out the proceeds of the first two years' rice crop and to obtain the negroes' agreement to new contracts, both of which processes were met with extreme suspicion and hostility. She tackled even the most recalcitrant with determination and courage and most in the end accepted the new order.

When, fifteen years later, Fan published the story of her efforts to rehabilitate the Butler plantations, she added a postscript defining her attitude to slavery. In the old days, she wrote, the slaves had been clothed, fed and housed at their master's expense, medicines supplied and a doctor always available. What were such provisions but wages? she asked. 'It is quite true that they were not free to leave their place or choose their masters, but, until a few years ago were the majority of English labourers much better off? Far less well off in point of food, clothing and houses. The low wages and large families of the English labourer tied him to the soil as effectively as ever slavery did the negroes. . . . As far as the masters are concerned, they are far better off [since emancipation] relieved from the terrible load of responsibility which slavery entailed, and I have always been thankful that before the property came into my hands the slaves were freed. But for the negroes, I cannot help thinking things are worse than when they were disciplined and controlled by a superior race, notwithstanding the drawbacks of the situation and, in some cases, grave abuses attending it. If slavery made a Legree, it also made an Uncle Tom.'

Concern about her daughter's present struggles and future prospects did not prevent Fanny making an extensive tour reading Shakespeare in Washington, through New England and in Chicago and Detroit; and in the summer of 1868 she wrote to Arthur Malkin from a house she had never expected to enter again.

Butler Place, Sunday, August 30th, 1868

My dear Arthur, I am writing to you now in the room where my children were born – *my room*, as it is once more called, in the home of my very sad married life. It is full twenty-six years since I last inhabited it. When my children ceased to be amongst the richest girls in America (which they once were) and had to leave this place, to which they were extremely attached, to go and live in a Philadelphia boarding house, it was let to people who took no care of it; and so it remained, getting more and more dilapidated and desolate, until last April.

I remained at Lenox for the benefit of the mountain air until a week ago, when, upon Fan's invitation, I came hither and am quite amazed at the transformation the little woman has made in the place. I have spent a very peaceful and happy week in this my former purgatory and leave it with infinite reluctance tomorrow, to start on a three months' tour in the West, reading as I run, as far as Niagara, the great lakes and the Mississippi. Of course, with hard work and hard travelling before me, I shall be very thankful when my three months' tour is over, especially if it answers as well as my three months' spring labour did. A net result of four thousand four hundred pounds (all my expenses paid, three hundred given away and eleven hundred *read away gratis* for charities) is a good three months' job, don't you think so?

CHAPTER 19

Years of Rest
1874–1876

From January 1874 Fanny's life can again be followed week by week through her letters to Harriet, so mysteriously missing from the records of the previous twenty-five years. The indomitable Mrs. Kemble, now aged sixty-four, had at last retired and was about to move into her daughter Fan's summer home within sight and sound of Butler Place where Sarah and the Wister family were planning to install themselves.

1812 Rittenhouse Square, Saturday, January 10th, 1874
My beloved Harriet, . . . Mary [Fox][1] has sent me in a magnificent china flower pot a large Catalonia jasmine in full bloom. It was Mr. Butler's first gift to me before we were married; and on Christmas Day Mary, to whom I had given it years ago and in whose gardener's care it has been ever since, sent it back to me, covered with fragrant blossoms – a strange flowering again of former memories.

Dr. Wister and Sally and their boy dined with me on Christmas Day, and Ellen[2] insisted on hanging green garlands round the dining-room, but was unhappy because she could not find a sprig of holly with bright berries to send up on the plum pudding, for the honour of England. Dr. Wister gave me a very pretty pair of French candelsticks, and Sally gave me Horace Furness's *Variorum* Shakespeare, the *Romeo and Juliet* and *Macbeth*. Fan sent me up from the plantation a barrel of the most magnificent oranges I ever saw, a product of the estate.

February 14th, 1874
I have no intention of undertaking any literary work except my reminiscences. Looking over my letters and copying portions of

[1] Fanny's nearest neighbour and frequent companion during the next three years.

[2] Ellen was the devoted maid who had postponed her marriage for two years to go to America with her mistress. Fanny once told Henry James that 'if my servants can live with me for a week, they can live with me for ever', and that, although with some interruptions, was to be the case with Ellen.

them affords me a certain amount of quiet amusement and occupation. The letters which could have revived distressing associations were all destroyed when I received the box containing my
whole correspondence with you and though occasionally, in
going back over all my life in those I have preserved, I still find
details that sadden me, I have hitherto derived more interest and
entertainment than anything else from the whole retrospect.

February 18th, 1874

Hitherto my poor drunken negro servant has continued perfectly
sober since he took the pledge over a month ago. I feel much
concerned for the man, who was in the war during the Southern
secession and had three brothers killed. Of course the privations
and exposures and fatigues of a soldier's life must have made
drinkers if not absolute drunkards of many poor fellows who
were not so before. The brandy bottle was always at hand and
must often have supplied the place of food, shelter, fire and rest.
If the accident of his being in my service rescues this poor man
from his ruinous propensity, I shall rejoice greatly. He has a wife
and two children. He was born a slave in Maryland, cannot write
and can hardly be said to read, so there is every excuse for him.

March 9th, 1874

Fan writes in delight of the sunny warmth of the weather in
Georgia, the multitude of singing birds and abundance of exquisite flowers. Of the state and prospects of the plantation, she
writes less hopefully and cheerfully. She speaks of a large defection among their negro labourers under the influence of two
worthless fellows who had to be dismissed for idleness and
insubordination. Unless some method can be found of obtaining
labourers to work the estates, the rapid defection of the negroes
and their idleness will, I should fear, before long compel all the
planters to abandon any hope of successfully working their plantations. For my own part, I am not surprised at this aspect of the
present or prospect for the future. I have never been able to
believe in any return of prosperity for any part of the Southern
country till the whole generation of former planters and slaves
has died out. Can you reflect upon the condition of that plantation as it was within my experience and think it reasonable to
imagine that the sudden abolition of slavery by means of the war
and the President's proclamation could cancel the action of all the

previous influences that had reigned for a hundred years upon the place and people?

Fan had managed the plantation on her own for three years, with varying success. At one time the negroes were so restive that she had to sleep with a loaded pistol by her bed, and it was touch and go whether they or she would get the upper hand. But by March 1871, when she left for England to marry the Rev. James Wentworth Leigh, son of Lord Leigh of Stoneleigh Abbey in Warwickshire, she felt that at last all was going well: 'My little place has never looked so lovely and the negroes are behaving like angels . . . I have worked so hard and cared so much about this place that it is more to me than I can express to know that I have succeeded.'[3]

Fan's hopes for the continued smooth running of the plantation were disappointed. Reports reaching her in England were so bad that she felt she could 'do no more', but her new husband thought otherwise. He had visited Butler's Island – 'where a fair queen resided among her sable subjects and entertained strangers with royal grace'[4] *– before their engagement and had liked it, so now he persuaded his wife that they could together put the place in order again. Leigh took to the management of a Southern estate as if born to the job.*

March 31st, 1874

You ask me questions which I am by no means capable of answering with regard to the condition of politics here and the government of the country. Before the war the Southern slaveholders were undoubtedly the most influential politicians in the United States. The Democratic party was formed in the South and was led and supported by Southern statesmen who controlled the whole government until the war destroyed, for the time being, all Southern influence in the councils of the country. Since its termination the South has been politically annihilated: the slave-holders are gone and no class of men has come forward to represent in any way their influence. A territorial aristocracy, of course, always has some good elements out of which to make leaders and governors, and the power and capacity of the planters, as efficient political men and statesmen of ability, are a great loss in the working of the government. The great difficulty here at the north is that men of character and ability cannot afford to sacrifice their personal interests to becoming working politicans, and those who do the business of the state are, as a rule, inferior

[3] Frances Leigh: *op. cit.*, pp. 193 and 195.
[4] James Leigh: *Other Days*, p. 114.

in honesty and capacity to the great majority of the people they represent (or I should say misrepresent) and rule. It is the most extraordinary state of things, of which it is difficult to see the remedy or result.

Good Friday, April 3rd, 1874

The plantation is not doing well; the difficulty of obtaining steady labour is becoming so great as to make it almost doubtful whether the proprietors of such estates must not give up the attempt altogether. The negroes are gradually leaving the estates, buying morsels of land for themselves, where they knock up miserable shanties and do a day's work or a job here and there and now and then, but entirely decline the settled working by contract for the whole agricultural season which they have accepted for the last year or two since the war. One of the planters in the neighbourhood of Butler's Island is employing Chinese labourers and Fan writes thus about them: 'They are certainly not a pretty race; they have such low, cunning, ignoble countenances. Nevertheless I should not be sorry to see about a hundred of them on this place working, for work they will, and do.'

Young Mr. Furness, the editor of Shakespeare, comes occasionally with his wife and passes an evening with me. I was so much pleased with the enthusiastic devotion to his laborious task of his *Variorum* Shakespeare that I gave him the pair of Shakespeare's gloves Cecilia Combe left me in her will and which had come to her mother, Mrs. Siddons, from Mrs. Garrick.

The precious bequest of Shakespeare's gloves reached me one evening while I was giving a reading in Boston and occasioned me such surprise and delight that one of the few times when I made blunders in my text was when I resumed my reading after finding them when I retired to rest in the middle of my performance.[5]

April 27th, 1874

My dear Ellen, after whom you so kindly ask, has been very unwell indeed with the same miserable influenza from which I am suffering; but she is the bravest and least selfish creature I ever saw and has never given way or absolutely laid up. My

[5] An old friend who was in the audience thought her so inspired that he wrote to her the next morning: 'Compared with your usual readings it was flying instead of walking. Something extraordinary must have happened.' Lee, *Atlantic Monthly*, May 1893.

whole house depends upon her and if she is disabled complete confusion must ensue.

My negro manservant has left me. I am afraid he found it impossible to endure the strain of enforced sobriety any longer. He took an absurd offence to give me warning and has gone off.

May 4th, 1874

The small country house where I am to spend the summer is a tiny old Pennsylvania farmhouse, consisting originally of four rooms on each of three stories built round one central stack of chimneys. There was formerly neither beauty nor convenience of any sort, but by dint of alterations and additions a very sufficiently pleasant and commodious residence has been made out of it. It is bright and clean and Fan is intent upon putting it all in order for me herself, and deprecated my having anything to do with arranging it, which she wishes to have entirely left to her.

York Farm, June 2nd, 1874

I took up my abode here last week on my children's birthday. We are gradually getting things to rights in this tiny habitation and it begins to look homelike and pretty, with gay chintz furniture and our books and pictures. The rooms are rather undersized for me, who like large ones, but there are a sufficient number of them and when I am alone here, as I shall be in the winter, they will be quite large enough.

America, my dear Harriet, is a very strange country and the condition of its coloured population at this moment one of the strangest political phenomena. Not only are negroes members of a state legislature in South Carolina, while here in Philadelphia my coloured manservant (who is a citizen and has a vote) is turned from the door of the theatre because he is not white, but at present in this city there are coloured men eligible and elected members of the public school boards, while their children are not admitted to the white public schools. This, of course, not by any law but by the force of custom and prejudice, stronger than any law. Time alone will overcome this, though the removal of all legal disabilities will naturally at first intensify the repugnance on the part of the whites to any form of equality between them. The Catholic priests, who are zealously working to obtain influence over the blacks for the sake of their votes, are doing all in their power to bring them into friendly relations with the Roman

Catholic Irish, so as to make one political force of them. Altogether it is a very curious process to watch.

June 14th, 1874

The experiment of bringing out English labourers to the plantation has failed with all but two of the eight men. These have worked according to their contract all winter and are now engaged in the lumber business till next winter when they will return to work on the rice crop. Two of the men found life unendurable and ran away, and are still in debt to Mr. Leigh for their passage money which he advanced them. The other four insisted on coming north with him and finding employment here. Of course it could not be found immediately, and the cost of bringing them up and of maintaining them has been a severe tax on Mr. Leigh.

The recruitment of English agricultural workers was James Leigh's only failed experiment. He had thought to help these victims of severe agricultural depression and at the same time provide labour for such jobs as the negroes could not or would not do on the plantation. The men however proved incapable of adapting to a totally different environment. Except for one, who stayed on for years as a ploughman, they were, Fan said, so helpless that they were no better than troublesome children; moreover, they were drunk and discontented and thoroughly demoralised the negroes. After two years the Leighs were glad to pay their fares home and be rid of them.

July 4th, 1874

I had a little granddaughter born to me last night in a furious thunderstorm: the 'vital spark of heavenly flame,' the living soul, came to us between two tremendous flashes of lightning and peals of thunder, and I wonder it was not frightened back into pre-existence.

July 10th, 1874

Fan and her child are going on admirably well, God be thanked, and all is better with me than I could ever have dreamed it possible to be.

August 16th, 1874

Our baby is to be christened [Alice Dudley] today by her father, in our tiny village church. It is just eight o'clock in the morning and we have already received enough beautiful flowers to make a hay-cock.

Thus far, my dearest Harriet, I wrote before breakfast. An old friend of my children, who was to be godfather, came out to breakfast so there I stopped. The day was a very trying one to me, recalling with acute vividness memories of former days, and rendering the church service of my little grandchild's christening full of conflicting emotions. I had to entertain a large party at lunch and was glad when it was all over, for I was very much worn out.

I go on at a steady jog-trot with my Memoirs and have arrived at the period of my marriage and the first letters I wrote to you from Butler Place; and it is strange enough to raise my eyes from that record and look across the road to the trees and grass and garden walks at the back of that house, opposite to the windows of the room where I am now writing.

December 23rd, 1874

I had a charming account of my dear little granddaughter in her mother's last letter from the plantation. She says the little woman is carried down to the rick yard of a morning and thence *surveys* the rice planting, the orange gathering and all the agricultural operations with extreme excitement, and holds her little court, being idolised by all the negroes who, in spite of their newly-obtained freedom, perpetuate on her the title of Little Missis and are all her very devoted slaves. The account of everything is very prosperous. The orange harvest alone had proved very valuable, and Fan says that on dull days the profusion of golden oranges makes a perfect sunshine of its own.

February 2nd, 1875

I have just finished reading Charles Greville's memoirs and am amazed at the indifference to decency and propriety which the publication of such notices of the Queen's family exhibits. The book has rather raised my estimate of the author's ability, but greatly lowered my opinion of his character. Nor can I imagine how it could be thought by anybody fitting to publish such records of George and William IV while their niece, the Queen of England is alive. The slur upon that excellent woman, Queen Adelaide, is abominable; and the constant mention of persons whom the writer was meeting on apparently cordially friendly terms as 'bastards' and 'bastardly' is disgusting. I think the whole tone of the book painfully unworthy of a gentleman.

(*Records*) Mr. Greville was a person of highly cultivated taste and a most agreeable and entertaining talker, especially to those interested in personal gossip, which I am not. On my telling him one day that I had had an inordinate dose of it from him and that I did not care for it, he exclaimed with unfeigned amazement, 'Good gracious! What do you care for then?'

Mr. Greville gave me several of the first volumes of his manuscript diary to read and I was very much amused to find certain strictures upon the ugliness of my hands and feet and an indifferent opinion of my merit as an actress among the earliest entries. Moreover, a record of a Sunday dinner at Lansdowne House, where he expected to meet my father and myself, his notice of which was, 'Charles came, but not his daughter, Miss Fanny not approving of Sunday society. Methodism behind the scenes!' In the same volume was an incident of such atrocious Irish barbarity that I did not think he ought to have let me read it, and I was very curious to know if he had done so consciously. I asked him if he remembered the contents of the book and the uncomplimentary things he had said of my personal and professional defects. He seemed quite surprised and laughed a great deal, saying that he had entirely forgotten what he had given me to read. Neither the strictures upon my extremities, my acting, nor my sabbath-keeping appeared in the book, nor the horrible incident of Irish brutality either.[6]

February 12th, 1875

Dearest Harriet, . . . I have just been making up my yearly account, a thing I have done for a good many years past. I find that I have spent four hundred pounds more than I did during my last year in England, where I had the same number of servants – though I keep a gardener here, who costs me ninety-six pounds a

---

[6] This is strange because Greville's remarks on Fanny's appearance and performance are in fact included in the 1874 edition of the Memoirs. They were not as uncomplimentary as Fanny remembered: 'I saw Miss Fanny Kemble for the first time on Friday and was disappointed. She is short, ill made, with large hands and feet, an expressive countenance, though not handsome; fine eyes, teeth and hair; not devoid of grace though with great energy and spirit . . . she excites no emotion, but she is very young, clever and may become a good, perhaps a great actress. Mrs. Siddons was not so good at her age.' (November 9, 1829, Vol. I, p. 240.)

year. I had a larger house, I travelled for three months abroad in
the summer and bought myself an outfit of new clothes in Paris,
whereas during this year I have not stirred from this place, and
one winter bonnet (an old one that I bought from Fan) and three
pairs of gloves are the only articles of dress I have bought; and yet
I have spent four hundred pounds more. Such is the cost of living
in this country now.

Having a piano once more is a great resource to me, and I have
resumed my old habit of practising after breakfast for an hour
daily. I take up the old music I love and it carries me for the time
into a world of pleasant thoughts and delightful memories. In the
evening I play from memory all sorts of things. On Sunday I
never open my piano, not from any religious scruples of my own,
but out of respect for those of others; and therefore on Saturday
evening I always wind up my musical reminiscences like a good
Englishwoman, with God Save the Queen, which was the first
thing I played in token of respectful rejoicing as soon as I got my
piano.

About noon I walk out every day that the weather permits and
have for companion a very nice little Pomeranian Spitz dog that
Mary gave me on my birthday. When I return home I read. I
always have some coarse needlework on hand that does not try
my eyes. In the evening I knit fine little Shetland wool shirts or
socks for baby and play patience. I do my writing after I leave the
rooms downstairs at ten o'clock. I find writing by candlelight tries
my eyes less than reading or needlework, so it is in the couple of
hours before I go to bed that I write letters and go on with my
Memoirs, and so the hours go by and so I spend my days.

March 16th, 1875

I get on very slowly with my Memoirs and have only crept as far
as the year 1839 and our return from the plantation. The copying
of my letters (from which of course I omit very considerable
portions) is very tiresome and so I am lazy about it; but I have no
other occupation to demand my attention, and so I go plodding
on sleepily but steadily, and almost wonder if I had done with it,
what else I should do.

June 8th, 1875

My monetary affairs have now become settled again; my property has been reinvested but at a diminution of interest of nearly
three hundred pounds a year. Of course, as I spend every penny

of my income, this has caused me both vexation and anxiety and, being quite unable to betake myself again to my former industry or open my mouth to fill my pocket, I have very gladly accepted a most liberal offer from the publisher of the *Atlantic Monthly* magazine, who wrote me word from Boston that he would be glad of any article I would send him. This is an immense relief to me and I am going to publish my manuscripts in his magazine.[7] I am really thankful for this renewed supply of means just now because I know myself to be quite incapable of any such change in my mode of life as a lesser income would necessitate. Though I spend nothing on superfluities, the general comfort in which I live is in itself expensive.

We have just got through the tremendous process to which the extreme variations of this climate compel all housekeepers here. Every carpet has been taken up and every curtain taken down, and, together with every woollen table-cover, rug, blanket, fur or similar object, packed with pepper and camphor in receptacles lined with cedar wood, having previously been sewn up in linen covers. Our floors are now covered with matting, our windows with white muslin draperies, our furniture with brown holland, and every picture, looking glass and engraving with coarse gauze to protect them from the swarms of flies; all of which of course gives an appearance of coolness and really adds to what little can be obtained by keeping the shutters shut and the rooms darkened all day.

June 25th, 1875

I have now had Fan and her baby with me for upwards of a week. The little girl is the most delicate looking creature I ever saw. She is so thin that one can see and feel all her little bones. She is as white as ivory, with dark shadows under her eyes and has not a single tooth yet, in spite of which she never cries or frets, and is habitually bright and lively. She takes as nearly as possible two quarts of milk in the four and twenty hours, and has had with them as much as six teaspoonfuls of brandy, which seems quite enormous for an infant but is in accordance with the medical treatment of the present day.

Certainly this is the most trying climate in the world. It is not a

---

[7] The first of some twenty instalments of Fanny's memoirs appeared in August 1875 under the title of *Old Women's Gossip*. When they were later brought out in book form in England, the publisher did not like this title, and Fanny's own suggestion of *Elderly Female Twaddle* was turned down in favour of *Records of a Girlhood*.

week since it was so *cold* we were obliged to have fires; and this morning, walking in the shade at seven o'clock, the perspiration ran down my face like rain.

June 26th, 1875

Yesterday I made Ellen cut off the whole of my hair, which she did very unwillingly. The intolerable heat of such a mass of hair in such weather as we are now having, the impossibility of keeping it dry and free from perspiration, and the tendency to erysipelas which I thought quite likely to be the consequence of the rusting of the hair-pins used in putting it up, determined me to this shearing; and my hair is now a grizzled crop all round my head. Very dreadfully frightful indeed I look, but the relief is immense, and I only wish I ⌐ould be shaved and go about with only my skin for skull-cap, as Sydney Smith wished he could throw off his flesh and sit in his bones in hot weather.

July 5th, 1875

My child and her child were with me nearly three weeks, and left the day before yesterday for the seaside. I miss Fan very much; she is a very cheerful, pleasant companion, and I miss the dear little pale-faced quiet baby. Their departure with three servants and a noisy little pet dog from such a small house as mine makes a wonderful silence, stillness and *sadness* at first.

July 31st, 1875

My grandson, about whom you ask, is not at all a 'precocious American young man', but an uncommonly clever and gifted boy. Like most of his country people he is deficient in animal spirits, and this and a rather unusual reasonableness prevent him from appearing, or indeed being, young for his age; but he is thoroughly well-bred and has no pert unpleasant precocity at all.

August 17th, 1875

I have only been able to walk out twice since the beginning of June, except to church. Last Sunday I had the opportunity of observing a most disgusting phenomenon on my way thither and back. The road was literally *alive* with those horrible potato-bugs which have come all the way from the wild lands of Colorado. They were marching along the highway by scores and hundreds, in companies, like a disbanded army. They have so completely stripped a potato field of several acres that I walked through the

naked *twigs* the other day, wondering what strange kind of crop
the farmer had put in the ground.

September 2nd, 1875

The Colorado beetles have infested this part of Pennsylvania in
such numbers as to recall the terrible denunciation of the Old
Testament, 'I will send my great army of the palmer worm and
the caterpillar on you.' After devouring the potatoes they betake
themselves to the neighbouring vegetables, egg plants, tomatoes
etc. For the last few days they appear to be emigrating in a body.
The garden walks and highroad have swarmed with them and
thousands have been crawling up the walls of the house, so that I
have had dustpans full of them scraped off two or three times a
day.

October 1st, 1875

I wonder if I told you that at Mr. Leigh's instigation I had bought
myself a printing machine, by means of which I print, instead of
write, my daily task of copying. It is a very ingeniously contrived
machine which is worked merely by striking keys as one plays on
a piano, and it is a great relief from the fatigue of constant writing.
It is an admirable invention and affords me a great deal of satisfaction in the process of working it.[8]

October 16th, 1875

Among the letters I found waiting [after a visit to Lenox and
Boston] was one from one of the managing committees of the
centennial exhibition to be held next year in Philadelphia that I
would give a reading for money for some additional building they
propose putting up. I was to deliver it in the Opera House, an
enormous building where my strength was taxed to the utmost
ten years ago to make my voice heard. I have declined upon three
grounds: want of strength, want of voice and want of articulation
in consequence of loss of teeth.

November 25th, 1875

I got a letter from Sally yesterday from the plantation. [She had
gone to 'console and sustain' Fan who had had a miscarriage and

[8] Fanny must have been one of the earliest to type her manuscripts. The first
typewriters on the market were produced by E. Remington & Sons, Gunsmiths of
Ilion, New York, in 1874. These machines used only capital letters – the first
shift-key models appeared only in 1878.

been near death.] Besides the pleasure of seeing her sister and Mr. Leigh, she seems to be enjoying the delightfully mild climate. She bears admiring testimony to the homelike charm of the pretty, tidy, pleasant abode the Leighs have contrived to make on that most unlovely rice swamp. How different from the wooden overseer's shanty which I inhabited during my stay there.

March 8th, 1876
My printing machine is a most delightful creature and I use it now entirely for copying the matter I send to the *Atlantic Monthly*. It tires neither my eyes nor my back as writing does, and it must be an unspeakable comfort to my poor printers.

March 11th, 1876
Dear Harriet, you say you feel it an exertion to dictate [Harriet, now over eighty, had been blind for some time and was in increasingly poor health] and I cannot bear to think of your making a painful effort to communicate with me. I am sure Eliza will let me hear how it is faring with you, and I will continue to write and tell you all that concerns me as long as you care to hear it. Your intercourse with me, my dearest friend, must not become a burden to you – I could not endure the thought.

March 15th, 1876
You are mistaken, my beloved Harriet. I should have infinite satisfaction in seeing you again, even as you now, alas! describe yourself. It is not in the power of life so to change you as to make my being with you anything but a happiness to me, especially if I were able to minister to your sad infirmity and help your dear Eliza to cheer you and brighten your darkness. I cannot bear to dwell upon this or to say how I long to be with you and hear your voice again, my dear first and lifelong friend.

April 17th, 1876
I suppose the unusually powerful activity of your mind during so many years of your life is what constitutes to you the peculiar hardship of the gradual blunting of your faculties of which you complain so sadly. It is curious to me how comfortably I endure the sense of gradually losing my faculties and becoming *stupid*. My memory is quite gone for any useful daily purpose. I hardly know what I read and invariably fall asleep no matter what time of day I take up a book; and when I have dozed through one of my

solitary evenings, I am as well satisfied with the employment of my time as if I had been working out logarithms.

I do not like physical decay quite as well as my growing imbecility. I have not been able to walk more than two or three times in the last three weeks, fearing exposure to damp and cold, and wet and wind, and dry and dust, as I have never done heretofore; and I am sorry to think I must soon have abiding falsehood in my mouth, as all my front teeth are more or less loose in their sockets. The only thing I regret to have lost is my voice and power of singing.

Lenox, April 27th, 1876

I am shocked and sorry to hear of poor Dr. Trench's accident and of his being disabled as you describe him.

(*Records*) Richard Chenevix Trench [Archbiship of Dublin] was one of my brother's early intimate friends, one of the most remarkable of that circle of brilliant young men with whom I had the good fortune to be in frequent intercourse in my girlhood. Whenever I returned to England I received kindly proofs of his constant and friendly remembrance. I stayed with him while reading at Winchester, and in Dublin, after his episcopal elevation, was honoured by his courteous notice and invitations.

This rendered not a little distressing a letter I received from Dr. Trench after the publication of my *Records of a Girlhood*, in which he expressed himself displeased and hurt at my mention of his participation with John Sterling and my brother in their Spanish adventure and sympathy with the revolutionary attempt of Torrijos. Dr. Trench complained of my having (as he appeared to think) held up the Spanish enthusiasm of his youth to ridicule, saying 'it was surely not an unworthy cause'. No indeed, had it been so I should neither have held it nor my brother nor his best friends up to ridicule in my account of it. But it was Dr. Trench himself who was ashamed of the young Englishmen's Spanish crusade, for I found to my astonishment that he had made such a complete secret of his part in the affair that, until the publication of my book, his own family and children knew nothing of that episode in his life. It was an absolute revelation to them and caused them considerable amusement and him, I am sorry to say, much annoyance.

Champlost [home of Mary Fox, near York Farm], June 13th, 1876
I left my small house at Branchtown [on her way to Lenox]

yesterday with a profound sense of heartfelt thankfulness for two and a half years of peace and pleasant comfort which I have enjoyed there and for which I do not think I have been half grateful enough. The little snug rooms have already put on something of a different appearance and no longer look *mine*. How completely characteristic of its habitual inhabitant a room becomes in its order and disorder, its look, sound and smell. Russia leather, you know, is always an element of the atmosphere in my rooms, as all the shades of violet and purple are of their colouring, so that my familiar friends associate the two with their notions of my habitat.

I have a feeling of rest and relief in finding myself free from all domestic duties and responsibilities. No breakfast, no dinner, no nothing to provide for and order. Neither have I my mocking-bird and canary to clean, for I have left them with Fan. I have an astonished sense of nothing to do and unlimited leisure to do it in. But I have lost my dear little granddaughter Alice's trotting feet in the nursery over my head and her sweet little bird's voice calling 'Go see Ganny', which she used to say very plainly.

Lenox, July 26th, 1876

The Perch, my former property and home in Lenox, is called a mile from the village. It never seemed to me more than three quarters of that distance, if so much. I walked down there and found it looking very pretty, the trees grown and the whole place much improved. It is the only place in this neighbourhood where there are any oak trees, and there are about half a dozen fine ones round the house. I was assured the other day that it was always supposed that my English love for the English tree had made me select that particular place, whereas it was bought without my having seen it, because it was a ready furnished house for sale, which I wanted at once. I find myself in consequence of that purchase invested with a dignity which none of my more distinguished kinsfolk achieved. Not only is the little 'Perch' designated as the Kemble place, but the road that leads from the village to it is set down on the maps as Kemble Street or Road, which struck me as strange and comical and melancholy enough.

August 2nd, 1876

Mr. Leigh intends returning with his wife and child to his own country in January and I at present purpose to accompany them. One of the livings offered to him lately was at Stratford-upon-Avon, and I cannot help thinking what a delight it would have been to me to sit in that church and hear him preach opposite Shakespeare's monument. This is the merest childishness, however. He has a special gift for dealing with what are called *rough* people. He has admirable common sense, excellent moral sense, great liberality of thought and sensibility of feeling, and true sympathy with the poor and hard-working folk of his country.

Boston, September 3rd, 1876

I left Lenox last Thursday. Of course it is *possible* that I may live to see it again, but very highly improbable, and so I looked my farewell at it with tender affection.

Some time ago I commissioned a Boston friend to have a stone placed on the grave of my aunt Dall in the Boston cemetery at Mount Auburn and went with him yesterday to see it. When first I came to Boston, forty years ago, Mount Auburn was a wild and picturesque piece of irregular ground, where only here and there a monument glimmered through the woodland. When I was engaged to be married Pierce and I used to ride out there and sit together under a group of trees on a pretty hillside, and I chose this spot for Dall's burial place. I intended to put a memorial stone over it, but my unsettled wandering life prevented me till I gave the necessary directions last year.

The whole place is now a *marble wilderness* of tombstones and monuments and mausoleums – terrace upon terrace rising all over the hill – a perfect stone labyrinth set in a flaming framework of scarlet geranium, scarlet salvia and yellow calceolaria. This, under the fiercest blaze I ever endured, was really the most terribly suggestive place of rest for the dead I ever saw. But I recognised the hillside and crest of trees where I used to come and walked through perfect lanes of memorial stones to my dear Dall's grave.

The inevitable emotions occasioned by the associations of the place and the oppression of the terrific heat quite knocked me up, and all day yesterday I suffered from the fatigue and excitement of the expedition.

York Farm, December 23rd, 1876

Yesterday evening my grandson Owen came home from school and Fan and I went over to sup with him. Coming away I and Dr. Wister, who was holding me, both slipped down the

broad doorsteps of the verandah which were entirely coated with
ice, and sat ourselves down on the gravel walk at the bottom
which was also one smooth sheet of ice – and there we sat
laughing so that neither of us could get up again, while Sally and
Fan and young Owen stood at the top, afraid to set their feet on
the treacherous steps lest they should fall upon us, crying out,
'Oh, mother! Oh, Owen! Are you hurt?' and then shrieking with
laughter at our absurd appearance as we sat on the ice. Between
the Owens, father and son, I was got on my feet again and Fan,
with frightful slipping, sliding, sliddering, ejaculations and
exclamations, was brought after me and we got safely home.

*It cannot have been an easy operation. Fanny, always stout, now
weighed some fourteen stone; and as for Fan, her mother had written a
month or two previously to Arthur Malkin: 'The lady you call "dear
little Fan" is no more. She is represented by a portly personable body,
little inferior to me in size and weight, and with a comely double chin,
which I somehow or other have avoided among my many signs of
elderliness.'*

Butler Place, January 13th, 1877
The Southern estate has been brought into the most beautiful
order by James's exertions or good judgment. He has worked
energetically and successfully as a clergyman among the people,
and has been mainly instrumental in having a decent church built
and consecrated. He has devoted himself to the schools and has
done good in every way among the inhabitants of the place and
the whole neighbourhood. Then I think he has enjoyed the life,
full of manly activity and occupation, of supervising this large
property and all its operations. He likes the mild soft winter
climate, he is a keen sportsman and finds a great deal of game in
the woods and swamps of the Altamaha. The whole region has a
wild, weird, picturesque beauty to which he is keenly alive.

We sail from New York this day week. Goodbye, my dearest
friend, I trust soon to see you again. I am, as ever
Your
Fanny Kemble
as you will be to the last, ever *as* ever, my Harriet St. Leger.

Epilogue
1877–1893

Always a bad sailor, Fanny was not spared her usual qualms on her last transatlantic crossing in the January of 1877. Her extrovert son-in-law, though, enjoyed every minute of it: 'We had a wonderful trip in the White Star steamer *Britannic*. The first three days the weather was fine and calm; the rest of the journey it blew a perfect hurricane. Fortunately the wind was with us and carried us along. We . . . accomplished the journey in less than eight days.'[1] At least the agony was short: earlier passages in sailing ships had lasted as long as a month.

Fanny settled in London – if settled is the word for one who constantly changed her abode. The Leighs took a fourteenth century manor house at Stratford-on-Avon where she joined them for the first Christmas after the homecoming. Fan was harassed; James, who had to officiate at his church in Leamington Spa, was only briefly there; but for Fanny and her little granddaughter Alice the occasion was an altogether joyful one. 'I went to kiss her in her crib,' she told Harriet, 'and her eager little face looked up from the pillow as she said, "only one more night more and tomorrow Chistmas Day".' When she was disposed of, her mother and I, Henry James, the American author, and all the servants took possession of the nursery and dressed it all up with Christmas wreaths and trimmed her tree that really looked extremely pretty. The nursery is a very fine room with an open arch roof of oak rafters and a huge chimney piece and a great oak table in the middle, so that, when dressed up and lighted by a bright brass gas chandelier, it looked quite picturesque, as did our band of maidens standing on steps, mounted on ladders, kneeling round the tree, with the young negro man-servant and our dark-bearded American friend helping to make a series of pictures which (with my lap full of bonbons with which I was diligently filling small bags, boxes and baskets to be tied to the tree) I took great pleasure in observing.

[1] J. W. Leigh, *op. cit.*, p. 191.

'Christmas day itself was delightful, Alice was in absolute ecstasies, the servants all beaming with delight at their small gifts. In the afternoon there was tea and plum cake for a table full of little children belonging to the coachman, gardener, etc. and their mothers. Our American friend seemed well pleased with all the ceremonies of the day, including Church service at Shakespeare's church.'

The American friend, for his part, was not unreservedly enthusiastic when he came to give his account of the day: 'I have kept [Christmas] by going to spend it with Mrs. James Leigh at Stratford on Avon. Her mother was there and the weather was brilliant; these circumstances and the picturesque old house with its hangings of holly and mistletoe helped me through my thirty-six hours. Likewise a Christmas tree for the little girl and a tea-party for the children of the people around the place; large, red-cheeked *infants* who kept bobbing curtseys and pulling their forelocks. But the Leighs themselves are not interesting. J.L. is an excellent, liberal, hard-working parson, but with the intellect and manners of a boy of seven; and his wife who (except for strength of will) is inferior to both her mother and sister, is a sort of perverted Helen Perkins, hating her position in England, detesting the English, alluding to it invidiously five times a minute and rubbing it unmercifully into her good-natured husband. She has a certain charm of honesty and freshness, and her fault is in the absurd anomaly of her position. I cannot imagine a stranger marriage.'[2]

Henry James had first encountered 'the terrific Kemble' in Rome five years earlier and been a little overawed by her magnificent presence. Clad on one occasion in purple velvet and venetian lace and on another 'draped in lavender satin lavishly décolleté', she had outshone even her handsome daughter Mrs. Wister for whom James at the time had a *tendresse*.[3] He had seen something of Fanny in London since her return from America, and the Christmas festivities at Stratford cemented a friendship that was to last until her death fifteen years later.

Many evenings were spent together, sometimes at the theatre, more often round the fire in her drawing-room. 'My sublime Fanny', James called her, relishing the exuberance of her personality no less than her wonderfully wide-ranging, dramatic, humorous flow of talk and anecdote. 'She is certainly one of the

[2] *Letters:* ed. Edel, Vol. II, pp. 147–8.
[3] *Op. cit.*, Vol. I, pp. 318, 322, 328.

women I know and like best,' he wrote two years later. 'I confess I find people in general very vulgar-minded and superficial. . . . It is therefore a kind of rest and refreshment to see a woman who (extremely annoying as she is sometimes) gives one a positive sense of having a deep, rich human nature and cast off all its vulgarities. The people of this world seem to me for the most part nothing but surface, and sometimes – Oh, ye Gods! – such desperately poor surface. Mrs. Kemble has no surface at all; she is like a straight deep cistern without a cover, or even, sometimes, without a bucket, into which, as a mode of intercourse, one must tumble with a splash.'[4]

In her last letters from York Farm Fanny had often given the impression of approaching decrepitude – lamenting the loss of mental and physical powers and gloomily insisting that she was becoming too old and fat ever again to tread her beloved Alps. She exaggerated. Every year until her eightieth she was able to travel to Switzerland where she still, as she had predicted, rode on mule-back or was carried up the mountains when she could no longer climb or walk. Although she had once vowed, after crossing the Mer de Glace with Fan, never to set foot on it again, she nevertheless fifteen years later ventured on the traverse of another glacier, the Aletsch, in the company of the eminent Victorian scientist and mountaineer, John Tyndall. It was an alarming experience: 'I was glad I was near to comfort and encourage her,' Tyndall wrote, 'for she was greatly terrified by the roughness of the passage.'[5] Fanny gratefully gave the famous climber a brooch for his wife; but she knew that this was to be her last visit to the Alps. At Brig, on the way home, she bade farewell to 'her' mountains in a long melancholy poem beginning,

> The angel walking took me by the hand,
> And said: no longer here may'st thou abide.
> To the soft valleys and smooth level land
> Come down, and humbly looking up, reside.
> 'My mountains! Oh, my mountains! Fare ye well,'
> Weeping, 'Oh, look on me once more,' I cried.

No wonder she wept. The annual pilgrimage to Switzerland had become a ritual. Grumble she might about the tourists, or about the new 'flashy, glaring, showy gin palaces' of hotels, or the disagreeable Swiss, but – 'their country is my earthly paradise.' Among the Alps she seemed in some way liberated – by the

---

[4] *Op. cit.*, Vol. II, p. 212.
[5] Eve and Creasey: *Life and Work of John Tyndall*, p. 264.

tiny, fragile flowers clinging to the rocks in ice and snow no less than by the great mountains themselves. 'Those who had not seen her in Switzerland,' wrote Henry James, 'never knew what admirable nonsense she could talk, nor with what originality and gaiety she could invite the spirit of mirth, flinging herself, in the joy of high places, on the pianos of mountain inns, joking, punning, botanising, encouraging the lowly and abasing the proud, making stupidity gape (that was almost her mission in life) and startling infallibly all primness of propriety.'[6]

Fanny never suffered fools gladly, nor for that matter those whom she arbitrarily dismissed as such. Taken to task by her son-in-law for having sat in silence next to the great Dean Stanley while dining with him in Westminster, she retorted, 'A very stupid man, my dear.' 'No, he's a very clever man. You must have said something to him. What was it?' 'As he was taking me in to dinner he remarked, "A very fine day, Mrs. Kemble," and I said, "I should have expected a less commonplace remark from the great Dean of Christchurch!" (*sic*) And he never spoke to me again.'[7]

The less eminent younger friends who came to take the place of the old ones as they vanished were put in their place as firmly as the Dean. One young man who brought roses from her publisher was aghast at her fury when he diffidently praised her *Records of a Girlhood*. 'She rounded upon me like a lioness; her form dilated, and her ever mobile features were all at work in an instant. *I had dared to pay a compliment to her book!* In the course of three minutes I was completely pulverised. Dr. Johnson was quoted to awful purpose, and I arose to take leave, feeling about as sneaky and idiotic as ever man felt in his life. She saw the effect of the explosion before I was out of the room, and by the time I had got half-way downstairs sent a swiftly flying messenger for my recall. On re-entering the room I found her sitting, both arms outstretched and with tears in her mellow voice and eyes, asking for pardon. From that moment we were firm friends.'[8]

Fanny's publisher might well send roses. Two further volumes of memoirs followed the *Records of a Girlhood*, an immediate success in 1878; her percipient but sometimes wayward *Notes upon Some of Shakespeare's Plays* came out in 1882; poems and

[6] *Essays in London*, p. 122.
[7] *Op. cit.*, p. 218. Stanley was, of course, Dean of Westminster.
[8] *Some Recollections of Yesterday* from *Temple Bar* magazine, Vol. 102, pp. 238–9.

articles appeared from time to time in *Temple Bar* magazine. A five-act farce which she jokingly prefixed with the words 'stolen from the French of Tartarin de Tarrascon' caused a tempest which it took some time to calm: 'My name is *Frances Anne Kemble*, and ought to be affixed to everything Mr. Bentley publishes for me. I wrote the 'stolen' to my farce for fun, and had no idea that it would be printed, whereas I expected that my name would be. I sent a Dedication to my story of *Far Away and Long Ago* and beg that it may be prefixed to it. Always truly yours, Frances Anne Kemble. (Her mark.)'[9]

Far Away and Long Ago – 'my tiresome novel in fifty chapters' – was Fanny's last work, appearing in her eightieth year. Inspired by loving memories of the Berkshire Hills in Massachussetts, it is a gently meandering tale with an improbably melodramatic climax, some mildly humorous observation of New England characters and occasional revealing autobiographical glimpses of past joys and sorrows: she speaks, for example, of her heroine's 'blessed year of nursing her child – alone sufficient in its exquisite happiness to atone for the misery of the most miserable of marriages, to atone for every earthly sorrow.'

Whatever the quality of Fanny's writing during those last years – as ever exceedingly verbose and now occasionally slipshod – this was a formidable output for a woman of her age. She achieved it only by strict self-discipline. A life-long habit of absolutely regulating her life by the clock ensured that certain hours every day were set aside for writing. Anne Ritchie, her old friend Thackeray's daughter, would find her 'with her watch open before her, reading, writing, working to rule. . . . She carried her love of method into everything, even to her games of patience. She always played the appointed number of games, whether she was tired or not, whether she was inclined or not.'[10]

Tired or not, inclined or not, she always had time for her friends. They would find her 'dressed in her black Paris dress, upright by the window, with flowers on the table beside her, while birds are pecking in their cage' – the bird-cage she still insisted on cleaning out herself, not choosing to leave so unpleasant a job to her servants – 'stately, ruddy and brown of complexion, almost to the very last mobile and expressive, reproachful, mocking and humorous, uplifting, heroic in turn.'[11]

[9] *Temple Bar*, Vol. 102, p. 337.   [10] *Chapters from some Memoirs*, p. 212.
[11] *Op. cit.*, p. 204.

Nathaniel Beard, the young man from the publishers, was one of those acute enough to realise that beneath the fun and drama of Fanny's dazzling conversation lay a lasting sadness: 'She seldom allowed herself to talk sadly, but I think that in her last years she seldom felt other than sad.'[12]

That Fanny should not have been entirely happy is not surprising. She did not like – never had liked – living in London; she was ill at ease with new customs, new manners, new fashions; her friend Harriet and her sister Adelaide were both dead, her elder daughter was far away in America, and with the other she was no longer as close as she had been. The friendly, easy companionship with Fan was no more. Fanny had refused to attend the baptism of her short-lived grandson since he was to be christened Pierce Butler and she could not bear to hear 'that evil name' uttered. Then Fan had objected furiously to the publication of the *Records of a Later Life*: 'She would never forgive [her mother],' she had said, 'she would never see her or speak to her again if there were a single disparaging word in the book concerning the man for whom she had named her child.'[13]

There was no open breach but, the old lady wrote to her other daughter, 'Fanny and I have very little intercourse. She comes to see me from a sense of duty and is kind and affectionately indifferent in her manner to me, but I have never been able to forget her furious outbreak of temper in Paris and am too much afraid of challenging another of the same sort to speak to her with freedom about anything. Her servants and her clothes are the principal subjects of our conversation – when it is not the rice crop – and I say but little of what I think and feel about anything to her. . . . Our intercourse is one of the most tragical consequences of life – to me the most tragical.'[14]

It cannot have been altogether easy, when Fanny could no longer live on her own, for her to make her home with the Leighs who had by then moved to a London parish; but at least there was help and comfort from her granddaughter Alice and the faithful maid Ellen who had left home and husband in Italy to be with her mistress in her increasing infirmity.

Fan was in America when, on January 15, 1893, as Ellen was helping her to bed, Frances Anne Kemble fell suddenly dead. It was not the death she had wished herself long ago on the Georgian plantation – 'to break my neck off the back of my horse at full

[12] *Temple Bar*, p. 335.   [13] Wright, *op. cit.*, pp. 206–7.
[14] Wright, *op. cit.*, pp. 208–9.

gallop on a fine day' – but it was quick and merciful. She was in her eighty-fourth year.

Henry James, though suffering from an acute attack of gout, rallied round at once to deal with a crowd of newspaper reporters on James Leigh's front doorstep; and five days later, still so lame that his shoe had to be split before he could put it on, he could only hobble to the graveside, conscious that the terrific Kemble should have rested, not in Kensal Rise cemetery but 'in some fold of the Alps – which she adored – and which in some ways she resembled.'

Among the small band of mourners was one whose home was in those beloved Alps – a former man-servant who had hurried from Switzerland on hearing of her death, to arrive barely in time to be present at the burial.

In the evening, when it was all over, Fanny's dark-bearded American friend sat down in his Kensington study to write a characteristically Jamesian letter to her daughter Sarah across the Atlantic in Philadelphia.

'Dear Mrs. Wister,[15] . . . I stood by your mother's grave this morning – a soft, kind, balmy day, with your brother-in-law and tall, pale, handsome Alice, and a few of those of her friends who have survived her, and were in town, and were not ill – as all the world lately has been. The number is inevitably small for of her generation she is the last, and she had made no new friends, naturally, in these last years. She was laid in the same earth as her father – and buried under a mountain of flowers – which I don't like – but which many people, most people do. It was all bright, somehow, and public and slightly pompous. I thought of you and Mrs. Leigh "far away on the billow," as it were – and hoped you felt, with us here, the great beneficence and good fortune of your mother's instantaneous and painless extinction. Everything of the condition, at the last, that she had longed for was there – and nothing that she dreaded was. And the devotion of her old restored maid, Mrs. Brianzoni, appears to have been absolute – of every moment and every hour. She stood there this morning with a very white face and her hands full of flowers. Your mother looked, after death, extraordinarily like her sister. . . . I mention these things – to bring everything a little nearer to you. I am conscious of a strange bareness and a kind of evening chill as it were in the air, as if some great object that had filled it for long

[15] *Selected Letters*, ed. Edel, pp. 213–14.

had left an emptiness – from displacement – to all the senses. It seemed – this morning – her laying to rest – not but what I think, I must frankly say, the act of *burial* anything but unacceptably horrible, a hideous old imposition of the church – it seemed quite like the end of some reign or the fall of some empire. But she wanted to go – and she went when she could, at last, without a pang. She was very touching in her infirmity all these last months – and yet with her wonderful air of smouldering embers under ashes. She leaves a great image – a great memory.'

Bibliography

Agate, James: *These were Actors*. London, 1943.

Armstrong, Margaret: *Fanny Kemble, A Passionate Victorian*. London, 1938.

Beard, Nathaniel: *Some Recollections of Yesterday*. *Temple Bar* Magazine, Vol. 102. London, 1894.

Bobbé, Dorothie: *Fanny Kemble*. New York, 1931.

Browning, Elizabeth Barrett: *Letters*, ed. Frederic G. Kenyon. London, 1897.

Browning: *The Letters of Robert Browning and Elizabeth Barrett Barrett*. London, 1899.

Butler, Pierce: *Mr. Butler's Statement*. Philadelphia, 1850.

Cooper, James Fenimore: *Correspondence*, ed. James Fenimore Cooper. Yale, 1922.

Craven, Mme. Auguste: *La Jeunesse de Fanny Kemble*. Paris, 1880.

Driver, Leotia S. *Fanny Kemble*. Chapel Hill, 1933.

Edel, Leon: *Henry James – the Middle Years*. London, 1963.

Eve, A. S. and Creasey, C. H.: *The Life and Works of John Tyndall*. With a chapter on Tyndall as a Mountaineer by Lord Schuster. London, 1945.

Fisher, Sidney George: *A Philadelphia Perspective: The Diary of Sidney George Fisher*, ed. N. B. Wainwright. Philadelphia, 1967.

Fitzgerald, Edward: *Letters to Fanny Kemble 1871–1883*. London, 1895.

Fitzgerald, Percy: *The Kembles*. London, 1871.

FitzSimons, Raymund: *Edmund Kean – Fire from Heaven*. London, 1976.

Forbes, John Murray: *Letters and Recollections*, ed. Sarah Forbes Hughes. Boston, 1899.

Gibbs, Henry: *Affectionately Yours, Fanny*. London, 1945.

Greville, Charles: *A Journal of the Reigns of King George IV and King William IV*, ed. Henry Reeve. London, 1874.

Greville, Charles: *A Journal of the Reign of Queen Victoria, 1837–1852*, ed. Henry Reeve. London, 1885.

Greville, Charles: *The Greville Memoirs*, ed. Lytton Strachey and Roger Fulford. London, 1938.

Greville, Henry: *Leaves from the Diary of Henry Greville*, ed. Viscountess Enfield. London, 1883.

Hone, Philip: *The Diary of Philip Hone, 1828–1851*, ed. Bayard Tuckerman. New York, 1889.

Hosmer, Harriet: *Letters and Memories*, ed. Cornelia Carr. London, 1913.

Hunt, Leigh: *Autobiography*, ed. Roger Ingpen. London, 1903.

Hunt, Leigh: *Dramatic Criticism*, ed. Lawrence Huston Houtchens and Carolyn Washburn Houtchens. London, 1950.

James, Henry: *Essays in London and Elsewhere*. London, 1893.

James, Henry: *Letters*, Vol. I, 1843–1874, ed. Leon Edel. London, 1974.

James, Henry: *Letters*, Vol. II, 1875–1883, ed. Leon Edel. Cambridge, Mass,, 1975.

James, Henry: *Notebooks*, ed. F. O. Matthiessen and Kenneth B. Murdock. New York, 1947.

James, Henry: *Selected Letters*, ed. Leon Edel. London, 1956.

Jameson, Anna: *Letters and Friendships*, ed. Mrs. Steuart Erskine. London, 1915.

Kemble, Frances Anne:

Letters, Journals, etc.:

Journal of Frances Anne Butler. London, 1835.

A Year of Consolation. London, 1847.

Journal of a Residence on a Georgian Plantation, 1838–9. London, 1863. Also ed. John A. Scott. London, 1961.

Records of A Girlhood. London, 1878.

Records of a Later Life. London, 1882.

Further Records. London, 1890.

Other writings:

Answer of Frances Anne Butler to the Libel of Pierce Butler praying for a Divorce. 1848.

The Adventures of Timothy John Homespun in Switzerland. London, 1889.

Far Away and Long Ago. London, 1889.

Francis I. London, 1832.

Notes upon Some of Shakespeare's Plays. London, 1882.

Plays. London, 1863. (Including *An English Tragedy*, and translations of Schiller's *Maria Stuart* and Dumas' *Mademoiselle de Belle Isle*.)

Poems. Philadelphia, 1844.

Poems. London, 1865.

Poems. London, 1883.

The Star of Seville. London, 1837.

Lee, Henry: *Frances Anne Kemble*. *Atlantic Monthly*, May 1893.

Leech, C. and Craik, T. W.: *The* Revels *History of Drama in English*, Vol. VI, 1750–1880. London, 1975.

Leigh, Frances Butler: *Ten Years on a Georgian Plantation after the War*. London, 1883.

Leigh, James Wentworth: *Other Days*. London, 1921.

Longfellow, Fanny Appleton: *Mrs. Longfellow – Selected Letters and Journals*, ed. Edward Wagenknecht. London, 1959.

Longfellow, Samuel: *Life of Henry Wadsworth Longfellow*. New York, 1886.

Macready, William Charles: *Journal*, ed. J. C. Trewin. London, 1967.

Macready, William Charles: *Diaries*, ed. William Toynbee. London, 1892.

Marshall, Dorothy: *Fanny Kemble*. London, 1977.

Moore, Thomas: *Journal*, ed. Peter Quennell. London, 1964.

Nicolson, Harold: *Tennyson*. London, 1923.

Odell, George C. D.: *Annals of the New York Stage*. New York, 1928.

Pope-Hennessy, Una: *Three English Women in America*. London, 1929.

Ritchie, Lady (Anne Thackeray): *Chapters from Some Memoirs*. London, 1894.

Rushmore, Robert: *Fanny Kemble*. London, 1970.

Sartoris, Adelaide: *A Week in a French Country House*. (With introduction by Lady Ritchie.) London, 1902.

Terry, Ellen: *Ellen Terry's Memoirs*, ed. Edith Craig and Christopher St. John. London, 1933.

Thackeray, William Makepeace: *Letters and Private Papers*, ed. Gordon N. Ray. London, 1946.

Thomas, Clara: *Love and Work Enough – the Life of Anna Jameson*. London, 1967.

Victoria: *The Girlhood of Queen Victoria*. A Selection from her Diaries, 1832–40, ed. Viscount Esher. London, 1912.

Wister, Fanny Kemble: *Fanny – the American Kemble*. Tallahassee, 1972.

Whitman, Walt: *Specimen Days*. Glasgow, 1883.

Wright, Constance: *Fanny Kemble and the Lovely Land*. London, 1974.

Index

264

Dickens, Charles, 117n.
Domestic Manners of the Americans (Frances Trollope), 60
Drury Lane, Theatre Royal, 18, 22, 30n., Royal Patent, 48
Dumas, Alexandre, 169

Edinburgh: Fanny spends year there, 23–4; theatre, 23, 39–41; frigidity of the public, 40, 41
Edward VII, (Prince of Wales), in America, 230
Egerton, Lord and Lady Francis, 46
Ellesmere, Lady, 116, 225
Ellesmere, Lord, 116, 200
Elssler, Fanny, 14 and n.
English Tragedy, An, play by Fanny, 124–5
Euphrasia (*The Grecian Daughter*), 38
Everett, Edward, 169 and n.
Exeter: cathedral, 202; nursery gardens, 202

Far Away and Long Ago, novel by Fanny, 258
Faudier, Madame, 8
Fergusson, Sir Adam, 40, 41, 203
Ferrier, Susan, 40
Fisher, Sidney, 230n., 231–2
Fitzclarence, Rev. Adolphus, 35–6
Fitzgerald, Edward, 5n., 161n.; Fanny's comments on him, 223 and n.
Fitzhugh, Emily, 203n.; letter from Fanny, 135 and n.
Fitzhugh, Lady, 203n.
Fleury, M. de, Fanny's great-grandfather, 3
Forbes, John, 233
Forrester, Fanny's horse, 181
Forster, John, 200 and n.
Foscari (Mitford), 20
Fox, Mary, 237, 245, 250
Fozzard, Captain, riding master, 37
Francis I, play by Fanny, 20–1, 49 and n., 54; produced, 56
Franklin, Benjamin, 89
Frascati, 191–3, 195
Frederick VII, King of Spain, 46
Freischütz, Der (Weber), 18
Frost, Mr., of Hull, 205–6
Fry, Elizabeth, 51 and n.
Fugitive Slave Bill, 156
Furness, Horace, editor of Shakespeare, 237, 240
Further Records (Fanny Kemble), xiii, xiv, 217, 218

Gamester, The (Moore), 38, 75
Garrick, David, xiii, 27
Garrick, Mrs., 240
Genlis, Madame de, and juvenile dramas, 4
George IV, 4–5, 243; death, 39
Georgia, 151n., 157, 158, 231; Butler family plantations, 107, 111, 125, 126, 133–4; pinelanders, 144
see also Butler's Island *and* St. Simon's Island
Glasgow, Fanny plays in, 40
Great Russell Street, the Kembles' home in, 46
Grecian Daughter, The (Murphy), 27, 38
Greville, Charles, 158 and n., 159, 164 and n., 202, 232; on the Butlers' relationship, 172; his memoirs, 243–4
Greville, Henry, 5n., 158n., 196, 197, 198n., 201, 202, 204, 224
Grey, Countess, and Grey family, 210 and n., 211

Hallam, Arthur Henry, 46, 50n.
Hamilton, Alexander, 151n.
Hamlet, 66, 83, 215, 228
Harley Street, Butlers rent house in, 164
Harness, Rev. William, 165 and n., 166
Harrisburg, 119, 120
Harvard College, Fanny's reading at, 218–19
Haydn, 84
Heath Farm, Hertfordshire, 17–19
Hernani (Hugo), 200
Highgate, Fanny's reading at, 205n.
Hill, Lord, Commander-in-Chief, 55
Hoboken, 63, 64; Turtle Club, 63
Holland House, 117n., 118
Holland, Lady, 117–18, 163–4; Fanny's description of her, 117–18
Holland, Lord, 117, 164
Holmes, doctor on Butler's Island, 141, 142, 145
Hone, Philip, 64–5, 91, 122n., description of Fanny, 65; on her Journal, 104n.; and her readings, 220
Honeymoon, The, 198
Hosmer, Harriet, 226
Housatonic valley, 109
Hudson river, Fanny's journeys on, 78–9, 91
Hugo, Victor, 8, 200; Fanny's review of, 170
Hull, 205–7; Fanny's readings, 205; Station Hotel and station, 205